THINKING FUNCTIONALLY WITH HASKELL

Richard Bird is famed for the clarity and rigour of his writing. His new textbook, which introduces functional programming to students, emphasises fundamental techniques for reasoning mathematically about functional programs. By studying the underlying equational laws, the book enables students to apply calculational reasoning to their programs, both to understand their properties and to make them more efficient.

The book has been designed to fit a first- or second-year undergraduate course and is a thorough overhaul and replacement of his earlier textbooks. It features case studies in Sudoku and pretty-printing, and over 100 carefully selected exercises with solutions. This engaging text will be welcomed by students and teachers alike.

THINKING FUNCTIONALLY
WITH HASKELL

RICHARD BIRD

University of Oxford

CAMBRIDGE
UNIVERSITY PRESS

CAMBRIDGE
UNIVERSITY PRESS

University Printing House, Cambridge CB2 8BS, United Kingdom

One Liberty Plaza, 20th Floor, New York, NY 10006, USA

477 Williamstown Road, Port Melbourne, VIC 3207, Australia

314-321, 3rd Floor, Plot 3, Splendor Forum, Jasola District Centre, New Delhi - 110025, India

79 Anson Road, #06-04/06, Singapore 079906

Cambridge University Press is part of the University of Cambridge.

It furthers the University's mission by disseminating knowledge in the pursuit of education, learning and research at the highest international levels of excellence.

www.cambridge.org
Information on this title: www.cambridge.org/9781107087200

First published 2015
4th printing 2016

A catalogue record for this publication is available from the British Library

Library of Congress Cataloging in Publication data
Bird, Richard, 1943-
Thinking functionally with Haskell / Richard Bird, University of Oxford.
pages . cm
ISBN 978-1-107-08720-0 (hardback) – ISBN 978-1-107-45264-0 (paperback)
1. Functional programming (Computer science) I. Title.
QA76.62.B573 2014
005.1´14–dc23
2014024954

ISBN 978-1-107-08720-0 Hardback
ISBN 978-1-107-45264-0 Paperback

Additional resources for this publication at www.cambridge.org/9781107087200

Contents

Preface

The present book is a completely rewritten version of the second edition of my *Introduction to Functional Programming using Haskell* (Prentice Hall). The main changes are: a reorganisation of some introductory material to reflect the needs of a one or two term lecture course; a fresh set of case studies; and a collection of over 100 exercises that now actually contain answers. As before, no knowledge of computers or programming is assumed, so the material is suitable as a first course in computing.

Every author has his or her own drum to beat when writing a textbook, and the present one is no different. While there are now numerous books, tutorials, articles and blogs devoted to Haskell, few of them emphasise what seems to me the main reason why functional programming is the best thing since sliced bread: the ability to think mathematically about functional programs. And the mathematics involved is neither new nor difficult. Any student who has come to grips with, say, high-school trigonometry and has applied simple trigonometric laws and identities to simplify expressions involving sines and cosines (a typical example: express $\sin 3\alpha$ in terms of $\sin \alpha$) will quickly appreciate that a similar activity is being proposed for programming problems. And the payoff is there at the terminal: faster computations. Even after 30 years I still get a great deal of pleasure from writing down a simple, obvious, but inefficient way to solve a problem, applying some well-known equational laws, and coming up with another solution that is ten times faster. Well, if I'm lucky.

If the message of the last paragraph turns you off, if you are perpetually running away from the Mordor of Mathematics, then the present book is probably not for you. Probably, but not necessarily so (nobody likes to lose customers). There is still pleasure to be gained in learning a novel and exciting way to write programs. Even programmers who for one reason or another do not or cannot use Haskell in their daily work, and certainly do not have the time to spend calculating better answers to their problems, have still been inspired by the enjoyment of learning Haskell and are hugely appreciative of its ability to express computational ideas and methods simply and briefly. In fact, the ability to express programming ideas in a purely functional style has been slowly incorporated into mainstream imperative programming languages, such as Python, Visual Basic, and C#.

One final but important point: Haskell is a large language and this book by no means covers all of it. It is not a reference guide to Haskell. Although details of the language appear on almost every page, especially in the earlier chapters, my primary intention is to convey the essence of functional programming, the idea of thinking functionally about programs, not to dwell too much on the particulars of one specific language. But over the years Haskell has absorbed and codified most of the ideas of functional programming expressed in earlier functional languages, such as SASL, KRC, Miranda, Orwell and Gofer, and it is difficult to resist the temptation to explain everything in terms of this one super-cool language.

Most of the programs recorded in this book can be found on the website

```
www.cs.ox.ac.uk/publications/books/functional
```

It is hoped to add more exercises (and answers), suggestions for projects, and so on, in due course. For more information about Haskell, the site www.haskell.org should be your first port of call.

Acknowledgements

The present book arose out of lecture notes I prepared based on the second edition. It has benefited enormously from the comments and suggestions by tutors and students. Others have emailed me with constructive comments and criticisms, or simply to point out typos and silly mistakes. These include: Nils Andersen, Ani Calinescu, Franklin Chen, Sharon Curtis, Martin Filby, Simon Finn, Jeroen Fokker, Maarten Fokkinga, Jeremy Gibbons, Robert Giegerich, Kevin Hammond, Ralf Hinze, Gerard Huet, Michael Hinchey, Tony Hoare, Iain Houston, John Hughes, Graham Hutton, Cezar Ionescu, Stephen Jarvis, Geraint Jones, Mark Jones, John Launchbury, Paul Licameli, David Lester, Iain MacCullum, Ursula Martin, Lambert Meertens, Erik Meijer, Quentin Miller, Oege de Moor, Chris Okasaki, Oskar Permvall, Simon Peyton Jones, Mark Ramaer, Hamilton Richards, Dan Russell, Don Sannella, Antony Simmons, Deepak D'Souza, John Spanondakis, Mike Spivey, Joe Stoy, Bernard Sufrin, Masato Takeichi, Peter Thiemann, David Turner, Colin Watson, and Stephen Wilson. In particular, Jeremy Gibbons, Bernard Sufrin and José Pedro Magalhães have read drafts of the manuscript and suggested a number of corrections.

I would also like to thank David Tranah, my editor at CUP, for continued advice and support. My status now is emeritus professor at the Department of Computer Science at Oxford, and I would like to thank the department and its head, Bill Roscoe, for continuing to make facilities available.

Richard Bird

Exercises

Exercise A

Express $\sin 3\alpha$ in terms of $\sin \alpha$.

Answers

Answer to Exercise A

$$\sin 3\alpha$$
$$= \quad \{\text{arithmetic}\}$$
$$\sin(2\alpha + \alpha)$$
$$= \quad \{\text{since } \sin(\alpha + \beta) = \sin \alpha \cos \beta + \cos \alpha \sin \beta\}$$
$$\sin 2\alpha \cos \alpha + \cos 2\alpha \sin \alpha$$
$$= \quad \{\text{since } \sin 2\alpha = 2 \sin \alpha \cos \alpha\}$$
$$2 \sin \alpha \cos^2 \alpha + \cos 2\alpha \sin \alpha$$
$$= \quad \{\text{since } \cos 2\alpha = \cos^2 \alpha - \sin^2 \alpha\}$$
$$2 \sin \alpha \cos^2 \alpha + (\cos^2 \alpha - \sin^2 \alpha) \sin \alpha$$
$$= \quad \{\text{since } \sin^2 \alpha + \cos^2 \alpha = 1\}$$
$$\sin \alpha (3 - 4 \sin^2 \alpha)$$

The above proof format was, I believe, invented by Wim Feijen. It will be used throughout the book.

Chapter 1

What is functional programming?

In a nutshell:

- Functional programming is a method of program construction that emphasises functions and their application rather than commands and their execution.

- Functional programming uses simple mathematical notation that allows problems to be described clearly and concisely.

- Functional programming has a simple mathematical basis that supports equational reasoning about the properties of programs.

Our aim in this book is to illustrate these three key points, using a specific functional language called Haskell.

1.1 Functions and types

We will use the Haskell notation

```
f :: X -> Y
```

to assert that f is a function taking arguments of type X and returning results of type Y. For example,

```
sin     :: Float -> Float
age     :: Person -> Int
add     :: (Integer,Integer) -> Integer
logBase :: Float -> (Float -> Float)
```

Float is the type of floating-point numbers, things like 3.14159, and Int is the type of limited-precision integers, integers n that lie in a restricted range such as

$-2^{29} \le n < 2^{29}$. The restriction is lifted with the type `Integer`, which is the type of unlimited-precision integers. As we will see in Chapter 3, numbers in Haskell come in many flavours.

In mathematics one usually writes $f(x)$ to denote the application of the function f to the argument x. But we also write, for example, $\sin\theta$ rather than $\sin(\theta)$. In Haskell we can always write `f x` for the application of `f` to the argument `x`. The operation of application can be denoted using a space. If there are no parentheses the space is necessary to avoid confusion with multi-letter names: `latex` is a name but `late x` denotes the application of a function `late` to an argument `x`.

As examples, `sin 3.14` or `sin (3.14)` or `sin(3.14)` are three legitimate ways of writing the application of the function `sin` to the argument `3.14`.

Similarly, `logBase 2 10` or `(logBase 2) 10` or `(logBase 2)(10)` are all legitimate ways of writing the logarithm to base 2 of the number 10. But the expression `logBase (2 10)` is incorrect. Parentheses are needed in writing `add (3,4)` for the sum of 3 and 4 because the argument of `add` is declared above as a pair of integers and pairs are expressed with parentheses and commas.

Look again at the type of `logBase`. It takes a floating point number as argument, and returns a function as result. At first sight that might seem strange, but at second sight it shouldn't: the mathematical functions $\log_2$ and $\log_e$ are exactly what is provided by `logBase 2` and `logBase e`.

In mathematics one can encounter expressions like $\log\sin x$. To the mathematician that means $\log(\sin x)$, since the alternative $(\log\sin)\, x$ doesn't make sense. But in Haskell one has to say what one means, and one has to write `log (sin x)` because `log sin x` is read by Haskell as `(log sin) x`. Functional application in Haskell *associates* to the left in expressions and also has the highest *binding power*. (By the way, `log` is the Haskell abbreviation for `logBase e`.)

Here is another example. In trigonometry one can write

$$\sin 2\theta = 2\sin\theta\cos\theta.$$

In Haskell one has to write

```
sin (2*theta) = 2 * sin theta * cos theta
```

Not only do we have to make the multiplications explicit, we also have to put in parentheses to say exactly what we mean. We could have added a couple more and written

```
sin (2*theta) = 2 * (sin theta) * (cos theta)
```

but the additional parentheses are not necessary because functional application binds tighter than multiplication.

1.2 Functional composition

Suppose f :: Y -> Z and g :: X -> Y are two given functions. We can combine them into a new function

    f . g :: X -> Z

that first applies g to an argument of type X, giving a result of type Y, and then applies f to this result, giving a final result of type Z. We always say that functions take *arguments* and return *results*. In fact we have

    (f . g) x = f (g x)

The order of composition is from right to left because we write functions to the left of the arguments to which they are applied. In English we write 'green pig' and interpret adjectives such as 'green' as functions taking noun phrases to noun phrases. Of course, in French . . .

1.3 Example: common words

Let us illustrate the importance of functional composition by solving a problem. What are the 100 most common words in *War and Peace*? What are the 50 most common words in *Love's Labours Lost*? We will write a functional program to find out. Well, perhaps we are not yet ready for a complete program, but we can construct enough of one to capture the essential spirit of functional programming.

What is given? Answer: a *text*, which is a list of characters, containing visible characters like 'B' and ',', and blank characters like spaces and newlines (' ' and '\n'). Note that individual characters are denoted using single quotes. Thus 'f' is a character, while f is a name. The Haskell type Char is the type of characters, and the type of lists whose elements are of type Char is denoted by [Char]. This notation is not special to characters, so [Int] denotes a list of integers, and [Float -> Float] a list of functions.

What is wanted as output? Answer: something like

    the: 154
    of: 50

```
a: 18
and: 12
in: 11
```

This display is also a list of characters, in fact it is the list

```
"  the: 154\n  of: 50\n  a: 18\n  and: 12\n  in: 11\n"
```

Lists of characters are denoted using double quotes. More on this in the exercises.

So we want to design a function, `commonWords` say, with type

```
commonWords :: Int -> [Char] -> [Char]
```

The function `commonWords n` takes a list of characters and returns a list of the n most common words in the list as a *string* (another name for a list of characters) in the form described above. The type of `commonWords` is written without parentheses, though we can put them in:

```
commonWords :: Int -> ([Char] -> [Char])
```

Whenever two `->` signs are adjacent in a type, the order of association is from right to left, exactly the opposite convention of functional application. So `A -> B -> C` means `A -> (B -> C)`. If you want to describe the type `(A -> B) -> C` you have to put in the parentheses. More on this in the next chapter.

Having understood precisely what is given and what is wanted, different people come up with different ways of solving the problem, and express different worries about various parts of the problem. For example, what is a 'word' and how do you convert a list of characters into a list of words? Are the words `"Hello"`, `"hello"` and `"Hello!"` distinct words or the same word? How do you count words? Do you count all the words or just the most common ones? And so on. Some find these details daunting and overwhelming. Most seem to agree that at some intermediate point in the computation we have to come up with a list of words and their frequencies, but how do we get from there to the final destination? Do we go through the list n times, extracting the word with the next highest frequency at each pass, or is there something better?

Let's start with what a word is, and just assert that a word is a maximal sequence of characters not containing spaces or newline characters. That allows words like `"Hello!"`, or `"3*4"` or `"Thelma&Louise"` but never mind. In a text a word is identified by being surrounded by blank characters, so `"Thelma and Louise"` contains three words.

We are not going to worry about how to split a text up into a list of its component words. Instead we just assume the existence of a function

```
words :: [Char] -> [[Char]]
```

that does the job. Types like `[[Char]]` can be difficult to comprehend, but in Haskell we can always introduce *type synonyms*:

```
type Text = [Char]
type Word = [Char]
```

So now we have `words :: Text -> [Word]`, which is much easier on the brain. Of course, a text is different from a word in that the former can contain blank characters and the latter cannot, but type synonyms in Haskell do not support such subtle distinctions. In fact, `words` is a library function in Haskell, so we don't have to define it ourselves.

There is still the issue of whether `"The"` and `"the"` denote the same or different words. They really should be the same word, and one way of achieving this is to convert all the letters in the text to lowercase, leaving everything else unchanged. To this end, we need a function `toLower :: Char -> Char` that converts upper-case letters to lowercase and leaves everything else unchanged. In order to apply this function to every character in the text we need a general function

```
map :: (a -> b) -> [a] -> [b]
```

such that `map f` applied to a list applies `f` to every element of the list. So, converting everything to lowercase is done by the function

```
map toLower :: Text -> Text
```

Good. At this point we have `words . map toLower` as the function which converts a text into a list of words in lowercase. The next task is to count the number of occurrences of each word. We could go through the list of words, checking to see whether the next word is new or has been seen before, and either starting a new count for a new word or incrementing the count for an existing word. But there is a conceptually simpler method, namely to *sort* the list of words into alphabetical order, thereby bringing all duplicated words together in the list. Humans would not do it this way, but the idea of sorting a list to make information available is probably the single most important algorithmic idea in computing. So, let us assume the existence of a function

```
sortWords :: [Word] -> [Word]
```

that sorts the list of words into alphabetical order. For example,

```
sortWords ["to","be","or","not","to","be"]
        = ["be","be","not","or","to","to"]
```

Now we want to count the runs of adjacent occurrences of each word in the sorted list. Suppose we have a function

```
countRuns :: [Word] -> [(Int,Word)]
```

that counts the words. For example,

```
countRuns ["be","be","not","or","to","to"]
   = [(2,"be"),(1,"not"),(1,"or"),(2,"to")]
```

The result is a list of words and their counts in alphabetical order of the words.

Now comes the key idea: we want the information in the list to be ordered not by word, but by decreasing order of count. Rather than thinking of something more clever, we see that this is just another version of sorting. As we said above, sorting is a *really* useful method in programming. So suppose we have a function

```
sortRuns :: [(Int,Word)] -> [(Int,Word)]
```

that sorts the list of runs into descending order of count (the first component of each element). For example,

```
sortRuns [(2,"be"),(1,"not"),(1,"or"),(2,"to")]
       = [(2,"be"),(2,"to"),(1,"not"),(1,"or")]
```

The next step is simply to take the first n elements of the result. For this we need a function

```
take :: Int -> [a] -> [a]
```

so that `take n` takes the first n elements of a list of things. As far as `take` is concerned it doesn't matter what a 'thing' is, which is why there is an a in the type signature rather than `(Int,Word)`. We will explain this idea in the next chapter.

The final steps are just tidying up. We first need to convert each element into a string so that, for example, `(2,"be")` is replaced by `"be   2\n"`. Call this function

```
showRun :: (Int,Word) -> String
```

The type `String` is a predeclared Haskell type synonym for `[Char]`. That means

```
map showRun :: [(Int,Word)] -> [String]
```

is a function that converts a list of runs into a list of strings.

The final step is to use a function

```
concat :: [[a]] -> [a]
```

that concatenates a list of lists of things together. Again, it doesn't matter what the 'thing' is as far as concatenation is concerned, which is why there is an a in the type signature.

Now we can define

```
commonWords :: Int -> Text -> String
commonWords n = concat . map showRun . take n .
                sortRuns . countRuns . sortWords .
                words . map toLower
```

The definition of commonWords is given as a pipeline of eight component functions glued together by functional composition. Not every problem can be decomposed into component tasks in quite such a straightforward manner, but when it can, the resulting program is simple, attractive and effective.

Notice how the process of decomposing the problem was governed by the declared types of the subsidiary functions. Lesson Two (Lesson One being the importance of functional composition) is that deciding on the type of a function is the very first step in finding a suitable definition of the function.

We said above that we were going to write a *program* for the common words problem. What we actually did was to write a functional definition of commonWords, using subsidiary definitions that we either can construct ourselves or else import from a suitable Haskell library. A list of definitions is called a *script*, so what we constructed was a script. The order in which the functions are presented in a script is not important. We could place the definition of commonWords first, and then define the subsidiary functions, or else define all these functions first, and end up with the definition of the main function of interest. In other words we can tell the story of the script in any order we choose. We will see how to compute with scripts later on.

1.4 Example: numbers into words

Here is another example, one for which we will provide a complete solution. The example demonstrates another fundamental aspect of problem solving, namely that a good way to solve a tricky problem is to first simplify the problem and then see how to solve the simpler problem.

Sometimes we need to write numbers as words. For instance

```
convert 308000 = "three hundred and eight thousand"
convert 369027 = "three hundred and sixty-nine thousand and
                    twenty-seven"
convert 369401 = "three hundred and sixty-nine thousand
                    four hundred and one"
```

Our aim is to design a function

```
convert :: Int -> String
```

that, given a nonnegative number less than one million, returns a string that represents the number in words. As we said above, `String` is a predeclared type synonym in Haskell for `[Char]`.

We will need the names of the component numbers. One way is to give these as three lists of strings:

```
> units, teens, tens :: [String]
> units = ["zero","one","two","three","four","five",
>          "six","seven","eight","nine"]
> teens = ["ten","eleven","twelve","thirteen","fourteen",
>          "fifteen","sixteen","seventeen","eighteen",
>          "nineteen"]
> tens  = ["twenty","thirty","forty","fifty","sixty",
>          "seventy","eighty","ninety"]
```

Oh, what is the > character doing at the beginning of each line above? The answer is that, in a script, it indicates a line of Haskell code, not a line of comment. In Haskell, a file ending with the suffix .lhs is called a *Literate Haskell Script* and the convention is that every line in such a script is interpreted as a comment unless it begins with a > sign, when it is interpreted as a line of program. Program lines are not allowed next to comments, so there has to be at least one blank line separating the two. In fact, the whole chapter you are now reading forms a legitimate .lhs file, one that can be loaded into a Haskell system and interacted with. We won't carry on with this convention in subsequent chapters (apart from anything else, it would force us to use different names for each version of a function that we may want to define) but the present chapter does illustrate *literate* programming in which we can present and discuss the definitions of functions in any order we wish.

Returning to the task in hand, a good way to tackle tricky problems is to solve a simpler problem first. The simplest version of our problem is when the given number *n* contains only one digit, so $0 \leq n < 10$. Let `convert1` deal with this version. We can immediately define

```
> convert1 :: Int -> String
> convert1 n = units!!n
```

This definition uses the list-indexing operation (!!). Given a list `xs` and an index `n`, the expression `xs!!n` returns the element of `xs` at position n, counting from 0. In particular, `units!!0` = `"zero"`. And, yes, `units!!10` is undefined because `units` contains just ten elements, indexed from 0 to 9. In general, the functions we define in a script are *partial* functions that may not return well-defined results for each argument.

The next simplest version of the problem is when the number n has up to two digits, so $0 \leq n < 100$. Let `convert2` deal with this case. We will need to know what the digits are, so we first define

```
> digits2 :: Int -> (Int,Int)
> digits2 n = (div n 10, mod n 10)
```

The number `div n k` is the whole number of times k divides into n, and `mod n k` is the remainder. We can also write

```
    digits2 n = (n `div` 10, n `mod` 10)
```

The operators `` `div` `` and `` `mod` `` are infix versions of `div` and `mod`, that is, they come between their two arguments rather than before them. This device is useful for improving readability. For instance a mathematician would write x div y and x mod y for these expressions. Note that the back-quote symbol `` ` `` is different from the single quote symbol `'` used for describing individual characters.

Now we can define

```
> convert2 :: Int -> String
> convert2 = combine2 . digits2
```

The definition of `combine2` uses the Haskell syntax for *guarded equations*:

```
> combine2 :: (Int,Int) -> String
> combine2 (t,u)
>    | t==0           = units!!u
>    | t==1           = teens!!u
>    | 2<=t && u==0 = tens!!(t-2)
>    | 2<=t && u/=0 = tens!!(t-2) ++ "-" ++ units!!u
```

To understand this code you need to know that the Haskell symbols for equality and comparison tests are as follows:

```
==   (equals to)
/=   (not equals to)
<=   (less than or equal to)
```

These functions have well-defined types that we will give later on.

You also need to know that the conjunction of two tests is denoted by &&. Thus a && b returns the boolean value True if both a and b do, and False otherwise. In fact

```
(&&) :: Bool -> Bool -> Bool
```

The type Bool will be described in more detail in the following chapter.

Finally, (++) denotes the operation of concatenating two lists. It doesn't matter what the type of the list elements is, so

```
(++) :: [a] -> [a] -> [a]
```

For example, in the equation

```
[sin,cos] ++ [tan] = [sin,cos,tan]
```

we are concatenating two lists of functions (each of type Float -> Float), while in

```
"sin cos" ++ " tan" = "sin cos tan"
```

we are concatenating two lists of characters.

The definition of combine2 is arrived at by carefully considering all the possible cases that can arise. A little reflection shows that there are three main cases, namely when the tens part t is 0, 1 or greater than 1. In the first two cases we can give the answer immediately, but the third case has to be divided into two subcases, namely when the units part u is 0 or not 0. The order in which we write the cases, that is, the order of the individual guarded equations, is unimportant as the guards are disjoint from one another (that is, no two guards can be true) and together they cover all cases.

We could also have written

```
combine2 :: (Int,Int) -> String
combine2 (t,u)
    | t==0      = units!!u
    | t==1      = teens!!u
    | u==0      = tens!!(t-2)
    | otherwise = tens!!(t-2) ++ "-" ++ units!!u
```

but now the order in which we write the equations is crucial. The guards are evaluated from top to bottom, taking the right-hand side corresponding to the first guard that evaluates to True. The identifier otherwise is just a synonym for True, so the last clause captures all the remaining cases.

There is yet another way of writing convert2:

```
convert2 :: Int -> String
convert2 n
   | t==0       = units!!u
   | t==1       = teens!!u
   | u==0       = tens!!(t-2)
   | otherwise = tens!!(t-2) ++ "-" ++ units!!u
   where (t,u) = (n `div` 10, n `mod` 10)
```

This makes use of a where *clause*. Such a clause introduces a *local* definition or definitions whose *context* or *scope* is the whole of the right-hand side of the definition of convert2. Such clauses are very useful in structuring definitions and making them more readable. In the present example, the where clause obviates the need for an explicit definition of digits2.

That was reasonably easy, so now let us consider convert3 which takes a number n in the range $0 \leq n < 1000$, so n has up to three digits. The definition is

```
> convert3 :: Int -> String
> convert3 n
>    | h==0       = convert2 t
>    | n==0       = units!!h ++ " hundred"
>    | otherwise = units!!h ++ " hundred and " ++ convert2 t
>    where (h,t) = (n `div` 100, n `mod` 100)
```

We break up the number in this way because we can make use of convert2 for numbers that are less than 100.

Now suppose n lies in the range $0 \leq n < 1,000,000$, so n can have up to six digits. Following exactly the same pattern as before, we can define

```
> convert6 :: Int -> String
> convert6 n
>    | m==0       = convert3 h
>    | h==0       = convert3 m ++ " thousand"
>    | otherwise = convert3 m ++ " thousand" ++ link h ++
>                   convert3 h
>    where (m,h) = (n `div` 1000,n `mod` 1000)
```

There will be a connecting word 'and' between the words for *m* and *h* just in the case that $0 < m$ and $0 < h < 100$. Thus

```
> link :: Int -> String
> link h = if h < 100 then " and " else " "
```

This definition makes use of a conditional expression

```
    if <test> then <expr1> else <expr2>
```

We could also have used guarded equations:

```
    link h | h < 100   = " and "
           | otherwise = " "
```

Sometimes one is more readable, sometimes the other. The names `if`, `then` and `else`, along with some others, are *reserved words* in Haskell, which means that we cannot use them as names for things we want to define.

Notice how the definition of `convert6` has been constructed in terms of the simpler function `convert3`, which in turn has been defined in terms of the even simpler function `convert2`. That is often the way with function definitions. In this example consideration of the simpler cases is not wasted because these simple cases can be used in the final definition.

One more thing: we have now named the function we are after as `convert6`, but we started off by saying the name should be `convert`. No problem:

```
> convert :: Int -> String
> convert = convert6
```

What we would like to do now is actually use the computer to apply `convert` to some arguments. How?

1.5 The Haskell Platform

If you visit the site `www.haskell.org`, you will see how to download *The Haskell Platform*. This is a large collection of tools and packages that can be used to run Haskell scripts. The platform comes in three versions, one for each of Windows, Mac and Linux. We deal only with the Windows version, the others being similar.

One of the tools is an interactive calculator, called GHCi. This is short for *Glasgow Haskell Compiler Interpreter*. The calculator is available as a Windows system called WinGHCi. If you open this window, you will get something like

```
GHCi, version 7.6.3: http://www.haskell.org/ghc/  :? for help
Loading package ghc-prim ... linking ... done.
Loading package integer-gmp ... linking ... done.
Loading package base ... linking ... done.
Prelude>
```

The prompt `Prelude>` means that the standard library of prelude functions, pre-declared types and other values is loaded. You can now use GHCi as a super-calculator:

```
Prelude> 3^5
243
Prelude> import Data.Char
Prelude Data.Char> map toLower "HELLO WORLD!"
"hello world!"
Prelude Data.Char>
```

The function `toLower` resides in the library `Data.Char`. After importing this library you have access to the functions defined in the library. Note that the prompt changes and now indicates the libraries that have been loaded. Such prompts can grow in size very quickly. But we can always change the prompt:

```
Prelude> :set prompt ghci>
ghci>
```

For brevity we will use this prompt throughout the book.

You can load a script, `Numbers2Words.lhs` say, that contains the definition of convert as follows:

```
ghci> :load "Numbers2Words.lhs"
[1 of 1] Compiling Main    ( Numbers2Words.lhs, interpreted )
Ok, modules loaded: Main.
ghci>
```

We will explain what modules are in the next chapter. Now you can type, for example,

```
ghci> convert 301123
"three hundred and one thousand one hundred and twenty-three"
ghci>
```

We end the chapter with some exercises. These contain additional points of interest and should be regarded as an integral part of the text. The same is true for all subsequent chapters, so please read the questions even if you do not answer them. The answers are given afterwards.

1.6 Exercises

Exercise A

Consider the function

```
double :: Integer -> Integer
double x = 2*x
```

that doubles an integer. What are the values of the following expressions?

```
map double [1,4,4,3]
map (double . double) [1,4,4,3]
map double []
```

Suppose sum :: [Integer] -> Integer is a function that sums a list of integers. Which of the following assertions are true and why?

```
sum . map double = double . sum
sum . map sum    = sum . concat
sum . sort       = sum
```

You will need to recall what the function concat does. The function sort sorts a list of numbers into ascending order.

Exercise B

In Haskell, functional application takes precedence over every other operator, so double 3+4 means (double 3)+4, not double (3+4). Which of the following expressions is a rendering of $\sin^2 \theta$ into Haskell?

```
sin^2 theta          sin theta^2      (sin theta)^2
```

(Exponentiation is denoted by (^).) How would you express $\sin 2\theta / 2\pi$ as a well-formed Haskell expression?

Exercise C

As we said in the text, a character, i.e. an element of Char, is denoted using single quotes, and a string is denoted using double quotes. In particular the string "Hello World!" is just a much shorter way of writing the list

```
['H','e','l','l','o',' ','W','o','r','l','d','!']
```

General lists can be written with brackets and commas. (By the way, parentheses are round, brackets are square, and braces are curly.) The expressions 'H' and "H" therefore have different types. What are they? What is the difference between 2001 and "2001"?

The operation ++ concatenates two lists. Simplify

```
[1,2,3] ++ [3,2,1]
"Hello" ++ " World!"
[1,2,3] ++ []
"Hello" ++ "" ++ "World!"
```

Exercise D

In the common words example we started off by converting every letter in the text to lowercase, and then we computed the words in the text. An alternative is to do things the other way round, first computing the words and then converting each letter in each word to lowercase. The first method is expressed by words . map toLower. Give a similar expression for the second method.

Exercise E

An operator $\oplus$ is said to be *associative* if $x \oplus (y \oplus z) = (x \oplus y) \oplus z$. Is numerical addition associative? Is list concatenation associative? Is functional composition associative? Give an example of an operator on numbers that is not associative.

An element e is said to be an *identity element* of $\oplus$ if $x \oplus e = e \oplus x = x$ for all x. What are the identity elements of addition, concatenation and functional composition?

Exercise F

My wife has a book with the title

EHT CDOORRSSW AAAGMNR ACDIINORTY.

It contains lists of entries like this:

```
6-letter words
--------------
...
eginor: ignore,region
eginrr: ringer
eginrs: resign,signer,singer
...
```

Yes, it is an anagram dictionary. The letters of the anagrams are sorted and the results are stored in dictionary order. Associated with each anagram are the English words with the same letters. Describe how you would go about designing a function

```
anagrams :: Int -> [Word] -> String
```

so that `anagrams n` takes a list of English words in alphabetical order, extracts just the *n*-letter words and produces a string that, when displayed, gives a list of the anagram entries for the *n*-letter words. You are not expected to be able to define the various functions; just give suitable names and types and describe what each of them is supposed to do.

Exercise G

Let's end with a song:

```
One man went to mow
Went to mow a meadow
One man and his dog
Went to mow a meadow

Two men went to mow
Went to mow a meadow
Two men, one man and his dog
Went to mow a meadow

Three men went to mow
Went to mow a meadow
Three men, two men, one man and his dog
Went to mow a meadow
```

Write a Haskell function `song :: Int -> String` so that `song n` is the song when there are n men. Assume n<10.

To print the song, type for example

```
ghci> putStrLn (song 5)
```

The function `putStrLn` will be explained in the following chapter. I suggest starting with

```
song n  = if n==0 then ""
            else song (n-1) ++ "\n" ++ verse n
verse n = line1 n ++ line2 n ++ line3 n ++ line4 n
```

This defines song *recursively*.

1.7 Answers

Answer to Exercise A

```
map double [1,4,4,3]               = [2,8,8,6]
map (double . double) [1,4,4,3] = [4,16,16,12]
map double []                      = []
```

You will gather from this that [] denotes the empty list.

All the following equations hold:

```
sum . map double = double . sum
sum . map sum    = sum . concat
sum . sort       = sum
```

In fact, each of these three equations are consequences of the three simpler laws:

```
a*(x+y) = a*x + a*y
x+(y+z) = (x+y)+z
x+y     = y+x
```

Of course, we don't know yet how to *prove* that the equations hold. (By the way, to avoid fuss we will often use a typewriter = sign to denote the equality of two Haskell expressions written in typewriter font. But a mathematical = sign is used in equations such as $\sin 2\theta = 2 \sin \theta \cos \theta$.)

Answer to Exercise B

Both sin theta^2 and (sin theta)^2 are okay, but not sin^2 theta.

Here is the rendering of $\sin 2\theta / 2\pi$ in Haskell:

```
sin (2*theta) / (2*pi)
```

Note that

```
sin (2*theta) / 2 * pi = (sin (2*theta) / 2) * pi
```

which is not what we want. The reason is that operators such as / and * at the same level of precedence associate to the left in expressions. More on this in the next chapter.

Answer to Exercise C

```
'H'     :: Char
"H"     :: [Char]
2001    :: Integer
"2001"  :: [Char]
```

By the way, `'\'` is used as an *escape* character, so `'\n'` is the newline character, and `'\t'` is the tab character. Also, `'\\'` is the backslash character, and `"\\n"` is a list of two characters, a backslash and the letter n. As a consequence, the file path `C:\firefox\stuff` is written as the Haskell string `"C:\\firefox\\stuff"`.

```
[1,2,3] ++ [3,2,1]       = [1,2,3,3,2,1]
"Hello" ++ " World!"     = "Hello World!"
[1,2,3] ++ []            = [1,2,3]
"Hello" ++ "" ++"World!" = "HelloWorld!"
```

If you got the last two right, you will have appreciated that `[]` is an empty list of anything, but `""` is an empty list of characters.

Answer to Exercise D

The clue is in the phrase 'converting each letter in each word to lowercase'. Converting each letter in a single word is expressed by `map toLower`, so the answer is `map (map toLower) . words`. That means the following equation holds:

```
words . map toLower = map (map toLower) . words
```

Answer to Exercise E

Numerical addition, list concatenation and functional composition are all associative. But of course, numerical subtraction isn't. Nor is exponentiation. The identity element of addition is 0, the identity element of concatenation is the empty list, and the identity element of functional composition is the identity function:

```
id :: a -> a
id x = x
```

Answer to Exercise F

This exercise follows Section 1.3 quite closely. One way of computing the function `anagrams n` is as follows:

1. Extract the words of length *n*, using a function

```
getWords :: Int -> [Word] -> [Word]
```

2. Take each word and add a label to it. The label consists of the characters of the word, sorted into alphabetical order. For example, word is turned into the pair ("dorw","word") This labelling is achieved by the function

```
addLabel :: Word -> (Label,Word)
```

where

```
type Label = [Char]
```

3. Sort the list of labelled words into alphabetical order of label, using the function

```
sortLabels :: [(Label,Word)] -> [(Label,Word)]
```

4. Replace each group of adjacent labelled words with the same label with a single entry consisting of a pair in which the first component is the common label and the second component is a list of words with that label. This uses a function

```
groupByLabel :: [(Label,Word)] -> [(Label,[Word])]
```

5. Replace each entry by a string using a function

```
showEntry :: [(Label,[Word])] -> String
```

and concatenate the results.

That gives

```
anagrams n = concat . map showEntry . groupByLabel .
             sortLabels . map addLabel . getWords n
```

Answer to Exercise G

One possible solution:

```
song n  = if n==0 then ""
          else song (n-1) ++ "\n" ++ verse n
verse n = line1 n ++ line2 n ++ line3 n ++ line4 n

line1 n = if n==1 then
             "One man went to mow\n"
          else
             numbers!!(n-2) ++ " men went to mow\n"
line2 n = "Went to mow a meadow\n"
line3 n = if n==1 then
             "One man and his dog\n"
          else
```

```
            numbers!!(n-2) ++ " men, " ++ count (n-2)
               ++ "one man and his dog\n"
  line4 n = "Went to mow a meadow\n\n"

  count n = if n==0 then ""
            else
            numbs!!(n-1) ++ " men, " ++ count (n-1)

  numbers = ["Two", "Three", "Four", "Five", "Six",
             "Seven", "Eight", "Nine"]
  numbs   = ["two", "three", "four", "five", "six",
             "seven", "eight"]
```

Notice that we have omitted to declare the types of the component functions and values in this script. Although Haskell will infer the correct types, it is usually a good idea to put them in for all functions and other values, however simple the types may be. Scripts with explicit type signatures are clearer to read and provide a useful check on the validity of definitions.

1.8 Chapter notes

If you are interested in the origins of Haskell, you should definitely read *The History of Haskell*, a copy of which is obtainable at

```
research.microsoft.com/~simonpj/papers/history-of-haskell
```

One of the abiding strengths of Haskell is that it wasn't designed to be a closed language, and researchers were encouraged to implement novel programming ideas and techniques by building language extensions or libraries. Consequently, Haskell is a large language and there are numerous books, tutorials and papers devoted to various aspects of the subject, including the recent *Parallel and Concurrent Programming in Haskell* by Simon Marlow (O'Reilly, 2013). Pointers to much of the material can be found at www.haskell.org. But three books in particular were open on my desk while writing this text. The first is *Haskell 98, Languages and Libraries, The Revised Report* (Cambridge University Press, 2003), edited by Simon Peyton Jones. This is an indispensable aid in understanding the nitty-gritty of the first standard version of Haskell, called Haskell 98. An online version of the report is available at

```
www.haskell.org/onlinereport
```

The present book mostly follows this standard, though it does not cover the whole language by any means.

Since then a new standard, Haskell 2010, has been released; see

```
haskell.org/onlinereport/haskell2010/
```

One change is that module names are now hierarchical, so we write `Data.List` rather than just `List` for the library of list utilities.

The second two are textbooks: *Real World Haskell* (O'Reilly, 2009) by Bryan O'Sullivan, John Goerzen and Don Stewart; and *Programming in Haskell* (Cambridge, 2007) by Graham Hutton. As its name implies, the former deals mostly with highly practical applications, while the latter is another introductory text. Graham Hutton did suggest to me, albeit with a grin, that my book should be called *Ivory Tower Haskell*.

There is a fascinating history concerning the common words problem. Jon Bentley invited one programmer, Don Knuth, to write a literate WEB program for the problem, and another programmer, Doug McIlroy, to write a literary review of it. The result was published in Bentley's *Programming Pearls* column in *Communications of the ACM*, vol. 29, no. 6 (June 1986).

Chapter 2

Expressions, types and values

In Haskell every *well-formed* expression has, by definition, a well-formed *type*. Each well-formed expression has, by definition, a *value*. Given an expression for evaluation,

- GHCi checks that the expression is *syntactically* correct, that is, it conforms to the rules of syntax laid down by Haskell.

- If it is, GHCi infers a type for the expression, or checks that the type supplied by the programmer is correct.

- Provided the expression is well-typed, GHCi evaluates the expression by reducing it to its simplest possible form to produce a value. Provided the value is printable, GHCi then prints it at the terminal.

In this chapter we continue the study of Haskell by taking a closer look at these processes.

2.1 A session with GHCi

One way of finding out whether or not an expression is well-formed is of course to use GHCi. There is a command `:type expr` which, provided `expr` is well-formed, will return its type. Here is a session with GHCi (with some of GHCi's responses abbreviated):

```
ghci> 3 +4)
<interactive>:1:5: parse error on input `)'
```

GHCi is complaining that on line 1 the character `')'` at position 5 is unexpected; in other words, the expression is not syntactically correct.

```
ghci> :type 3+4
3+4 :: Num a => a
```

GHCi is asserting that the type of 3+4 is a number. More on this below.

```
ghci> :type if 1==0 then 'a' else "a"
<interactive>:1:23:
Couldn't match expected type `Char' with actual type `[Char]'
In the expression: "a"
In the expression: if 1 == 0 then 'a' else "a"
```

GHCi expects the types of expr1 and expr2 in a conditional expression

```
    if test then expr1 else expr2
```

to be the same. But a character is not a list of characters so the conditional expression, though conforming to the rules of Haskell syntax, is not well-formed.

```
ghci> sin sin 0.5
<interactive>:1:1:
No instance for (Floating (a0 -> a0))
arising from a use of `sin'
Possible fix: add an instance declaration for
  (Floating (a0 -> a0))
In the expression: sin sin 0.5
In an equation for `it': it = sin sin 0.5
```

GHCi gives a rather opaque error message, complaining that the expression is not well-formed.

```
ghci> sin (sin 0.5)
0.4612695550331807
```

Ah, GHCi is happy with this one.

```
ghci> :type map
map :: (a -> b) -> [a] -> [b]
```

GHCi returns the type of the function map.

```
ghci> map
<interactive>:1:1:
No instance for (Show ((a0 -> b0) -> [a0] -> [b0]))
arising from a use of `print'
Possible fix:
add an instance declaration for
```

```
(Show ((a0 -> b0) -> [a0] -> [b0]))
```
In a stmt of an interactive GHCi command: print it

GHCi is saying that it doesn't know how to print a function.

```
ghci> :type 1 `div` 0
1 `div` 0 :: Integral a => a
```

GHCi is asserting that the type of 1 `div` 0 is an integral number. The expression
1 `div` 0 is therefore well-formed and possesses a value.

```
ghci> 1 `div` 0
*** Exception: divide by zero
```

GHCi returns an error message. So what is the value of 1 `div` 0? The answer
is that it is a special value, written mathematically as $\bot$ and pronounced 'bottom'.
In fact, Haskell provides a predeclared name for this value, except that it is called
undefined, not bottom.

```
ghci> :type undefined
undefined :: a
ghci> undefined
*** Exception: Prelude.undefined
```

Haskell is not expected to produce the value $\bot$. It may return with an error message, or remain perpetually silent, computing an infinite loop, until we interrupt the
computation. It may even cause GHCi to crash. Oh, yes.

```
ghci> x*x where x = 3
<interactive>:1:5: parse error on input `where'

ghci> let x = 3 in x*x
9
```

A where clause does *not* qualify an expression in Haskell, but the whole of the
right-hand side of a definition. Thus the first example is not a well-formed expression. On the other hand, a let expression

```
    let <defs> in <expr>
```

is well-formed, at least assuming the definitions in <defs> are and the expression
<expr> is. Let-expressions appear infrequently in what follows, but occasionally
they can be useful.

2.2 Names and operators

As we have seen, a script is a collection of names and their definitions. Names for functions and values begin with a lowercase letter, except for data constructors (see later on) which begin with an uppercase letter. Types (e.g. Int), type classes (e.g. Num) and modules (e.g. Prelude or Data.Char) also begin with an uppercase letter.

An operator is a special kind of function name that appears between its (two) arguments, such as the + in x + y or the ++ in xs ++ ys. Operator names begin with a symbol. Any (non-symbolic) function of two arguments can be converted into an operator by enclosing it in back quotes, and any operator can be converted to a prefix name by enclosing it in parentheses. For example,

```
3 + 4     is the same as   (+) 3 4
div 3 4   is the same as   3 `div` 4
```

Operators have different levels of precedence (binding power). For example,

```
3 * 4 + 2       means   (3 * 4) + 2
xs ++ yss !! 3  means   xs ++ (yss !! 3)
```

If in any doubt, add parentheses to remove possible ambiguity. By the way, we can use any names we like for lists, including x, y, goodylist, and so on. But a simple aid to memory is to use x for things, xs for lists of things, and xss for lists of lists of things. That explains why we wrote yss in the expression yss !! 3 in the last line above.

Operators with the same level of precedence normally have an order of association, either to the left or right. For example, the usual arithmetic operators associate to the left:

```
3 - 4 - 2  means   (3 - 4) - 2
3 - 4 + 2  means   (3 - 4) + 2
3 / 4 * 5  means   (3 / 4) * 5
```

Functional application, which has higher precedence than any other operator, also associates to the left:

```
eee bah gum     means   (eee bah) gum
eee bah gum*2   means   ((eee bah) gum)*2
```

Some operators associate to the right:

```
(a -> b) -> [a] -> [b]   means   (a -> b) -> ([a] -> [b])
x ^ y ^ z                means   x ^ (y ^ z)
eee . bah . gum          means   eee . (bah . gum)
```

Of course, if an operator, such as functional composition, is associative the order
has no effect on meaning (i.e. the value is the same). Again, one can always add
parentheses to remove possible ambiguity.

We can declare new operators; for example:

```
(+++) :: Int -> Int -> Int
x +++ y = if even x then y else x + y
```

The conditional expression has low binding power, so the expression above means

```
if even x then y else (x + y)
```

not (if even x then y else x) + y. Again, one can always use parentheses
to group differently.

If we like we can declare a precedence level and an order of association for (+++),
but we won't spell out how.

Sections and lambda expressions

It is a matter of style, but in the main we prefer to write scripts in which all the
little helper functions are named explicitly. Thus if we need a function that adds 1
to a number, or doubles a number, then we might choose to name such functions
explicitly:

```
succ, double :: Integer -> Integer
succ n   = n+1
double n = 2*n
```

However, Haskell provides alternative ways of naming these two functions, namely
(+1) and (2*). The device is called a *section*. In a section one of the arguments of
an operator is included along with the operator. Thus

```
(+1) n = n+1
(0<) n = 0<n
(<0) n = n<0
(1/) x = 1/x
```

Sections are certainly attractive ways of naming simple helper functions and we henceforth accept them onto our list of Good Things to Use in Moderation.

There is one important caveat about sections: although (+1) is the section that adds 1 to a number, (-1) is *not* the section that subtracts 1. Instead (-1) is just the number -1. Haskell uses the minus sign both as the binary operation of subtraction and as a prefix to denote negative numbers.

Now suppose we want a function that doubles a number and then adds 1 to the answer. This function is captured by the composition (+1) . (*2) of two sections. But the result is unsatisfying because it looks a little abstruse; anyone reading it would have to pause for a moment to see what it meant. The alternative seems to be to give the function a name, but what would be a suitable name? Nothing helpful really comes to mind.

The alternative is to use a *lambda expression* \n -> 2*n+1. It is called a lambda expression because mathematically the function would be written as $\lambda n.2*n+1$. Read the expression as 'that function of *n* which returns $2*n+1$'. For example,

```
ghci>  map (\n -> 2*n+1) [1..5]
[3,5,7,9,11]
```

Once in a while a lambda expression seems the best way to describe some function, but only once in a while and we will take them out of the box only on rare occasions.

2.3 Evaluation

Haskell evaluates an expression by reducing it to its simplest possible form and printing the result. For example, suppose we have defined

```
    sqr :: Integer -> Integer
    sqr x = x*x
```

There are basically two ways to reduce the expression sqr (3+4) to its simplest possible form, namely 49. Either we can evaluate 3+4 first, or else apply the definition of sqr first:

```
  sqr (3+4)                    sqr (3+4)
= sqr 7                      = let x = 3+4 in x*x
= let x = 7 in x*x           = let x = 7 in x*x
= 7*7                        = 7*7
= 49                         = 49
```

The number of reduction steps is the same in each case, but the order of the reduction steps is slightly different. The method on the left is called *innermost reduction* and also *eager evaluation*; the one on the right is called *outermost reduction* or *lazy evaluation*. With eager evaluation arguments are always evaluated before a function is applied. With lazy evaluation the definition of a function is installed at once and only when they are needed are the arguments to the function evaluated.

Doesn't seem much of a difference, does it? But consider the following (slightly abbreviated) evaluation sequences concerning the function `fst` that returns the first element of a pair, so `fst (x,y) = x`:

```
    fst (sqr 1,sqr 2)           fst (sqr 1,sqr 2)
  = fst (1*1,sqr 2)           = let p = (sqr 1,sqr 2)
  = fst (1,sqr 2)               in fst p
  = fst (1,2*2)               = sqr 1
  = fst (1,4)                 = 1*1
  = 1                         = 1
```

The point here is that under eager evaluation the value `sqr 2` is computed, while under lazy evaluation that value is not needed and is not computed.

Now suppose we add the definitions

```
infinity :: Integer
infinity = 1 + infinity

three :: Integer -> Integer
three x = 3
```

Evaluating `infinity` will cause GHCi to go into a long, silent think trying to compute 1 + (1 + (1 + (1 + (1 + ... until eventually it runs out of space and returns an error message. The value of `infinity` is ⊥.

Again there are two ways to evaluate `three infinity`:

```
    three infinity                 three infinity
  = three (1+infinity)           = let x = infinity in 3
  = three (1+(1+infinity))       = 3
  = ...
```

Here eager evaluation gets stuck in a loop trying to evaluate `infinity`, while lazy evaluation returns the answer 3 at once. We don't need to evaluate the argument of `three` in order to return 3.

One more definition, a version of the factorial function:

```
factorial :: Integer -> Integer
factorial n = fact (n,1)


fact :: (Integer,Integer) -> Integer
fact (x,y) = if x==0 then y else fact (x-1,x*y)
```

This is another example of a *recursive definition* (the definition of infinity was also recursive, and so was the function song in the previous chapter). Expressions involving recursive functions are evaluated like any other definition.

Here the two evaluation schemes result in the following sequence of reduction steps (we hide the steps involving simplification of the conditional expression to make another point):

```
   factorial 3                     factorial 3
 = fact (3,1)                    = fact (3,1)
 = fact (3-1,3*1)                = fact (3-1,3*1)
 = fact (2,3)                    = fact (2-1,2*(3*1))
 = fact (2-1,2*3)                = fact (1-1,1*(2*(3*1)))
 = fact (1,6)                    = 1*(2*(3*1))
 = fact (1-1,1*6)                = 1*(2*3)
 = fact (0,6)                    = 1*6
 = 6                             = 6
```

The point to appreciate is that, while the number of reduction steps is basically the same, lazy evaluation requires much more space to achieve the answer. The expression 1*(2*(3*1)) is built up in memory before being evaluated.

The pros and cons of lazy evaluation are briefly as follows. On the plus side, lazy evaluation terminates whenever *any* reduction order terminates; it never takes more steps than eager evaluation, and sometimes infinitely fewer. On the minus side, it can require a lot more space and it is more difficult to understand the precise order in which things happen.

Haskell uses lazy evaluation. ML (another popular functional language) uses eager evaluation. Exercise D explores why lazy evaluation is a Good Thing. Lazy evaluation is considered further in Chapter 7.

A Haskell function f is said to be *strict* if f undefined = undefined, and *non-strict* otherwise. The function three is non-strict, while (+) is strict in both arguments. Because Haskell uses lazy evaluation we can define non-strict functions. That is why Haskell is referred to as a *non-strict* functional language.

2.4 Types and type classes

Haskell has built-in (or primitive) types such as `Int`, `Float` and `Char`. The type `Bool` of boolean values is defined in the standard prelude:

```
data Bool = False | True
```

This is an example of a *data declaration*. The type `Bool` is declared to have two data *constructors*, `False` and `True`. The type `Bool` has three values, not two: `False`, `True` and `undefined :: Bool`. Why do we need that last value? Well, consider the function

```
to :: Bool -> Bool
to b = not (to b)
```

The prelude definition of `not` is

```
not :: Bool -> Bool
not True  = False
not False = True
```

The definition of `to` is perfectly well-formed, but evaluating `to True` causes GHCi to go into an infinite loop, so its value is ⊥ of type `Bool`. We will have much more to say about data declarations in future chapters.

Haskell has built-in compound types, such as

`[Int]`	a list of elements, all of type `Int`
`(Int,Char)`	a pair consisting of an `Int` and a `Char`
`(Int,Char,Bool)`	a triple
`()`	an empty tuple
`Int -> Int`	a function from `Int` to `Int`

The sole inhabitant of the type `()` is also denoted by `()`. Actually, there is a second member of `()`, namely `undefined :: ()`. Now we can appreciate that there is a value ⊥ for every type.

As we have already said, when defining values or functions it is always a good idea to include the type signature as part of the definition.

Consider next the function `take n` that takes the first n elements of a list. This function made its appearance in the previous chapter. For example,

```
take 3 [1,2,3,4,5] = [1,2,3]
take 3 "category"  = "cat"
take 3 [sin,cos]   = [sin,cos]
```

What type should we assign to `take`? It doesn't matter what the type of the elements of the list is, so `take` is what is called a *polymorphic* function and we denote its type by

```
take :: Int -> [a] -> [a]
```

The a is a *type variable*. Type variables begin with a lowercase letter. Type variables can be instantiated to any type.

Similarly,

```
(++) :: [a] -> [a] -> [a]
map  :: (a -> b) -> [a] -> [b]
(.)  :: (b -> c) -> (a -> b) -> (a -> c)
```

The last line declares the polymorphic type of functional composition.

Next, what is the type of `(+)`? Here are some suggestions:

```
(+) :: Int -> Int -> Int
(+) :: Float -> Float -> Float
(+) :: a -> a -> a
```

The first two types seem too specific, while the last seems too general: we can't add two functions or two characters or two booleans, at least not in any obvious way.

The answer is to introduce *type classes*:

```
(+) :: Num a => a -> a -> a
```

This declaration asserts that `(+)` is of type `a -> a -> a` for any *number type* a. A type class, such as `Num`, has a collection of named methods, such as `(+)`, which can be defined differently for each instance of the type class. Type classes therefore provide for *overloaded* functions, functions with the same name but different definitions. Overloading is another kind of polymorphism.

Numbers are rather complicated, and are explained in more detail in the following chapter, so we illustrate type classes with a simpler type class

```
class Eq a  where
  (==),(/=) :: a -> a -> Bool
  x /= y    = not (x == y)
```

This introduces the Equality type class, members of which can use one and the same equality test `(==)` and inequality test `(/=)`. There is a *default* definition of `(/=)` as part of the class, so we only have to provide a definition of `(==)`.

To become a member of the Eq club we have to define an *instance*. For example,

```
instance Eq Bool  where
   x == y  = if x then y else not y

instance Eq Person  where
   x == y  = (pin x == pin y)
```

If `pin :: Person -> Pin` then we need `Eq Pin` for the last instance to be correct. Of course, we don't have to make `Person` a member of the Equality club; we can always define

```
samePerson :: Person -> Person -> Bool
samePerson x y = (pin x == pin y)
```

But we can't use `(==)` instead of `samePerson` unless we make an instance declaration.

Here are simplified versions of two other type classes, `Ord` and `Show`:

```
class (Eq a) => Ord a  where
  (<),(<=),(>=),(>) :: a -> a -> Bool
  x < y  = not (x >= y)
  x <= y = x == y || x < y
  x >= y = x == y || x > y
  x > y  = not (x <= y)

class Show a  where
   show :: a -> String
```

The boolean operator `(||)` denotes disjunction: `a || b` is true only if at least one of a and b is true. We can define this operator by

```
(||) :: Bool -> Bool -> Bool
a || b = if a then True else b
```

The default definitions of the `Ord` methods are mutually dependent, so one has to provide a specific definition of at least one of them in any instance to break the dependency (unlike Eq where only `(/=)` was given a default definition). The type class `Ord` needs Eq as a *superclass* because it makes use of `(==)` in the default definitions of the four comparison operations.

The type class `Show` is used for displaying results. Haskell cannot display the result of a computation unless the type of the result is a member of `Show`. Let us explain this in a little more detail.

2.5 Printing values

We begin with a mystery:

```
ghci> "Hello ++"\n"++ "young" ++"\n"++ "lovers"
"Hello\nyoung\nlovers"
```

Oh. What we wanted was

```
Hello
young
lovers
```

Why didn't Haskell print that?

The reason is that after evaluating a well-formed expression to produce a value, Haskell applies show to the value to produce a string that can be printed at the terminal. Applying show to a value v produces a string that when printed looks exactly like v: Thus,

```
show 42        = "42"
show 42.3      = "42.3"
show 'a'       = "'a'"
show "hello\n" = "\"hello\\n\""
```

Printing the result involves the use of a Haskell *command*

```
putStrLn :: String -> IO ()
```

The type IO a is a special type, the type of input–output computations that when executed have some interaction with the outside world and return a value of type a. If the return value is uninteresting, as with putStrLn, we use the null-tuple value ().

So, Haskell uniformly applies a show-and-put strategy to print values. Since the greeting above is already a string, we really want to miss out the show step and go straight to the put:

```
ghci> putStrLn ("Hello ++"\n"++ "young" ++"\n"++ "lovers")
Hello
young
lovers
```

Haskell provides many more commands for input–output, for reading and writing to files, for displaying graphics, and so on. Such commands have to be sequenced correctly, and for this Haskell provides a special notation, called do-notation. Commands are the subject of Chapter 10, and what follows is simply a foretaste of things to come.

To see an example, consider the common words problem of the previous chapter. There we defined a function

```
commonWords :: Int -> String -> String
```

such that `commonWords n` took a text string and returned a string giving a table of the n most common words in the text. The following program reads the text from a file, and writes the output to a file. The type `FilePath` is another synonym for a list of characters:

```
cwords :: Int -> FilePath -> FilePath -> IO()
cwords n infile outfile
   = do {text <- readFile infile;
         writeFile outfile (commonWords n text);
         putStrLn "cwords done!"}
```

Evaluating, for example

```
ghci> cwords 100 "c:\\WarAndPeace" "c:\\Results"
```

on a Windows platform will cause the file c:\WarAndPeace to be read, and the results printed to c:\Results. The program also prints a message to the terminal. The two component functions of the definition above have types

```
readFile  :: FilePath -> IO String
writeFile :: FilePath -> String -> IO ()
```

Suppose that we didn't want to call `cwords` from within an interactive session, but to use it as a stand-alone program. Here is one way. We need to define a value for an identifier main of type IO (). Here is such a program:

```
main
  = do {putStrLn "Take text from where:";
        infile <- getLine;
        putStrLn "How many words:";
        n <- getLine;
        putStrLn "Put results where:";
        outfile <- getLine;
        text <- readFile infile;
        writeFile outfile (commonWords (read n) text);
        putStrLn "cwords done!" }
```

For an explanation of read see Exercise H. Suppose the common words script is stored in the file cwords.lhs. We can compile it with GHC, the Glasgow Haskell Compiler:

```
$ ghc cwords.lhs
```

The compiled program will be stored in the file cwords.exe. To run the program under Windows, type

```
$ cwords
```

and follow the instructions.

2.6 Modules

Suppose we thought that the function commonWords was sufficiently useful that we wanted to incorporate it into other scripts. The way to do this is to turn the common words script into a *module*. First, we rewrite the script in the following way:

```
module CommonWords (commonWords) where
import Data.Char (toLower)
import Data.List (sort,words)
...
commonWords :: Int -> String -> String
...
```

The module declaration is followed by the name of the module, which must begin with a capital letter. Furthermore, the script has to be stored in a file called CommonWords.lhs to enable Haskell to find the module (at least, if you are using literate scripts; otherwise it would be CommonWords.hs). Following the name of the module is a list of *exports*, the functions, types and other values you want to be able to export to other scripts. The list of exports has to be enclosed in parentheses. Here we just export one function, commonWords. The exports are the only things defined in the module that are visible in other modules. Omitting the export list, and the surrounding parentheses, means that everything in the module is exported.

We can then compile the module using GHC and then import it into other scripts with the declaration

```
import CommonWords (commonWords)
```

There are two major advantages of Haskell modules. One is we can structure our scripts into bite-sized chunks, separating out little groups of related functions into

separate modules. The other advantage is that the functions in a compiled module
are much faster to evaluate because their definitions are compiled into machine-
specific code, leading to a much slicker reduction process. GHCi is an *interpreter*
rather than a compiler; it evaluates internal forms of expression that are much closer
to the source language of Haskell.

2.7 Haskell layout

The examples of do-notation used braces ({ and }) and semicolons; these are examples of *explicit layout*. Braces and semicolons are used only to control layout
and have no meaning as part of the language of Haskell expressions. We can use
them in other places too:

```
roots :: (Float,Float,Float) -> (Float,Float)
roots (a,b,c)
  | a == 0        = error "not quadratic"
  | disc < 0      = error "complex roots"
  | otherwise     = ((-b-r)/e, (-b+r)/e)
  where {disc = b*b - 4*a*c; r = sqrt d; e = 2*a}
```

Here the where clause uses explicit braces and semicolons rather than appealing
to Haskell's layout rules. Instead, we could have written

```
where disc = b*b - 4*a*c
      r     = sqrt d
      e     = 2*a
```

But we couldn't have written

```
where disc = b*b - 4*a*c
         r = sqrt d
         e = 2*a
```

The layout (or *offside*) rule takes effect whenever the opening brace is omitted after
the keyword where or do (and also after let). When this happens the indentation
of the next item, whether or not on a new line, is remembered. For each subsequent
line, if it is indented more, then the previous line is continued; if it is indented the
same amount, then a new item begins; and if it is indented less, then the layout list
is ended. At least, that's roughly the offside rule.

The offside rule explains why there is an indentation in the declarations of type
classes and instances:

```
class Foo a  where
   I am part of the class declaration.
   So am I.
Now the class declaration has ended.
```

You can always put in braces and semicolons if in any doubt. Actually the offside rule can still cause confusion when used with do-notation. So the recommendation is belts, braces and semicolons.

And you thought the football offside rule was complicated.

2.8 Exercises

Exercise A

On the subject of precedence, this question comes from Chris Maslanka's puzzle page in the *Guardian* newspaper:

'Is a half of two plus two equal to two or three?'

Exercise B

Some of the following expressions are not syntactically correct, while others are syntactically correct but do not have sensible types. Some are well-formed. Which is which? In the case of a well-formed expression, give a suitable type. Assume `double :: Int -> Int`. I suggest you don't use a computer to check your answers, but if you do, be prepared for some strange error messages.

The expressions are:

```
[0,1)
double -3
double (-3)
double double 0
if 1==0 then 2==1
"++" == "+" ++ "+"
[(+),(-)]
[[],[[]],[[[]]]]
concat ["tea","for",'2']
concat ["tea","for","2"]
```

Exercise C

In the good old days, one could write papers with titles such as

'The morphology of prex – an essay in meta-algorithmics'

These days, journals seem to want all words capitalised:

'The Morphology Of Prex – An Essay In Meta-algorithmics'

Write a function `modernise :: String -> String` which ensures that paper titles are capitalised as above. Here are some helpful questions to answer first:

1. The function `toLower :: Char -> Char` converts a letter to lowercase. What do you think is the name of the prelude function that converts a letter to upper-case?

2. The function `words :: String -> [Word]` was used in the previous chapter. What do you think the prelude function

   ```
   unwords :: [Word] -> String
   ```

   does? Hint: which, if either, of the following equations should hold?

   ```
   words . unwords = id
   unwords . words = id
   ```

3. The function `head :: [a] -> a` returns the head of a nonempty list, and `tail :: [a] -> [a]` returns the list that remains when the head is removed. Suppose a list has head `x` and tail `xs`. How would you reconstruct the list?

Exercise D

Beaver is an eager evaluator, while Susan is a lazy one.[1] How many times would Beaver evaluate `f` in computing `head (map f xs)` when `xs` is a list of length n? How many times would Susan? What alternative to `head . map f` would Beaver prefer?

The function `filter p` filters a list, retaining only those elements that satisfy the boolean test `p`. The type of `filter` is

```
filter :: (a -> Bool) -> [a] -> [a]
```

Susan would happily use `head . filter p` for a function that finds the first element of a list satisfying `p`. Why would Beaver not use the same expression?

Instead, Beaver would probably define something like

---

[1] If you don't know, google 'lazy susan' to discover what a lazy susan is.

```
first :: (a -> Bool) -> [a] -> a
first p xs | null xs    = error "Empty list"
           | p x        = ...
           | otherwise  = ...
           where x = head xs
```

The function `null` returns `True` on an empty list, and `False` otherwise. When evaluated, the expression `error message` stops execution and prints the string `message` at the terminal, so its value is ⊥. Complete the right-hand side of Beaver's definition.

What alternative might Beaver prefer to `head . filter p . map f`?

Exercise E

The type `Maybe` is declared in the standard prelude as follows:

```
data Maybe a = Nothing | Just a
                 deriving (Eq, Ord)
```

This declaration uses a `deriving` clause. Haskell can automatically generate instances of some standard type classes for some data declarations. In the present case the deriving clause means that we don't have to go through the tedium of writing

```
instance (Eq a) => Eq (Maybe a)
   Nothing == Nothing = True
   Nothing == Just y  = False
   Just x == Nothing  = False
   Just x == Just y   = (x == y)

instance (Ord a) => Ord (Maybe a)
   Nothing <= Nothing = True
   Nothing <= Just y  = True
   Just x <= Nothing  = False
   Just x <= Just y   = (x <= y)
```

The reason why `Nothing` is declared to be less than `Just y` is simply because the constructor `Nothing` comes before the constructor `Just` in the data declaration for `Maybe`.

The reason why the `Maybe` type is useful is that it provides a systematic way of handling failure. Consider again the function

```
first p = head . filter p
```

of the previous exercise. Both Eager Beaver and Lazy Susan produced versions of this function that stopped execution and returned an error message when `first p` was applied to the empty list. That's not very satisfactory. Much better is to define

```
first :: (a -> Bool) -> [a] -> Maybe a
```

Now failure is handled gracefully by returning `Nothing` if there is no element of the list that satisfies the test.

Give a suitable definition of this version of `first`.

Finally, count the number of functions with type `Maybe a -> Maybe a`.

Exercise F

Here is a function for computing x to the power n, where $n \geq 0$:

```
exp :: Integer -> Integer -> Integer
exp x n | n == 0    = 1
        | n == 1    = x
        | otherwise = x*exp x (n-1)
```

How many multiplications does it take to evaluate `exp x n`?

Dick, a clever programmer, claims he can compute `exp x n` with far fewer multiplications:

```
exp x n | n == 0  = 1
        | n == 1  = x
        | even n   = ...
        | odd n    = ...
```

Fill in the dots and say how many multiplications it takes to evaluate the expression `exp x n` by Dick's method, assuming $2^p \leq n < 2^{p+1}$.

Exercise G

Suppose a date is represented by three integers $(day, month, year)$. Define a function `showDate :: Date -> String` so that, for example,

```
showDate (10,12,2013) = "10th December, 2013"
showDate (21,11,2020) = "21st November, 2020"
```

You need to know that `Int` is a member of the type class `Show`, so that `show n` produces a string that is the decimal representation of the integer n.

Exercise H

The credit card company Foxy issues cards with ten-digit card-identification numbers (CINs). The first eight digits are arbitrary but the number formed from the last two digits is a checksum equal to the sum of the first eight digits. For example, "6324513428" is a valid CIN because the sum of the first eight digits is 28.

Construct a function `addSum :: CIN -> CIN` that takes a string consisting of eight digits and returns a string of ten digits that includes the checksum. Thus `CIN` is a type synonym for `String`, though restricted to strings of digits. (Note that Haskell type synonyms cannot enforce type constraints such as this.) You will need to convert between a digit character and the corresponding number. One direction is easy: just use `show`. The other direction is also fairly easy:

```
getDigit :: Char -> Int
getDigit c = read [c]
```

The function `read` is a method of the type class `Read` and has type

```
read :: Read a => String -> a
```

The type class `Read` is dual to `Show` and `read` is dual to `show`. For example,

```
ghci> read "123" :: Int
123
ghci> read "123" :: Float
123.0
```

The function `read` has to be supplied with the type of the result. One can always add *type annotations* to expressions in this way.

Now construct a function `valid :: CIN -> Bool` that checks whether an identification number is valid. The function `take` might prove useful.

Exercise I

By definition a *palindrome* is a string that, ignoring punctuation symbols, blank characters and whether or not a letter is in lowercase or uppercase, reads the same forwards and backwards. Write an interactive program

```
palindrome :: IO ()
```

which, when run, conducts an interactive session, such as

```
ghci> palindrome
Enter a string:
```

```
Madam, I'm Adam
Yes!

ghci> palindrome
Enter a string:
A Man, a plan, a canal - Suez!
No!

ghci> palindrome
Enter a string:
Doc, note I dissent. A fast never prevents a fatness.
I diet on cod.
Yes!
```

The function isAlpha :: Char -> Bool tests whether a character is a letter, and reverse :: [a] -> [a] reverses a list. The function reverse is provided in the standard prelude and isAlpha can be imported from the library Data.Char.

2.9 Answers

Answer to Exercise A

The answer to Maslanka's puzzle is 'Yes!' This little puzzle has fooled a number of distinguished computer scientists.

Answer to Exercise B

My GHCi session produced (with explanations added):

```
ghci> :type [0,1)
<interactive>:1:5: parse error on input `)'
```

GHCi knows that ')' is wrong, though it is not smart enough to suggest ']'.

```
ghci> :type double -3
<interactive>:1:9:
No instance for (Num (Int -> Int))
arising from the literal `3'
Possible fix: add an instance declaration for
  (Num (Int -> Int))
```

```
In the second argument of `(-)', namely `3'
In the expression: double - 3
```

The explanation of the error message is that numerical subtraction (-) has type
Num a => a -> a. For double - 3 to be well-formed (yes, it was typed as
double -3 but the spaces are not significant here), double has to be a number, so
the class instance Num (Int -> Int) is required. But there isn't one: you cannot
sensibly subtract a number from a function.

```
ghci> double (-3)
-6
ghci> double double 0
<interactive>:1:1:
The function `double' is applied to two arguments,
but its type `Int -> Int' has only one
In the expression: double double 0
In an equation for `it': it = double double 0
```

Most of GHCi's error message is clear.

```
ghci> if 1==0 then 2==1

<interactive>:1:18:
parse error (possibly incorrect indentation)
```

Conditional expressions are incomplete without an 'else' clause.

```
ghci> "++" == "+" ++ "+"
True
```

Both sides are well-formed and denote the same list.

```
ghci> [(+),(-)]
<interactive>:1:1:
No instance for (Show (a0 -> a0 -> a0))
arising from a use of `print'
Possible fix:
add an instance declaration for
  (Show (a0 -> a0 -> a0))
In a stmt of an interactive GHCi command: print it
```

To display the value [(+),(-)] we have to be able to show its elements. But no
way of showing functions has been provided.

```
ghci> :type [[],[[]],[[[]]]]
```

```
[[],[[]],[[[]]]] :: [[[[a]]]]
```

To explain, let the main list have type [b]. The first element is a list, so b=[c].
The second element is a list of lists, so c=[d]. The third element is a list of lists of
lists, so d=[a].

```
ghci> concat ["tea","for",'2']
<interactive>:1:21:
Couldn't match expected type `[Char]'
with actual type `Char'
In the expression: '2'
In the first argument of `concat',
namely `["tea", "for", '2']'
In the expression: concat ["tea", "for", '2']
```

The first two elements of the list have type [Char], but the last has type Char and
that is not allowed.

```
ghci> concat ["tea","for","2"]
"teafor2"
```

Answer to Exercise C ·

1. toUpper, of course.

2. Concatenates the words, putting a single space between them. We have

    ```
    words . unwords = id
    ```

   but not unwords . words = id.

3. [x] ++ xs.

    ```
    modernise :: String -> String
    modernise = unwords . map capitalise . words

    capitalise :: Word -> Word
    capitalise xs = [toUpper (head xs)] ++ tail xs
    ```

We will see another way of writing capitalise in Chapter 4.

Answer to Exercise D

Computing head (map f xs) takes *n* evaluations of f under eager evaluation,
but only one under lazy evaluation. Beaver would have to exploit the identity
head . map f = f . head.

Instead of defining `first p = head . filter p`, Beaver might define

```
first :: (a -> Bool) -> [a] -> a
first p xs | null xs   = error "Empty list"
           | p x       = x
           | otherwise = first p (tail xs)
           where x = head xs
```

Instead of defining `first p f = head . filter p . map f`, Beaver might define

```
first :: (b -> Bool) -> (a -> b) -> [a] -> b
first p f xs | null xs   = error "Empty list"
             | p x       = x
             | otherwise = first p f (tail xs)
             where x = f (head xs)
```

The point is that with eager evaluation most functions have to be defined using explicit recursion, not in terms of useful component functions like `map` and `filter`.

Answer to Exercise E

Lazy Susan would probably write

```
first p xs = if null ys then Nothing
                        else Just (head ys)
             where ys = filter p xs
```

As to the number of functions of type `Maybe a -> Maybe a`, there are just six. Applied to `Nothing` the function can only return `Nothing` or `undefined`. Applied to `Just x` the function can only return `Nothing` or `Just x` or `undefined`. The point is that we know absolutely nothing about the underlying type, so no new values can be invented. That makes six possible functions in all.

Answer to Exercise F

It takes `n-1` multiplications to evaluate `exp x n`. Dick's method is to exploit the identities $x^{2m} = (x^2)^m$ and $x^{2m+1} = x(x^2)^m$ to obtain a recursive definition:

```
exp x n | n == 0 = 1
        | n == 1 = x
        | even n = exp (x*x) m
        | odd n  = x*exp (x*x) (m-1)
        where m = n `div` 2
```

This is an example of a *divide and conquer* algorithm. Dick's program takes p multiplications, where $2^p \leq n < 2^{p+1}$. Thus $p = \lfloor \log n \rfloor$, where $\lfloor x \rfloor$ returns the *floor* of a number, the greatest integer no bigger than the number. We will consider the floor function in more detail in the following chapter.

Answer to Exercise G

```
showDate :: Date -> String
showDate (d,m,y) = show d ++ suffix d ++ " " ++
                   months !! (m-1) ++ ", " ++ show y
```

The function `suffix` computes the right suffix:

```
suffix d = if d==1 || d==21 || d==31 then "st" else
           if d==2 || d==22 then "nd" else
           if d==3 || d==23 then "rd" else
           "th"

months = ["January",.......]
```

If you indulged in clever arithmetic to compute `suffix`, then you should realise that Sometimes a Simple Solution is Best.

Answer to Exercise H

One solution is as follows:

```
addSum :: CIN -> CIN
addSum cin =
   cin ++ show (n `div` 10) ++ show (n `mod` 10)
   where n = sum (map fromDigit cin)

valid :: CIN -> Bool
valid cin = cin == addSum (take 8 cin)

fromDigit :: Char -> Int
fromDigit c = read [c]
```

The function `fromDigit` will return a numerical digit given a digit character.

Answer to Exercise I

Here is one solution:

```
import Data.Char (toLower,isAlpha)

palindrome :: IO()
palindrome
  = do {putStrLn "Enter a string:";
        xs <- getLine;
        if isPalindrome xs then putStrLn "Yes!"
        else putStrLn "No!"}

isPalindrome :: String -> Bool
isPalindrome xs = (ys == reverse ys)
  where ys = map toLower (filter isAlpha xs)
```

2.10 Chapter notes

The chapter has referred a number of times to the Haskell 'standard prelude'. This is a collection of basic types, type classes, functions and other values that are indispensible in many programming tasks. For a complete description of the standard prelude, see Chapter 8 of the Haskell report; alternatively, visit

> www.haskell.org/onlinereport/standard-prelude.html

See www.haskell.org for more information on the implementation of functional languages and of Haskell in particular. An older book, *The Implementation of Functional Programming Languages* (Prentice Hall, 1987) by Simon Peyton Jones, is no longer in print, but an online version can be found at

> research.microsoft.com/~simonpj/papers/slpj-book-1987

Apart from GHC there are other maintained compilers for Haskell, including UHC, the Utrecht Haskell Compiler. See the home page cs.uu.nl/wiki/UHC.

On the eager-versus-lazy evaluation debate, read Bob Harper's blog article *The point of laziness*, which can be found at

> existentialtype.wordpress.com/2011/04/24/

In the blog Harper enumerates some of the reasons why he prefers a strict language. But also read Lennart Augustsson's reply to the post. Augustsson's main point, emphasised in Exercise D, is that under strict evaluation you are forced for efficiency reasons to define most functions by explicit recursion, and therefore lose the ability to build definitions out of simple standard functions. That undercuts our ability to reason about functions by applying general laws about their component functions.

Bob Harper is one of the authors of *The Definition of Standard ML (Revised)* (MIT Press, 1989). ML is a strict functional language. You can find an introduction to ML at

```
www.cs.cmu.edu/~rwh/smlbook/book.pdf
```

Another increasingly popular language is Agda, which is both a dependently-typed functional language and also a proof assistant; see the Agda home page

```
wiki.portal.chalmers.se/agda/pmwiki.php
```

Chris Maslanka writes a regular column in the Saturday edition of the *Guardian* newspaper.

Chapter 3

Numbers

Numbers in Haskell are complicated because in the Haskell world there are many different kinds of number, including:

Int   limited-precision integers in at least the range
             $[-2^{29}, 2^{29})$. Integer overflow is not detected.
Integer   arbitrary-precision integers
Rational   arbitrary-precision rational numbers
Float   single-precision floating-point numbers
Double   double-precision floating-point numbers
Complex   complex numbers (defined in Data.Complex)

Most programs make use of numbers in one way or another, so we have to get at least a working idea of what Haskell offers us and how to convert between the different kinds. That is what the present chapter is about.

3.1 The type class Num

In Haskell all numbers are instances of the type class Num:

```
class (Eq a, Show a) => Num a where
    (+),(-),(*) :: a -> a -> a
    negate      :: a -> a
    abs, signum :: a -> a
    fromInteger :: Integer -> a
```

The class Num is a subclass of both Eq and Show. That means every number can be printed and any two numbers can be compared for equality. Any number can be added to, subtracted from or multiplied by another number. Any number can be negated. Haskell allows -x to denote `negate x`; this is the only prefix operator in Haskell.

The functions `abs` and `signum` return the absolute value of a number and its sign. If ordering operations were allowed in `Num` (and they aren't because, for example, complex numbers cannot be ordered), we could define

```
abs x      = if x < 0 then -x else x
signum x | x < 0   = -1
         | x == 0 = 0
         | x > 0   = 1
```

The function `fromInteger` is a conversion function. An integer literal such as 42 represents the application of `fromInteger` to the appropriate value of type `Integer`, so such literals have type `Num a => a`. This choice is explained further below after we have considered some other classes of number and the conversion functions between them.

3.2 Other numeric type classes

The `Num` class has two subclasses, the real numbers and the fractional numbers:

```
class (Num a,Ord a) => Real a where
  toRational :: a -> Rational

class (Num a) => Fractional a where
  (/) :: a -> a -> a
  fromRational :: Rational -> a
```

Real numbers can be ordered. The only new method in the class `Real`, apart from the comparison operations which are inherited from the superclass `Ord`, is a conversion function from elements in the class to elements of `Rational`. The type `Rational` is essentially a synonym for pairs of integers. The real number π is not rational, so `toRational` can only convert to an approximate rational number:

```
ghci> toRational pi
884279719003555 % 281474976710656
```

Not quite as memorable as 22 % 7, but more accurate. The symbol % is used to separate the numerator and denominator of a rational number.

The fractional numbers are those on which division is defined. A complex number cannot be real but it can be fractional. A floating-point literal such as 3.149 represents the application of fromRational to an appropriate rational number. Thus

```
3.149 ::  Fractional a => a
```

This type and the earlier type Num a => a for 42 explains why we can form a legitimate expression such as 42 + 3.149, adding an integer to a floating-point number. Both types are members of the Num class and all numbers can be added. Consideration of

```
ghci> :type 42 + 3.149
42 + 3.149 :: Fractional a => a
```

shows that the result of the addition is also a fractional number.

One of the subclasses of the real numbers is the integral numbers. A simplified version of this class is:

```
class (Real a, Enum a) => Integral a where
   divMod :: a -> a -> (a,a)
   toInteger :: a -> Integer
```

The class Integral is a subclass of Enum, those types whose elements can be enumerated in sequence. Every integral number can be converted into an Integer through the conversion function toInteger. That means we can convert an integral number into any other type of number in two steps:

```
fromIntegral :: (Integral a, Num b) => a -> b
fromIntegral = fromInteger . toInteger
```

Application of divMod returns two values:

```
x `div` y  = fst (x `divMod` y)
x `mod` y  = snd (x `divMod` y)
```

The standard prelude functions fst and snd return the first and second components of a pair:

```
fst :: (a,b) -> a
fst (x,y) = x

snd :: (a,b) -> b
snd (x,y) = y
```

Mathematically, $x \operatorname{div} y = \lfloor x/y \rfloor$. We will see how to compute $\lfloor x \rfloor$ in the following section. And $x \bmod y$ is defined by

$$x = (x \operatorname{div} y) * y + x \bmod y$$

For positive x and y we have $0 \leq x \bmod y < x$.

Recall the function `digits2` from the first chapter, where we defined

```
digits2 n = (n `div` 10, n `mod` 10)
```

It is more efficient to say `digits2 n = n `divMod` 10` because then only one invocation of `divMod` is required. Even more briefly, we can use a section and write `digits2 = (`divMod` 10)`.

There are also other numeric classes, including the subclass `Floating` of the class `Fractional` that contains, among others, the logarithmic and trigonometric functions. But enough is enough.

3.3 Computing floors

The value $\lfloor x \rfloor$, the *floor* of x, is defined to be the largest integer m such that $m \leq x$. We define a function `floor :: Float -> Integer` for computing floors. Haskell provides such a function in the standard prelude, but it is instructive to consider our own version.

One student, call him Clever Dick, to whom this task was given came up with the following solution:

```
floor :: Float -> Integer
floor = read . takeWhile (/= '.') . show
```

In words, the number is shown as a string, the string is truncated by taking only the digits up to the decimal point, and the result is read again as an integer. We haven't met `takeWhile` yet, though Clever Dick evidently had. Clever Dick's solution is wrong on a number of counts, and Exercise D asks you to list them.

Instead we will find the floor of a number with the help of an explicit search, and for that we will need a loop:

```
until :: (a -> Bool) -> (a -> a) -> a -> a
until p f x = if p x then x else until p f (f x)
```

The function `until` is also provided in the standard prelude. Here is an example:

```
ghci> until (>100) (*7) 1
343
```

Essentially until f p x computes the first element y in the infinite list

```
[x, f x, f (f x), f (f (f x)), ...]
```

for which p y = True. See the following chapter where this interpretation of until is made precise.

Thinking now about the design of floor it is tempting to start off with a case analysis, distinguishing between the cases $x < 0$ and $x \geq 0$. In the case $x < 0$ we have to find the first number m in the sequence $-1, -2, \ldots$ for which $m \leq x$. That leads to – in the case of a negative argument –

```
floor x = until (`leq` x) (subtract 1) (-1)
          where m `leq` x = fromInteger m <= x
```

There are a number of instructive points about this definition. Firstly, note the use of the prelude function subtract whose definition is

```
subtract x y = y-x
```

We have to use subtract 1 because (-1) is *not* a section but the number -1 (look at the third argument of until).

Secondly, why have we used `leq` when the alternative (<=) seems perfectly adequate? The answer is that (<=) has the type

```
(<=) :: Num a => a -> a -> Bool
```

In particular the two arguments of (<=) have to have the same type. But we want

```
leq :: Integer -> Float -> Bool
```

and the two arguments have different numeric types. We therefore need to convert integers to floats using fromInteger. Appreciation of the need for conversion functions in some situations is one of the key points to understand about Haskell arithmetic.

Finally, note that (`leq` x) is not the same as (leq x):

```
(leq x)   y = leq x y
(`leq` x) y = y `leq` x = leq y x
```

It is easy to make this mistake.

If you don't like the subsidiary definition, you can always write

```
    floor x = until ((<=x) . fromInteger) (subtract 1) (-1)
```

In this version we have *inlined* the definition of (`leq` x).

We still have to deal with the case $x \geq 0$. In this case we have to look for the first
integer n such that $x < n+1$. We can do this by finding the first integer n such that
$x < n$ and subtracting 1 from the answer. That leads to

```
    floor x = until (x `lt` ) (+1) 1 - 1
             where x `lt` n = x < fromInteger n
```

Putting the two pieces together, we obtain

```
    floor x = if x < 0
             then until (`leq` x) (subtract 1) (-1)
             else until (x `lt`) (+1) 1 - 1
```

(Question: why do we not have to write x < fromInteger 0 in the first line?)
The real problem with this definition, apart from the general ugliness of a case
distinction and the asymmetry of the two cases, is that it is very slow: it takes about
$|x|$ steps ($|x|$ is the mathematician's way of writing abs x) to deliver the result.

Binary search

A better method for computing floor is to first find integers m and n such that
$m \leq x < n$ and then shrink the interval (m,n) to a unit interval (one with $m+1 = n$)
that contains x. Then the left-hand bound of the interval can be returned as the
result. That leads to

```
    floor :: Float -> Integer
    floor x = fst (until unit (shrink x) (bound x))
             where unit (m,n) = (m+1 == n)
```

The value bound x is some pair (m,n) of integers such that $m \leq x < n$. If (m,n) is
not a unit interval, then shrink x (m,n) returns a new interval of strictly smaller
size that still bounds x.

Let us first consider how to shrink a non-unit interval (m,n) containing x, so $m \leq
x < n$. Suppose p is any integer that satisfies $m < p < n$. Such a p exists since (m,n)
is not a unit interval. Then we can define

```
    type Interval = (Integer,Integer)

    shrink :: Float -> Interval -> Interval
```

```
shrink x (m,n) = if p `leq` x then (p,n) else (m,p)
                 where p = choose (m,n)
```

How should we define choose?

Two possible choices are `choose (m,n) = m+1` or `choose (m,n) = n-1` for both reduce the size of an interval. But a better choice is

```
choose :: Interval -> Integer
choose (m,n) = (m+n) `div` 2
```

With this choice the size of the interval is halved at each step rather than reduced by 1.

However, we need to check that $m < (m+n) \operatorname{div} 2 < n$ in the case $m+1 \neq n$. The reasoning is:

$$m < (m+n) \operatorname{div} 2 < n$$
$$\equiv \quad \{\text{ordering on integers}\}$$
$$m+1 \leq (m+n) \operatorname{div} 2 < n$$
$$\equiv \quad \{\text{since } (m+n) \operatorname{div} 2 = \lfloor (m+n)/2 \rfloor\}$$
$$m+1 \leq (m+n)/2 < n$$
$$\equiv \quad \{\text{arithmetic}\}$$
$$m+2 \leq n \wedge m < n$$
$$\equiv \quad \{\text{arithmetic}\}$$
$$m+1 < n$$

Finally, how should we define bound? We can start off by defining

```
bound :: Float -> Interval
bound x = (lower x, upper x)
```

The value `lower x` is some integer less than or equal to x, and `upper x` some integer greater than x. Instead of using linear search to discover these values, it is better to use

```
lower :: Float -> Integer
lower x = until (`leq` x) (*2) (-1)

upper :: Float -> Integer
upper x = until (x `lt`) (*2) 1
```

For a fast version of bound it is better to double at each step rather than increase or decrease by 1. For example, with $x = 17.3$ it takes only seven comparisons to compute the surrounding interval $(-1, 32)$, which is then reduced to $(17, 18)$ in a further five steps. In fact, evaluating both the upper and lower bounds takes time proportional to $\log |x|$ steps, and the whole algorithm takes at most twice this time. An algorithm that takes logarithmic time is much faster than one that takes linear time.

The standard prelude defines floor in the following way:

```
floor x = if r < 0 then n-1 else n
          where (n,r) = properFraction x
```

The function properFraction is a method in the RealFrac type class (a class we haven't discussed and whose methods deal with truncating and rounding numbers). It splits a number x into its integer part n and its fractional part r, so $x = n + r$. Now you know.

3.4 Natural numbers

Haskell does not provide a type for the natural numbers, that is, the nonnegative integers. But we can always define such a type ourselves:

```
data Nat = Zero | Succ Nat
```

This is an example of a *data declaration*. The declaration says that Zero is a value of Nat and that Succ n is also a value of Nat whenever n is. Both Zero and Succ are called *data constructors* and begin with a capital letter. The type of Zero is Nat and the type of Succ is Nat -> Nat. Thus each of

```
Zero, Succ Zero, Succ (Succ Zero), Succ (Succ (Succ Zero))
```

is an element of Nat.

Let us see how to program the basic arithmetical operations by making Nat a fully paid-up member of the Num class. First, we have to make Nat an instance of Eq and Show:

```
instance Eq Nat where
  Zero   == Zero   = True
  Zero   == Succ n = False
  Succ m == Zero   = False
  Succ m == Succ n = (m == n)
```

```
instance Show Nat where
  show Zero               = "Zero"
  show (Succ Zero)        = "Succ Zero"
  show (Succ (Succ n)) = "Succ (" ++ show (Succ n) ++ ")"
```

These definitions make use of *pattern matching*. In particular, the definition of show makes use of three patterns, Zero, Succ Zero and Succ (Succ n). These patterns are different from one another and together cover all the elements of Nat apart from ⊥.

Alternatively, we could have declared

```
data Nat = Zero | Succ Nat  deriving (Eq,Ord,Show)
```

As we said in Exercise E of the previous chapter, Haskell is smart enough to construct automatically instances of some standard classes, including Eq, Ord and Show.

Now we can install Nat as a numeric type:

```
instance Num Nat where
  m + Zero      = m
  m + Succ n    = Succ (m+n)

  m * Zero      = Zero
  m * (Succ n) = m * n + m

  abs n              = n
  signum Zero        = Zero
  signum (Succ n) = Succ Zero

  m - Zero           = m
  Zero - Succ n      = Zero
  Succ m - Succ n = m - n

  fromInteger x
    | x <= 0      = Zero
    | otherwise = Succ (fromInteger (x-1))
```

We have defined subtraction as a total operation: $m - n = 0$ if $m \leq n$. Of course, the arithmetic operations on Nat are horribly slow. And each number takes up a lot of space.

Partial numbers

We have said that there is a value $\perp$ of every type. Thus undefined :: a for all types a. Since Succ is, by definition, a non-strict function, the values

        undefined, Succ undefined, Succ (Succ undefined), ...

are all different and all members of Nat. To be honest, these partial numbers are not very useful, but they are there. You can think of Succ undefined as being a number about which we know only that it is at least 1:

```
ghci> Zero == Succ undefined
False
ghci> Succ Zero == Succ undefined
*** Exception: Prelude.undefined
```

There is also one further number in Nat:

        infinity :: Nat
        infinity = Succ infinity

Thus

```
ghci> Zero == infinity
False
ghci> Succ Zero == infinity
False
```

and so on.

In summary, the elements of Nat consist of the finite numbers, the partial numbers and the infinite numbers (of which there is only one). We shall see that this is true of other data types: there are the finite elements of the type, the partial elements and the infinite elements.

We could have chosen to make the constructor Succ strict. This is achieved by declaring

        data Nat = Zero | Succ !Nat

The annotation ! is known as *strictness flag*. With such a declaration, we have for example

```
ghci> Zero == Succ undefined
*** Exception: Prelude.undefined
```

This time, evaluating the equality test forces the evaluation of both sides, and the evaluation of `Succ undefined` raises an error message. Making `Succ` strict collapses the natural numbers into just the finite numbers and one undefined number.

3.5 Exercises

Exercise A

Which of the following expressions denote 1?

```
-2 + 3, 3 + -2, 3 + (-2), subtract 2 3, 2 + subtract 3
```

In the standard prelude there is a function `flip` defined by

```
flip f x y = f y x
```

Express `subtract` using `flip`.

Exercise B

Haskell provides no fewer than three ways to define exponentiation:

```
(^)  :: (Num a, Integral b) => a -> b -> a
(^^) :: (Fractional a, Integral b) => a -> b -> a
(**) :: (Floating a) => a -> a -> a
```

The operation (`^`) raises any number to a nonnegative integral power; (`^^`) raises any number to any integral power (including negative integers); and (`**`) takes two fractional arguments. The definition of (`^`) basically follows Dick's method of the previous chapter (see Exercise E). How would you define (`^^`)?

Exercise C

Could you define `div` in the following way?

```
div :: Integral a => a -> a -> a
div x y = floor (x/y)
```

Exercise D

Consider again Clever Dick's solution for computing `floor`:

```
floor :: Float -> Integer
floor = read . (takeWhile (/= '.') . show
```

Why doesn't it work?

Consider the following mini-interaction with GHCi:

```
ghci> 12345678.0 :: Float
1.2345678e7
```

Haskell allows the use of so-called *scientific notation*, also called *exponent notation*, to describe certain floating-point numbers. For example the number above denotes $1.2345678 * 10^7$. When the number of digits of a floating-point number is sufficiently large, the number is printed in this notation. Now give another reason why Clever Dick's solution doesn't work.

Exercise E

The function `isqrt :: Float -> Integer` returns the floor of the square root of a (nonnegative) number. Following the strategy of Section 3.3, construct an implementation of `isqrt x` that takes time proportional to $\log x$ steps.

Exercise F

Haskell provides a function `sqrt :: Floating a => a -> a` that gives a reasonable approximation to the square root of a (nonnegative) number. But, let's define our own version. If y is an approximation to $\sqrt{x}$, then so is x/y. Moreover, either $y \leq \sqrt{x} \leq x/y$ or $x/y \leq \sqrt{x} \leq y$. What is a better approximation to $\sqrt{x}$ than either y or x/y? (Yes, you have just rediscovered Newton's method for finding square roots.)

The only remaining problem is to decide when an approximation y is good enough. One possible test is $|y^2 - x| < \varepsilon$, where $|x|$ returns the absolute value of x and ε is a suitably small number. This test guarantees an *absolute* error of at most ε. Another test is $|y^2 - x| < \varepsilon * x$, which guarantees a *relative* error of at most ε. Assuming that numbers of type `Float` are accurate only to six significant figures, which of these two is the more sensible test, and what is a sensible value for ε?

Hence construct a definition of `sqrt`.

Exercise G

Give an explicit instance of `Nat` as a member of the type class `Ord`. Hence construct a definition of

```
divMod :: Nat -> Nat -> (Nat,Nat)
```

3.6 Answers

Answer to Exercise A

All except 2 + -3 and 2 + subtract 3, neither of which are well-formed. We have subtract = flip (-).

Answer to Exercise B

```
x ^^ n = if 0 <= n then x^n else 1/(x ^ (negate n))
```

Answer to Exercise C

No. You would have to write

```
div :: Integral a => a -> a -> a
div x y = floor (fromInteger x / fromInteger y)
```

Answer to Exercise D

Clever Dick's function gives floor (-3.1) = -3 when the answer should be -4. And if you tried to repair his solution by subtracting 1 if the solution was negative, you would have floor (-3.0) = -4 when the answer should be -3. Ugh!

Also, Clever Dick's solution has floor 12345678.0 = 1 because the argument is shown as 1.2345678e7.

Answer to Exercise E

```
isqrt :: Float -> Integer
isqrt x = fst (until unit (shrink x) (bound x))
          where unit (m,n) = (m+1 == n)


shrink :: Float -> Interval -> Interval
shrink x (m,n) = if (p*p) `leq` x then (p,n) else (m,p)
                 where p = (m+n) `div` 2


bound :: Float -> Interval
bound x = (0,until above (*2) 1)
          where above n = x `lt` (n*n)
```

The functions `leq` and `lt` were defined in Section 3.3. Note the parentheses in the expressions (p*p) `leq` x and x `lt` (n*n). We didn't state an order of association for `leq` and `lt`, so without parentheses these two expressions would have been interpreted as the ill-formed expressions p * (p `leq` x) and (x `lt` n) * n. (I made just this mistake when first typing in the solution.)

Answer to Exercise F

A better approximation to $\sqrt{x}$ than either y or x/y is $(y+x/y)/2$. The relative-error test is the more sensible one, and the program is

```
sqrt :: Float -> Float
sqrt x = until goodenough improve x
         where goodenough y = abs (y*y-x) < eps*x
               improve y    = (y+x/y)/2
               eps          = 0.000001
```

Answer to Exercise G

It is sufficient to define (<):

```
instance Ord Nat where
   Zero < Zero     = False
   Zero < Succ n   = True
   Succ m < Zero   = False
   Succ m < Succ n = (m < n)
```

Now we can define

```
divMod :: Nat -> Nat -> (Nat,Nat)
divMod x y = if x < y then (Zero,x)
             else (Succ q,r)
             where (q,r) = divMod (x-y) y
```

3.7 Chapter notes

The primary source book for computer arithmetic is *The Art of Computer Programming, Volume 2: Semi-numerical Algorithms* (Addison-Wesley, 1998) by Don Knuth. The arithmetic of floors and other simple numerical functions is studied in depth in *Concrete Mathematics* (Addison-Wesley, 1989) by Don Knuth, Ronald Graham and Oren Patashnik.

Chapter 4

Lists

Lists are the workhorses of functional programming. They can be used to fetch and carry data from one function to another; they can be taken apart, rearranged and combined with other lists to make new lists. Lists of numbers can be summed and multiplied; lists of characters can be read and printed; and so on. The list of useful operations on lists is a long one. This chapter describes some of the operations that occur most frequently, though one particularly important class will be introduced only in Chapter 6.

4.1 List notation

As we have seen, the type [a] denotes lists of elements of type a. The empty list is denoted by []. We can have lists over any type but we cannot mix different types in the same list. As examples,

```
[undefined,undefined]  :: [a]
[sin,cos,tan]          :: Floating a => [a -> a]
[[1,2,3],[4,5]]        :: Num a => [[a]]
["tea","for",2]        not valid
```

List notation, such as [1,2,3], is in fact an abbreviation for a more basic form

```
1:2:3:[]
```

The operator (:) :: a -> [a] -> [a], pronounced 'cons', is a constructor for lists. It associates to the right so there is no need for parentheses in the above expression. It has no associated definition, which is why it is a constructor. In other words, there are no rules for simplifying an expression such as 1:2:[]. The operator (:) is non-strict in both arguments – more precisely, it is non-strict and returns a non-strict function. The expression

```
undefined : undefined
```

may not be very interesting, but we do know it is not the empty list. In fact, that is the only thing we do know about it. Note that the two occurrences of undefined have different types in this expression.

The empty list [] is also a constructor. Lists can be introduced as a Haskell data type with the declaration

```
data List a = Nil | Cons a (List a)
```

The only difference is that List a is written [a], Nil is written [] and Cons is written (:).

According to this declaration, every list of type [a] takes one of three forms:

- The undefined list undefined :: [a];

- The empty list [] :: [a];

- A list of the form x:xs where x :: a and xs :: [a].

As a result there are three kinds of list:

- A *finite* list, which is built from (:) and []; for example, 1:2:3:[]

- A *partial* list, which is built from (:) and undefined; for example, the list filter (<4) [1..] is the partial list 1:2:3:undefined. We know there is no integer after 3 that is less than 4, but Haskell is an evaluator, not a theorem prover, so it ploughs away without success looking for more answers.

- An *infinite* list, which is built from (:) alone; for example, [1..] is the infinite list of the nonnegative integers.

All three kinds of list arise in everyday programming. Chapter 9 is devoted to exploring the world of infinite lists and their uses. For example, the prelude function iterate returns an infinite list:

```
iterate :: (a -> a) -> a -> [a]
iterate f x = x:iterate f (f x)
```

In particular, iterate (+1) 1 is an infinite list of the positive integers, a value we can also write as [1..] (see the following section).

As another example,

```
head (filter perfect [1..])
  where perfect n = (n == sum (divisors n))
```

returns the first perfect number, namely 6, even though nobody currently knows whether `filter perfect [1..]` is an infinite or partial list.

Finally, we can define

```
until p f = head . filter p . iterate f
```

The function `until` was used to compute floors in the previous chapter. As this example demonstrates, functions that seem basic in programming are often composed of even simpler functions. A bit like protons and quarks.

4.2 Enumerations

Haskell provides useful notation for enumerating lists of integers. When m and n are integers we can write

`[m..n]`	for the list $[m, m+1, \ldots, n]$
`[m..]`	for the infinite list $[m, m+1, m+2, \ldots]$
`[m,n..p]`	for the list $[m, m+(n-m), m+2(n-m), \ldots, p]$
`[m,n..]`	for the infinite list $[m, m+(n-m), m+2(n-m), \ldots]$

The first two notations crop up frequently in practice, the second two less so. As examples,

```
ghci> [0,2..11]
[0,2,4,6,8,10]
ghci> [1,3..]
[1,3,5,7,9,11 {Interrupted}
```

In the first example the enumeration stops at 10 because 11 isn't even. In the second example we quickly interrupted the evaluation of an infinite list.

As a matter of fact, enumerations are not restricted to integers, but to members of yet another type class Enum. We won't elaborate more on this class, except to say that Char is also a member:

```
ghci> ['a'..'z']
"abcdefghijklmnopqrstuvwxyz"
```

4.3 List comprehensions

Haskell provides another useful and very attractive piece of notation, called *list comprehensions*, for constructing lists out of other lists. We illustrate with a few examples:

```
ghci> [x*x | x <- [1..5]]
[1,4,9,16,25]
ghci> [x*x | x <- [1..5], isPrime x]
[4,9,25]
ghci> [(i,j) | i <- [1..5], even i, j <- [i..5]]
[(2,2),(2,3),(2,4),(2,5),(4,4),(4,5)]
ghci> [x | xs <- [[(3,4)],[(5,4),(3,2)]], (3,x) <- xs]
[4,2]
```

Here is another example. Suppose we wanted to generate all Pythagorean triads in a given range. These are triples of numbers (x,y,z) such that $x^2 + y^2 = z^2$ and $1 \leq x, y, z \leq n$ for some given n. We can define

```
    triads :: Int -> [(Int,Int,Int)]
    triads n = [(x,y,z) | x <- [1..n], y <- [1..n],
                    z <- [1..n], x*x+y*y==z*z]
```

Hence

```
ghci> triads 15
[(3,4,5),(4,3,5),(5,12,13),(6,8,10),
 (8,6,10),(9,12,15),(12,5,13),(12,9,15)]
```

That's probably not what we want: each essentially distinct triad is generated in two different ways. Moreover, the list contains redundant triads consisting of multiples of basic triads.

To improve the definition of `triad` we can restrict x and y so that $x < y$ and x and y are coprime, meaning they have no divisors in common. As mathematicians we know that $2x^2$ cannot be the square of an integer, so the first restriction is valid. The divisors of a number can be computed by

```
    divisors x = [d | d <- [2..x-1], x `mod` d == 0]
```

Hence

```
    coprime x y = disjoint (divisors x) (divisors y)
```

We will leave the definition of `disjoint` as an exercise.

That means we can define

```
triads n = [(x,y,z) | x <- [1..n], y <- [x+1..n],
                      coprime x y,
                      z <- [y+1..n], x*x+y*y==z*z]
```

This definition is better than before, but let us try to make it a little faster, mainly to illustrate an important point. Since $2x^2 < x^2 + y^2 = z^2 \leq n^2$ we see that $x < n/\sqrt{2}$. So $x \leq \lfloor n/\sqrt{2} \rfloor$. That suggests we can write

```
triads n = [(x,y,z) | x <- [1..m], y <- [x+1..n],
                      coprime x y,
                      z <- [y+1..n], x*x+y*y==z*z]
            where m = floor (n / sqrt 2)
```

But the expression for m is incorrect: n is an Int and we cannot divide integers. We need an explicit conversion function, and the one to use is fromIntegral (not fromInteger because n is an Int not an Integer). We need to replace the definition of m by m = floor (fromIntegral n / sqrt 2). Once again we have to be careful about what kinds of number we are dealing with and aware of the available conversion functions between them.

List comprehensions can be used to define some common functions on lists. For example,

```
map f xs    = [f x | x <- xs]
filter p xs = [x | x <- xs, p x]
concat xss  = [x | xs <- xss, x <- xs]
```

Actually, in Haskell it is the other way around: list comprehensions are translated into equivalent definitions in terms of map, and concat. The translation rules are:

```
[e |True]        = [e]
[e | q]          = [e | q, True]
[e | b, Q]       = if b then [e | Q] else []
[e | p <- xs, Q] = let ok p = [e | Q]
                       ok _ = []
                   in concat (map ok xs)
```

The definition of ok in the fourth rule uses a *don't care* pattern, also called a *wild card*. The p in the fourth rule is a pattern, and the definition of ok says that the empty list is returned on any argument that doesn't match the pattern p.

Another useful rule is

```
[e | Q1, Q2] = concat [[e | Q2] | Q1]
```

4.4 Some basic operations

We can define functions over lists by pattern matching. For example,

```
null :: [a] -> Bool
null []     = True
null (x:xs) = False
```

The patterns [] and x:xs are disjoint and exhaustive, so we can write the two equations for null in either order. The function null is strict because Haskell has to know which equation to apply and that requires evaluation of the argument, at least to the extent of discovering whether it is the empty list or not. (A question: why not simply define null = (==[])?) We could also have written

```
null [] = True
null _  = False
```

This definition uses a don't care pattern.

Here are two other definitions using pattern matching:

```
head :: [a] -> a
head (x:xs) = x

tail :: [a] -> [a]
tail (x:xs) = xs
```

There is no equation for the pattern [], so Haskell reports an error if we try to evaluate head [] or tail [].

We can use [x] as shorthand for x:[] in a pattern:

```
last :: [a] -> a
last [x]     = x
last (x:y:ys) = last (y:ys)
```

The first equation has a pattern that matches a singleton list; the second has a pattern that matches a list that contains at least two elements. The standard prelude definition of last is slightly different:

```
last [x]    = x
last (_:xs) = last xs
```

This definition uses a don't care pattern. The two equations have to be written in this order because x: [] matches both patterns.

4.5 Concatenation

Here is the definition of (++), the concatenation operation:

```
(++) :: [a] -> [a] -> [a]
[] ++ ys     = ys
(x:xs) ++ ys = x:(xs ++ ys)
```

The definition uses pattern matching on the first argument but not on the second. The second equation for (++) is very succinct and requires some thought, but once you have got it, you have understood a lot about how lists work in functional programming. Here is a simple evaluation sequence:

```
        [1,2] ++ [3,4,5]
    =   {notation}
        (1:(2:[])) ++ (3:(4:(5:[])))
    =   {second equation for ++}
        1:((2:[]) ++ (3:(4:(5:[]))))
    =   {and again}
        1:(2:([] ++ (3:(4:(5:[])))))
    =   {first equation for ++}
        1:(2:(3:(4:(5:[]))))
    =   {notation}
        [1,2,3,4,5]
```

As this example suggests, the cost of evaluating xs++ys is proportional to the length of xs, where

```
length :: [a] -> Int
length []     = 0
length (x:xs) = 1 + length xs
```

Note also that

```
undefined ++ [1,2] = undefined
[1,2] ++ undefined = 1:2:undefined
```

We know nothing about the first list, but we do know that the second list begins with 1 followed by 2.

Concatenation is an associative operation. Thus

```
(xs ++ ys) ++ zs = xs ++ (ys ++ zs)
```

for *all* lists xs, ys and zs. We will see how to prove assertions like these in Chapter 6.

4.6 concat, map and filter

Three very useful list operations that we have met already are concat, map and filter. Here are their definitions using pattern matching:

```
concat :: [[a]] -> [a]
concat []        = []
concat (xs:xss) = xs ++ concat xss

map :: (a -> b) -> [a] -> [b]
map f []      = []
map f (x:xs) = f x:map f xs

filter :: (a -> Bool) -> [a] -> [a]
filter p []      = []
filter p (x:xs) = if p x then x:filter p xs
                         else filter p xs
```

There is a common theme underlying these definitions that we will identify and exploit in Chapter 6. An alternative definition of filter is

```
filter p = concat . map (test p)
test p x = if p x then [x] else []
```

With this definition, filter p is implemented by converting each element of the list into a singleton list if it satisfies p, and the empty list otherwise. The results are then concatenated.

Two basic facts about map are that

```
map id      = id
map (f . g) = map f . map g
```

The first equation says that applying the identity function to each element of a list leaves the list unchanged. The two occurrence of id in this law have different types: on the left it is a -> a and on the right it is [a] -> [a]. The second equation says that applying g to every element of a list, and then applying f to every element of the result, gives the same list as applying f . g to every element. Read from right to left, the equation says that two traversals of a list can be replaced by one, with a corresponding gain in efficiency.

The two facts have a name: they are called the *functor* laws of map. The name is borrowed from a branch of mathematics called Category Theory. In fact, Haskell provides a type class Functor, whose definition is

```
class Functor f where
    fmap :: (a -> b) -> f a -> f b
```

The method fmap is expected to satisfy exactly the same laws as map. The reason for this type class is that the idea of mapping a function over a list can be generalised to one of mapping a function over an arbitrary data structure, such as trees of various kinds. For example, consider the type

```
data Tree a = Tip a | Fork (Tree a) (Tree a)
```

of binary trees with labels in their tips. Tree-structured data arise in a number of places, for example with the syntax of expressions of various kinds. We can define a mapping function over trees, but rather than calling it mapTree we can call it fmap by making trees a member of the Functor class:

```
instance Functor Tree where
    fmap f (Tip x)    = Tip (f x)
    fmap f (Fork u v) = Fork (fmap f u) (fmap f v)
```

In fact map is just a synonym for the instance fmap for lists:

```
ghci> fmap (+1) [2,3,4]
[3,4,5]
```

We mention the Functor type class here primarily to show that if ever you think some function on lists can be usefully generalised to other kinds of data structure, the chances are good that the designers of Haskell have already spotted it and introduced an appropriate type class. As we will see later on, and especially in Chapter 12, the functor laws of map appear in many calculations.

There is another group of laws that involve map, all of which have a common theme. Consider the equations

```
f . head        = head . map f
map f . tail    = tail . map f
map f . concat = concat . map (map f)
```

The first equation holds only if f is a strict function, but the others hold for arbitrary f. If we apply both sides of the equation to the empty list, we get

```
f (head []) = head (map f []) = head []
```

Since the head of an empty list is undefined, we require f to be strict to make the equation true.

Each of the laws has a simple interpretation. In each case you can apply the operation (head, tail, and so on) to a list and then change each element, or you can change each element first and then apply the operation. The common theme lies in the types of the operations involved:

```
head   :: [a] -> a
tail   :: [a] -> [a]
concat :: [[a]] -> [a]
```

The point about the operations is that they do not depend in any way on the nature of the list elements; they are simply functions that shuffle, discard or extract elements from lists. That is why they have polymorphic types. And functions with polymorphic types all satisfy some law that says you can change values before or after applying the function. In mathematics such functions are called *natural transformations* and the associated laws, *naturality* laws.

As another example, since reverse :: [a] -> [a] we would expect that

```
map f . reverse =  reverse . map f
```

Indeed this is the case. Of course, this naturality law still has to be proved.

Another law is

```
concat . map concat = concat . concat
```

The two sides assert that two ways of concatenating a list of lists of lists (either do the inner concatenations first, or do the outer concatenations first) give the same result.

Finally, here is just one property of filter:

```
filter p . map f = map f . filter (p . f)
```

We can prove this law by simple equational reasoning:

$$
\begin{aligned}
&\texttt{filter p . map f}\\
=\ &\{\text{second definition of } \texttt{filter}\}\\
&\texttt{concat . map (test p) . map f}\\
=\ &\{\text{functor property of } \texttt{map}\}\\
&\texttt{concat . map (test p . f)}\\
=\ &\{\text{since } \texttt{test p . f = map f . test (p . f)}\}\\
&\texttt{concat . map (map f . test (p . f))}\\
=\ &\{\text{functor property of } \texttt{map}\}\\
&\texttt{concat . map (map f) . map (test (p . f))}\\
=\ &\{\text{naturality of } \texttt{concat}\}\\
&\texttt{map f . concat . map (test (p . f))}\\
=\ &\{\text{second definition of } \texttt{filter}\}\\
&\texttt{map f . filter (p . f)}
\end{aligned}
$$

Laws like those above are not just of academic interest, but are deployed in finding new and better ways of expressing definitions. That's why functional programming is the best thing since sliced bread.

4.7 zip and zipWith

Finally, to complete a simple toolbox of useful operations, we consider the functions zip and zipWith. The definitions in the standard prelude are:

```
zip :: [a] -> [b] -> [(a,b)]
zip (x:xs) (y:ys) = (x,y): zip xs ys
zip _        _       = []

zipWith :: (a -> b -> c) -> [a] -> [b] -> [c]
zipWith f (x:xs) (y:ys) = f x y : zipWith f xs ys
zipWith f _       _       = []
```

A caring programmer (one who doesn't like 'don't care' patterns) would have written

```
zip [] ys       = []
zip (x:xs) []    = []
```

```
zip (x:xs) (y:ys) = (x,y):zip xs ys
```

Both definitions use pattern matching on both arguments. You have to know that
pattern matching is applied from top to bottom and from left to right. Thus

```
zip [] undefined = []
zip undefined [] = undefined
```

The definition of `zip` can be given another way:

```
zip = zipWith (,)
```

The operation `(,)` is a constructor for pairs: `(,) a b = (a,b)`.

Here is one example of the use of `zipWith`. Suppose we want to determine whether
a list is in nondecreasing order. A direct definition would have:

```
nondec :: (Ord a) => [a] -> Bool
nondec []       = True
nondec [x]      = True
nondec (x:y:xs) = (x <= y) && nondec (y:xs)
```

But another, equivalent and shorter definition is

```
nondec xs = and (zipWith (<=) xs (tail xs))
```

The function and is yet another useful function in the standard prelude. It takes a
list of booleans and returns `True` if all the elements are `True`, and `False` otherwise:

```
and :: [Bool] -> Bool
and []     = True
and (x:xs) = x && and xs
```

One final example. Consider the task of building a function `position` that takes a
value x and a finite list xs and returns the first position in xs (counting positions
from 0) at which x occurs. If x does not occur in the list, then -1 is returned. We
can define

```
position :: (Eq a) => a -> [a] -> Int
position x xs
   = head ([j | (j,y) <- zip [0..] xs, y==x] ++ [-1])
```

The expression `zip [0..] xs` pairs each element of xs with its position in xs.
Although the first argument of `zip` is an infinite list, the result is a finite list whenever xs is. Observe that the problem is solved by first computing the list of *all*
positions at which x is found, and then taking the first element. Under lazy evaluation it is not necessary to construct the value of every element of the list in order

to calculate the head of the list, so there is no great loss of efficiency in solving the problem this way. And there is a great deal of simplicity in defining one search result in terms of all search results.

4.8 Common words, completed

Let's now return to Section 1.3 and complete the definition of commonWords. Recall that we finished with

```
commonWords :: Int -> [Char] -> [Char]
commonWords n = concat . map showRun . take n .
                sortRuns . countRuns . sortWords .
                words . map toLower
```

The only functions we have still to give definitions for are

```
showRun    countRuns    sortRuns    sortWords
```

All the others, including words, are provided in the standard Haskell libraries.

The first one is easy:

```
showRun :: (Int,Word) -> [Char]
showRun (n,w) = w ++ ": " ++ show n ++ "\n"
```

The second one can be defined by

```
countRuns :: [Word] -> [(Int,Word)]
countRuns []     = []
countRuns (w:ws) = (1+length us,w):countRuns vs
                   where (us,vs) = span (==w) ws
```

The prelude function span p splits a list into two, the first being the longest prefix of the list all of whose elements satisfy the test p, and the second being the suffix that remains. Here is the definition:

```
span :: (a -> Bool) -> [a] -> ([a],[a])
span p []     = ([],[])
span p (x:xs) = if p x then (x:ys,zs)
                       else ([],x:xs)
                where (ys,zs) = span p xs
```

That leaves sortRuns and sortWords. We can import the function sort from Data.List by the command

```
import Data.List (sort)
```

Since `sort :: (Ord a) => [a] -> [a]` we can then define

```
sortWords :: [Word] -> [Word]
sortWords = sort

sortRuns :: [(Int,Word)] -> [(Int,Word)]
sortRuns = reverse . sort
```

To understand the second definition you have to know that Haskell automatically defines the comparison operation (`<=`) on pairs by

```
(x1,y1) <= (x2,y2) = (x1 < x2) || (x1 == x2 && y1 <= y2)
```

You also have to know that `sort` sorts into ascending order. Since we want the codes in descending order of count, we just sort into ascending order and reverse the result. That, by the way, is why we defined frequency counts by having the count before the word rather than afterwards.

Instead of relying on the library function for sorting, let us end by programming a sorting function ourselves. One good way to sort is to use a *divide and conquer* strategy: if the list has length at most one then it is already sorted; otherwise we can divide the list into two equal halves, sort each half by using the sorting algorithm recursively, and then merge the two sorted halves together. That leads to

```
sort :: (Ord a) => [a] -> [a]
sort []  = []
sort [x] = [x]
sort xs  = merge (sort ys) (sort zs)
           where (ys,zs) = halve xs

halve xs = (take n xs, drop n xs)
           where n = length xs `div` 2
```

That leaves us with the definition of `merge`, which merges two sorted lists together into one sorted list:

```
merge :: (Ord a) => [a] -> [a] -> [a]
merge [] ys = ys
merge xs [] = xs
merge (x:xs) (y:ys)
  | x <= y    = x:merge xs (y:ys)
  | otherwise = y:merge (x:xs) ys
```

In fact, many Haskell programmers wouldn't write the last clause of merge in quite this way. Instead they would write

```
merge xs'@(x:xs) ys'@(y:ys)
  | x <= y    = x:merge xs ys'
  | otherwise = y:merge xs' ys
```

This definition uses an *as-pattern*. You can see the point: rather than deconstructing a list and then reconstructing it again (a cheap but not free operation), it is better to reuse the value that we matched with. True, but it does obscure a simple mathematical equation, and we will use such patterns only very sparingly in this book.

Both sort and merge are defined recursively and it is worthwhile pointing out why the two recursions terminate. In the case of merge you have to see that one or other of the two arguments of merge decreases in size at each recursive call. Hence one of the base cases will eventually be reached. In the case of sort the critical observation is that if xs has length at least two, then both ys and zs have length strictly less than xs, and the same argument applies. But see what happens if we had omitted the clause sort [x] = [x]. Since $1 \operatorname{div} 2 = 0$ we would have,

```
sort [x] = merge (sort []) (sort [x])
```

That means evaluation of sort [x] requires evaluation of sort [x], and the whole definition of sort spins off into an infinite loop for nonempty arguments. Checking that you have all the necessary base cases is one of the most important parts of constructing a recursive function.

4.9 Exercises

Exercise A

Which of the following equations are true for all xs and which are false?

```
[]:xs = xs
[]:xs = [[],xs]
xs:[] = xs
xs:[] = [xs]
xs:xs = [xs,xs]
[[]] ++ xs = xs
[[]] ++ xs = [[],xs]
[[]] ++ [xs] = [[],xs]
```

```
[xs] ++ [] = [xs]
```

By the way, why didn't we define `null = (==[])`?

Exercise B

You want to produce an infinite list of all distinct pairs (x, y) of natural numbers. It doesn't matter in which order the pairs are enumerated, as long as they all are there. Say whether or not the definition

```
allPairs = [(x,y) | x <- [0..], y <- [0..]]
```

does the job. If you think it doesn't, can you give a version that does?

Exercise C

Give a definition of the function

```
disjoint :: (Ord a) => [a] -> [a] -> Bool
```

that takes two lists in ascending order, and determines whether or not they have an element in common.

Exercise D

Under what conditions do the following two list comprehensions deliver the same result?

```
[e | x <- xs, p x, y <- ys]
[e | x <- xs, y <- ys, p x]
```

Compare the costs of evaluating the two expressions.

Exercise E

When the great Indian mathematician Srinivasan Ramanujan was ill in a London hospital, he was visited by the English mathematician G.H. Hardy. Trying to find a subject of conversation, Hardy remarked that he had arrived in a taxi with the number 1729, a rather boring number it seemed to him. Not at all, Ramanujan instantly replied, it is the first number that can be expressed as two cubes in essentially different ways: $1^3 + 12^3 = 9^3 + 10^3 = 1729$. Write a program to find the second such number.

In fact, define a function that returns a list of all essentially different quadruples (a, b, c, d) in the range $0 < a, b, c, d \leq n$ such that $a^3 + b^3 = c^3 + d^3$. I suggest using a list comprehension, but only after thinking carefully about what it means to say two quadruples are essentially different. After all, $a^3 + b^3 = c^3 + d^3$ can be written in eight different ways.

Exercise F

The dual view of lists is to construct them by adding elements to the end of the list:

```
data List a = Nil | Snoc (List a) a
```

Snoc is, of course, Cons backwards. With this view of lists $[1, 2, 3]$ would be represented by

```
Snoc (Snoc (Snoc Nil 1) 2) 3
```

Exactly the same information is provided by the two views but it is organised differently. Give the definitions of head and last for the snoc-view of lists, and define two functions

```
toList :: [a] -> List a
fromList :: List a -> [a]
```

for converting efficiently from one view of lists to the other. (Hint: reverse is efficient, taking linear time to reverse a list.)

Exercise G

How much space is required to evaluate length xs? Consider the following alternative definition of length:

```
length :: [a] -> Int
length xs = loop (0,xs)
   where loop (n,[])   = n
         loop (n,x:xs) = loop (n+1,xs)
```

Does the space requirement change? Does it change if we switched to eager evaluation? These questions are taken up in much more detail in Chapter 7.

Exercise H

The prelude function take n takes the first n elements of a list, while drop n drops the first n elements. Give recursive definitions for these functions. What are the values of

```
take 0 undefined     take undefined []
```

according to your definition? A more tricky question: can you find a definition in which both the above expressions have the value []? If not, why not?

Which of the following equations are valid for all integers *m* and *n*? You don't have to justify your answers, just try to understand what they claim to say.

```
take n xs ++ drop n xs  =  xs
take m . drop n  =  drop n . take (m+n)
take m . take n  =  take (m `min` n)
drop m . drop n  =  drop (m+n)
```

The standard prelude function `splitAt` n can be defined by

```
splitAt n xs = (take n xs,drop n xs)
```

Though clear, the above definition is maybe a little inefficient as it involves processing xs twice. Give a definition of `splitAt` that traverses the list only once.

Exercise I

Which of the following statements about the equation

```
map (f . g) xs = map f (map g xs)
```

do you agree with, and which do you disagree with (again, no justification is required)?

1. It's not true for all xs; it depends on whether xs is a finite list or not.

2. It's not true for all f and g; it depends on whether f and g are strict functions or not.

3. It's true for all lists xs, finite, partial or infinite, and for all f and g of the appropriate type. In fact `map (f . g) = map f . map g` is a much neater alternative.

4. It looks true, but it has to be proved so from the definition of `map` and the definition of functional composition.

5. Used right-to-left, it expresses a program optimisation: two traversals of a list are replaced by one.

6. It's not an optimisation under lazy evaluation because `map g xs` is not computed in its entirety before evaluation of `map f` on the result begins.

7. Whether or not it is computed in pieces or as a whole, the right-hand side does produce an intermediate list, while the left-hand side doesn't. It is a rule for optimising a program even under lazy evaluation.

Exercise J

Here are some equations; at least one of them is false. Which are the true ones, and which are false? Once again, you do not have to provide any justification for your answers, the aim is just to look at some equations and appreciate what they are saying.

```
map f . take n      = take n . map f
map f . reverse     = reverse . map f
map f . sort        = sort . map f
map f . filter p    = map fst . filter snd . map (fork (f,p))
filter (p . g)      = map (invertg) . filter p . map g
reverse . concat    = concat . reverse . map reverse
filter p . concat = concat . map (filter p)
```

In the fifth equation assume `invertg` satisfies `invertg . g = id`. The function `fork` in the fourth equation is defined by

```
fork :: (a -> b,a -> c) -> a -> (b,c)
fork (f,g) x = (f x, g x)
```

Exercise K

Define `unzip` and `cross` by

```
unzip = fork (map fst, map snd)
cross (f,g) = fork (f . fst, g . snd)
```

What are the types of these functions?

Prove by simple equational reasoning that

```
cross (map f, map g) . unzip = unzip . map (cross (f,g))
```

You can use the functor laws of map and the following rules:

```
cross (f,g) . fork (h,k) = fork (f . h,g . k)
fork (f,g) . h           = fork (f . h,g . h)
fst . cross (f,g)        = f . fst
snd . cross (f,g)        = g . snd
```

Exercise L

Continuing from the previous exercise, prove that

```
cross (f,g) . cross (h,k) = cross (f . h,g . k)
```

We also have `cross (id,id) = id` (Why?). So it looks like `cross` has functor-like properties, except that it takes a pair of functions. Yes, it's a *bifunctor*. That suggests a generalisation:

```
class Bifunctor p where
    bimap :: (a -> b) -> (c -> d) -> p a c -> p b d
```

The arguments to `bimap` are given one by one rather than paired. Express `cross` in terms of `bimap` for the instance `Pair` of `Bifunctor`, where

```
type Pair a b = (a,b)
```

Now consider the data type

```
data Either a b = Left a | Right b
```

Construct the instance `Either` of `Bifunctor`.

4.10 Answers

Answer to Exercise A

Only the following three equations are true:

```
xs:[] = [xs]
[[]] ++ [xs] = [[],xs]
[xs] ++ [] = [xs]
```

If we defined `null` by `null = (==[])`, then its type would have to be the more restrictive

```
null :: (Eq a) => [a] -> Bool
```

That means you can only use an equality test on lists if the list elements can be compared for equality. Of course, the empty list contains no elements, so (==) is not needed.

Answer to Exercise B

No, `allPairs` produces the infinite list

```
allPairs = [(0,y) | y <- [0..]]
```

One alternative, which lists the pairs in ascending order of their sum, is

```
allPairs = [(x,d-x) | d <- [0..], x <- [0..d]]
```

Answer to Exercise C

The definition is

```
disjoint xs [] = True
disjoint [] ys = True
disjoint xs'@(x:xs) ys'@(y:ys)
  | x < y  = disjoint xs ys'
  | x == y = False
  | x > y  = disjoint xs' ys
```

We used an as-pattern, just to be clever.

Answer to Exercise D

They deliver the same result only if ys is a finite list:

```
ghci> [1 | x <- [1,3], even x, y <- undefined]
[]
ghci> [1 | x <- [1,3], y <- undefined, even x]
*** Exception: Prelude.undefined
ghci> [1 | x <- [1,3], even x, y <- [1..]]
[]
Prelude> [1 | x <- [1,3], y <- [1..], even x]
{Interrupted}
```

When they do deliver the same result, the former is more efficient.

Answer to Exercise E

One way of generating essentially different quadruples is to restrict the quadruple (a,b,c,d) to values satisfying $a \leq b$ and $c \leq d$ and $a < c$. Hence

```
quads n = [(a,b,c,d) | a <- [1..n],  b <- [a..n],
                       c <- [a+1..n],d <- [c..n],
                       a^3 + b^3 == c^3 + d^3]
```

The second such number is $4104 = 2^3 + 16^3 = 9^3 + 15^3$.

Answer to Exercise F

```
head :: List a -> a
head (Snoc Nil x) = x
head (Snoc xs x)  = head xs
```

```
last :: List a -> a
last (Snoc xs x) = x

toList :: [a] -> List a
toList = convert . reverse
   where convert []     = Nil
         convert (x:xs) = Snoc (convert xs) x
fromList :: List a -> [a]
fromList = reverse . convert
   where convert Nil          = []
         convert (Snoc xs x) = x:convert xs
```

Answer to Exercise G

It requires a linear amount of space since the expression

```
1 + (1 + (1 + ... (1 + 0)))
```

is built up in memory. The space requirement for the second definition of length does not change under lazy evaluation since the expression

```
loop ((((0 + 1) + 1) + 1 ... +1),[])
```

is built up in memory. But under eager evaluation the length of a list can be computed using constant extra space.

Answer to Exercise H

```
take, drop :: Int -> [a] -> [a]
take n []     = []
take n (x:xs) = if n==0 then [] else x:take (n-1) xs

drop n []     = []
drop n (x:xs) = if n==0 then x:xs else drop (n-1) xs
```

With this definition of take we have

```
take undefined [] = []    take 0 undefined = undefined
```

With the alternative

```
take n xs | n==0      = []
          | null xs   = []
          | otherwise = head xs: take (n-1) (tail xs)
```

we have

```
take undefined [] = undefined    take 0 undefined = []
```

The answer to the tricky question is: no. Either argument n or argument xs has to be examined and, whichever happens first, ⊥ is the result if ⊥ is the value of that argument.

All four equations are valid for all lists *xs* and for all *m, n* ≠ ⊥, under either definition.

The function splitAt n can be defined by

```
splitAt :: Int -> [a] -> ([a],[a])
splitAt n [] = ([],[])
splitAt n (x:xs) = if n==0 then ([],x:xs) else (x:ys,zs)
                   where (ys,zs) = splitAt (n-1) xs
```

Answer to Exercise I

I would agree with (3), (4), (5) and (7).

Answer to Exercise J

The only false equation is map f . sort = sort . map f which is true only if *f* is order-preserving, i.e. $x \le y \equiv f\, x \le f\, y$.

Answer to Exercise K

```
unzip :: [(a,b)] -> ([a],[b])
cross :: (a -> b, c -> d) -> (a,c) -> (b,d)
```

The calculation is

```
        cross (map f, map g) . unzip
    =   {definition of unzip}
        cross (map f, map g) . fork (map fst, map snd)
    =   {law of cross and fork}
        fork (map f . map fst, map g . map snd)
    =   {law of map}
        fork (map (f . fst), map (g . snd))
```

We seem to be stuck, as no law applies. Try the right-hand side:

```
      unzip . map (cross (f,g))
  =   {definition of unzip}
      fork (map fst, map snd) . map (cross (f,g))
  =   {law of fork}
      fork (map fst . map (cross (f,g)),
            map snd . map (cross (f,g)))
  =   {law of map}
      fork (map (fst . cross (f,g)),
            map (snd . cross (f,g)))
  =   {laws of fst and snd}
      fork (map (f . fst), map (g . snd))
```

Phew. Both sides have reduced to the same expression. That is often the way with calculations: one side doesn't always lead easily to the other, but both sides reduce to the same result.

The calculations we have seen so far have all been carried out at the function level. Such a style of definition and proof is called *point-free* (and also *pointless* by some jokers). Point-free proofs are what the automatic calculator of Chapter 12 produces. The point-free style is very slick, but it does necessitate the use of various *plumbing combinators*, such as `fork` and `cross`, to pass arguments to functions. Plumbing combinators push values around, duplicate them and even eliminate them. As an example of the last kind,

```
const :: a -> b -> a
const x y = x
```

This little combinator is in the standard prelude and can be quite useful on occasion.

Two more plumbing combinators, also defined in the standard prelude, are `curry` and `uncurry`:

```
curry :: ((a, b) -> c) -> a -> b -> c
curry f x y = f (x,y)

uncurry :: (a -> b -> c) -> (a,b) -> c
uncurry f (x,y) = f x y
```

A *curried* function is a function that takes its arguments one at a time, while a non-curried function takes a single, tupled argument. The key advantage of curried functions is that they can be *partially applied*. For instance, take n is a perfectly valid function in its own right, and so is map f. That is why we have used curried functions from the start.

By the way, curried functions are named after Haskell B. Curry, an American logician. And, yes, that is where Haskell got its name.

Answer to Exercise L

```
    cross (f,g) . cross (h,k)
=   {definition of cross}
    cross (f,g) . fork (h . fst, k . snd)
=   {law of cross and fork}
    fork (f . h . fst,g . k . snd)
=   {definition of cross}
    cross (f . h, g . k)
```

We have cross = uncurry bimap, where uncurry was defined in the previous answer.

Here is the instance of Either:

```
instance Bifunctor Either where
   bimap f g (Left x)  = Left (f x)
   bimap f g (Right y) = Right (g y)
```

4.11 Chapter notes

Most of the functions introduced in this chapter can be found in the Haskell standard prelude. Functors, bifunctors, and natural transformations are explained in books about Category Theory. Two such are *Basic Category Theory for Computer Scientists* (MIT Press, 1991) by Benjamin Pierce, and *The Algebra of Programming* (Prentice Hall, 1997) by Richard Bird and Oege de Moor.

Also on the subject of laws, read Phil Wadler's influential article *Theorems for free!* which can be found at

```
homepages.inf.ed.ac.uk/wadler/papers/free/
```

In mathematics, the so-called taxicab number taxicab(n) is the smallest number that can be expressed as the sum of two positive cubes in n distinct ways. So $1729 =$ taxicab(2). Google 'taxicab numbers' for more information.

Chapter 5

A simple Sudoku solver

> HOW TO PLAY: Fill in the grid so that every row,
> every column and every 3×3 box contains the
> digits 1–9. There's no maths involved. You
> solve the puzzle with reasoning and logic.
> *Advice on how to play Sudoku, the* Independent

This chapter is devoted to an extended exercise in the use of lists to solve problems, and in the use of equational reasoning to reason about them and to improve efficiency.

The game of Sudoku is played on a 9 by 9 grid, though other sizes are also possible. Given a matrix, such as that in Figure 5.1, the idea is to fill in the empty cells with the digits 1 to 9 so that each row, column and 3×3 box contains the numbers 1 to 9. In general there may be any number of solutions, though in a good Sudoku puzzle there should always be a unique solution. Our aim is to construct a program to solve Sudoku puzzles. Specifically, we will define a function `solve` for computing a list of all the ways a given grid may be completed. If only one solution is wanted, then we can take the head of the list. Lazy evaluation means that only the first result will then be computed.

We begin with a specification, then use equational reasoning to calculate a more efficient version. There's no maths involved, just reasoning and logic!

5.1 Specification

Here are the basic data types of interest, starting with matrices:

```
type Matrix a = [Row a]
```

		4		5	7			
				9	4			
3	6							8
7	2		6					
		4		2				
			8			9	3	
4						5	6	
		5	3					
		6	1		9			

Figure 5.1 A Sudoku grid

```
type Row a    = [a]
```

The two type synonyms say nothing more than that `Matrix a` is a synonym for
`[[a]]`. But the way it is said emphasises that a matrix is a list of *rows*; more
precisely, a $m \times n$ matrix is a list of m rows in which each row is a list with the
same length n. Haskell type synonyms cannot enforce such constraints, though
there are languages, called *dependently-typed* languages, that can.

A grid is a 9×9 matrix of digits:

```
type Grid  = Matrix Digit
type Digit = Char
```

The valid digits are 1 to 9 with 0 standing for a blank:

```
digits :: [Char]
digits = ['1' .. '9']

blank :: Digit -> Bool
blank = (== '0')
```

Recall that `Char` is also an instance of the type class `Enum`, so `['1' .. '9']` is a
valid expression and does indeed return the list of nonzero digits.

We will suppose for simplicity that the input grid contains only digits and blanks,
so we do not have to check for the input being well-formed. But should we also
insist that no non-blank digit is repeated in any row, column or box? If there were
such repetitions there would be no solution. We postpone this decision until after
we see how the rest of the algorithm pans out.

Now for the specification. The aim is to write down the simplest and clearest specification without regard to how efficient the result might be. That's a key difference between functional programming and other forms of program construction: we can always begin with a clear and simple, though possibly extremely inefficient definition of solve, and then use the laws of functional programming to massage the computation into one that takes acceptable time and space.

One possibility is first to construct a list of all possible correctly filled grids, a vastly long but still finite list, and then to test the given grid against each of them to identify those whose entries match the given non-blank ones. Certainly that approach takes the idea of an inefficient specification to the extreme. Another reasonable alternative is to start with the given grid and to complete it by filling in every possible choice for the blank entries. The result will be a list of filled grids. Then we can filter this list for those that don't contain duplicates in any row, box or column. This specification is implemented by

```
solve :: Grid -> [Grid]
solve = filter valid . completions
```

where the subsidiary functions have types

```
completions :: Grid -> [Grid]
valid    :: Grid -> Bool
```

Let us work on completions first and consider valid afterwards. One way of defining completions is by a two-step process:

```
completions = expand . choices
```

where

```
choices :: Grid -> Matrix [Digit]
expand  :: Matrix [Digit] -> [Grid]
```

The function choices installs the available digits for each cell:

```
choices = map (map choice)
choice d = if blank d then digits else [d]
```

If the cell is blank, then all digits are installed as possible choices; otherwise there is only one choice and a singleton is returned. If we want to apply f to every element of a matrix, then map (map f) is the function to use because, after all, a matrix is just a list of lists.

After applying choices we obtain a matrix each of whose entries is a list of digits. What we want to do next is to define expand to convert this matrix into a list of grids by installing all the choices in all possible ways. That seems a little difficult to think about, so let's consider a simpler problem first, namely when instead of a 9×9 matrix we have a list of length 3. Suppose we want to convert

```
[[1,2,3],[2],[1,3]]
```

into the list

```
[[1,2,1],[1,2,3],[2,2,1],[2,2,3],[3,2,1],[3,2,3]]
```

The second list of lists arises by taking, in all possible ways, one element from the first list, one element from the second list and one element from the third list. Let us call the function that does this cp (short for 'cartesian product', which is exactly what a mathematician would call it). There doesn't seem to be any clever way of computing cp in terms of other functions, so we adopt the default strategy of defining this function by breaking up its argument list into two possibilities, the empty list [] and a nonempty list xs:xss. You might guess the definition of cp [] but you would probably be wrong; the better alternative is to think about the second case first. Suppose we assume

```
cp [[2],[1,3]] = [[2,1],[2,3]]
```

How can we extend this definition to one for cp ([1,2,3]:[[2],[1,3]])? The answer is to prefix 1 to every element of cp [[2],[1,3]], then to prefix 2 to every element of the same list, and finally to prefix 3 to every element. That process can be expressed neatly using a list comprehension:

```
cp (xs:xss) = [x:ys | x <- xs, ys <- cp xss]
```

In words, prefix every element of xs to every element of cp xss in all possible ways.

If your nose is good at sniffing out inefficiencies, you might suspect that this one-liner is not the best possible, and you would be right. We will return to this point in Section 7.3, but let's just say that a more efficient definition is

```
cp (xs:xss) = [x:ys | x <- xs, ys <- yss]
              where yss = cp xss
```

This version guarantees that cp xss is computed just once.

Now, what is cp []? The answer is not [] but [[]]. To see why the first is wrong, consider a little calculation:

```
cp [xs] = cp (xs:[])
        = [x:ys | x <- xs, ys <- cp []]
```

```
    = [x:ys | x <- xs, ys <- []]
    = []
```

In fact with `cp [] = []` we can show that `cp xss = []` for all lists `xss`. So that definition is clearly wrong. You can check that the second alternative, `[[]]`, does give what is wanted.

Summarising, we can define `cp` by

```
cp :: [[a]] -> [[a]]
cp []       = [[]]
cp (xs:xss) = [x:ys | x <- xs, ys <- yss]
              where yss = cp xss
```

For example,

```
ghci> cp [[1],[2],[3]]
[[1,2,3]]

ghci> cp [[1,2],[],[4,5]]
[]
```

In the second example there is no possible choice from the middle list, so the empty list is returned.

But what about matrices and `expand`, which does the same thing on matrices as `cp` does on lists? You will have to think a bit before seeing that what is wanted is

```
expand :: Matrix [Digit] -> [Grid]
expand = cp . map cp
```

That looks a little cryptic, but `map cp` returns a list of all possible choices for each row, and so applying `cp` to the result installs each choice for the rows in all possible ways. The general type of the right-hand side is

```
cp . map cp :: [[[a]]] -> [[[a]]]
```

and the declared type of `expand` is just a restricted version of this type. Note that `expand` returns the empty list if any element in any row is the empty list.

Finally, a valid grid is one in which no row, column or box contains duplicates:

```
valid :: Grid -> Bool
valid g = all nodups (rows g) &&
          all nodups (cols g) &&
          all nodups (boxs g)
```

The prelude function `all` is defined by

```
all p = and . map p
```

Applied to a finite list `xs` the function `all p` returns `True` if all elements of `xs` satisfy p, and `False` otherwise. The function nodups can be defined by

```
nodups :: (Eq a) => [a] -> Bool
nodups []     = True
nodups (x:xs) = all (/=x) xs && nodups xs
```

Evaluation of nodups on a list of length n takes time proportional to n^2. As an alternative we could sort the list and check that it is strictly increasing. Sorting can be done in time proportional to $n \log n$ steps. That seems a big saving over n^2. However, with $n = 9$, it is not clear that using an efficient sorting algorithm is worthwhile. What would you prefer: $2n^2$ steps or $100n \log_2 n$ steps?

It remains to define `rows`, `cols` and `boxs`. If a matrix is given by a list of its rows, then `rows` is just the identity function on matrices:

```
rows :: Matrix a -> Matrix a
rows = id
```

The function `cols` computes the transpose of a matrix. Thus if a matrix consists of m rows, where each row has length n, the transpose is a list of n rows, where each row has length m. Assuming both m and n are not zero, we can define

```
cols :: Matrix a -> Matrix a
cols [xs]     = [[x] | x <- xs]
cols (xs:xss) = zipWith (:) xs (cols xss)
```

It is usual in matrix algebra to suppose that the matrix is nonempty, and that certainly suffices here, but it is interesting to consider what happens if we allow m or n to be zero. This point is taken up in the exercises.

The function `boxs` is a little more interesting. We give the definition first and explain it afterwards:

```
boxs :: Matrix a -> Matrix a
boxs = map ungroup . ungroup .
       map cols .
       group . map group
```

The function group splits a list into groups of three:

```
group :: [a] -> [[a]]
```

```
group [] = []
group xs = take 3 xs:group (drop 3 xs)
```

The function ungroup takes a grouped list and ungroups it:

```
ungroup :: [[a]] -> [a]
ungroup = concat
```

The action of boxs in the 4×4 case, when group splits a list into groups of two rather than three, is illustrated by the picture

$$
\begin{pmatrix} a & b & c & d \\ e & f & g & h \\ i & j & k & l \\ m & n & o & p \end{pmatrix} \longrightarrow \begin{pmatrix} \begin{pmatrix} ab & cd \\ ef & gh \end{pmatrix} \\ \begin{pmatrix} ij & kl \\ mn & op \end{pmatrix} \end{pmatrix}
$$

$$
\downarrow
$$

$$
\begin{pmatrix} a & b & e & f \\ c & d & g & h \\ i & j & m & n \\ k & l & o & p \end{pmatrix} \longleftarrow \begin{pmatrix} \begin{pmatrix} ab & ef \\ cd & gh \end{pmatrix} \\ \begin{pmatrix} ij & mn \\ kl & op \end{pmatrix} \end{pmatrix}
$$

Grouping produces a list of matrices; transposing each matrix and ungrouping yields the boxes, as a matrix whose rows are the boxes of the original matrix.

5.2 Lawful program construction

Observe that instead of thinking about matrices in terms of indices, and doing arithmetic on indices to identify the rows, columns and boxes, we have gone for definitions of these functions that treat the matrix as a complete entity in itself. This style has aptly been called *wholemeal programming*. Wholemeal programming is good for you: it helps to prevent a disease called indexitis, and encourages lawful program construction.

For example, here are three laws that are valid on Sudoku grids:

```
rows . rows = id
cols . cols = id
boxs . boxs = id
```

In other words, all three functions are involutions. The first two are valid on all matrices, and the third is valid on arbitrary $n^2 \times n^2$ matrices (provided we change the definition of `group` to group by *n*). Two are easy to prove, but one is more difficult. The difficult law is not the one about `boxs`, as you might expect, but the involution property of `cols`. Though it is intuitively obvious that transposing a matrix twice gets you back to the original matrix, proving it from the definition of `cols` is a little tricky and we won't go into details, basically because we haven't yet discussed the tools available to do the job.

By contrast, here is the proof of the involution property of `boxs`. The proof is by simple equational reasoning. It makes use of various laws, including the functor laws of `map`, the fact that `id` is the identity element of composition, and the facts that

```
ungroup . group = id
group . ungroup = id
```

The second equation is valid only on grouped lists, but that will be the case in the calculation to come.

We will talk through the proof rather than lay everything out in a long chain. The starting point is to use the definition of `boxs` to rewrite `boxs . boxs`:

```
map ungroup . ungroup . map cols . group . map group .
map ungroup . ungroup . map cols . group . map group
```

The middle expression `map group . map ungroup` simplifies to `id` using the functor law of `map` and the property that `group` and `ungroup` are inverses. That gives

```
map ungroup . ungroup . map cols . group .
ungroup . map cols . group . map group
```

An appeal to `group . ungroup = id` gets us to

```
map ungroup . ungroup . map cols .
map cols . group . map group
```

The functor law of `map` and the involution property of `cols` now gets us to

```
map ungroup . ungroup . group . map group
```

And the proof is finished off using `ungroup . group = id` twice more. As you can see, it's a very simple calculation.

Here are three more laws, valid on $N^2 \times N^2$ matrices of choices:

```
map rows . expand = expand . rows
map cols . expand = expand . cols
```

```
map boxs . expand = expand . boxs
```

We will make use of these laws in a short while.

Finally, here are two laws about cp:

```
map (map f) . cp     = cp . map (map f)
filter (all p) . cp = cp . map (filter p)
```

The first law, a naturality law, is suggested solely by the type of cp; we saw similar laws in the previous chapter. The second law says that as an alternative to taking the cartesian product of a list of lists, and then retaining only those lists all of whose elements satisfy p, we can first filter the original lists to retain only those elements that satisfy p and then take the cartesian product. As the previous sentence illustrates, one equation can be worth a thousand words.

5.3 Pruning the matrix of choices

Summarising what we have at the moment,

```
solve :: Grid -> [Grid]
solve = filter valid . expand . choices
```

Though executable in theory, this definition of solve is hopeless in practice. Assuming about 20 of the 81 entries are fixed initially, there are about 9^{61}, or

```
ghci> 9^61
16173092699229880893718618465586445357583280647840659957609
```

grids to check! We therefore need a better approach.

To make a more efficient solver, an obvious idea is to remove any choices from a cell c that already occur as singleton entries in the row, column and box containing c. A singleton entry corresponds to a fixed choice. We therefore seek a function

```
prune :: Matrix [Digit] -> Matrix [Digit]
```

so that

```
filter valid . expand = filter valid . expand . prune
```

How can we define prune? Well, since a matrix is a list of rows, a good place to start is by pruning a single row. The function pruneRow is defined by

```
pruneRow :: Row [Digit] -> Row [Digit]
pruneRow row = map (remove fixed) row
```

```
where fixed = [d | [d] <- row]
```

The fixed choices are the singleton entries in each row. The definition of `fixed` uses a list comprehension involving a pattern: all elements of `row` that are not singletons are discarded.

The function `remove` removes the fixed choices from any choice that is not fixed:

```
remove :: [Digit] -> [Digit] -> [Digit]
remove ds [x] = [x]
remove ds xs  = filter (`notElem` ds) xs
```

The standard prelude function `notElem` is defined by

```
notElem :: (Eq a) => a -> [a] -> Bool
notElem x xs = all (/= x) xs
```

Here are a couple of examples of the use of `pruneRow`:

```
ghci> pruneRow [[6],[1,2],[3],[1,3,4],[5,6]]
[[6],[1,2],[3],[1,4],[5]]

ghci> pruneRow [[6],[3,6],[3],[1,3,4],[4]]
[[6],[],[3],[1],[4]]
```

In the first example, `[6]` and `[3]` are the fixed choices; removing these choices from the other entries reduces the last entry to a fixed choice. In the second example, removing the fixed choices reduces the second entry to the empty list of choices.

The function `pruneRow` satisfies the equation

```
filter nodups . cp = filter nodups . cp . pruneRow
```

In words, this equation says that pruning a row will not throw away any list that contains no duplicates. We will also make use of this law in a short while.

We are now nearly ready for a calculation that will determine the function `prune`. Nearly, but not quite because we are going to need two more laws: If `f . f = id`, then

```
filter (p . f) = map f . filter p . map f
filter (p . f) . map f = map f . filter p
```

The second law follows from the first (Why?). Here is the proof of the first law:

```
    map f . filter p . map f
=   {we proved in the previous chapter that
            filter p . map f = map f . filter (p . f)}
    map f . map f . filter (p . f)
=   {functor law of map and f . f = id}
    filter (p . f)
```

Now for the main calculation. The starting point is to use the definition of valid to rewrite the expression filter valid . expand in the form

```
filter valid . expand
= filter (all nodups . boxs) .
  filter (all nodups . cols) .
  filter (all nodups . rows) . expand
```

The order in which the filters appear on the right is not important. The plan of attack is to send each of these filters into battle with expand. For example, in the boxs case we can calculate:

```
    filter (all nodups . boxs) . expand
=   {above law of filter, since boxs . boxs = id}
    map boxs . filter (all nodups) . map boxs . expand
=   {since map boxs . expand = expand . boxs}
    map boxs . filter (all nodups) . expand . boxs
=   {definition of expand}
    map boxs . filter (all nodups) . cp . map cp . boxs
=   {since filter (all p) . cp = cp . map (filter p)}
    map boxs . cp . map (filter nodups) . map cp . boxs
=   {functor law of map}
    map boxs . cp . map (filter nodups . cp) . boxs
```

Now we use the property

```
filter nodups . cp = filter nodups . cp . pruneRow
```

to rewrite the final expression in the form

```
map boxs . cp . map (filter nodups . cp . pruneRow) . boxs
```

The remaining steps essentially repeat the calculation above, but in the reverse direction:

```
map boxs . cp . map (filter nodups . cp . pruneRow) .
boxs
```
=   {functor law of map}
```
map boxs . cp . map (filter nodups) .
map (cp . pruneRow) . boxs
```
=   {since cp . map (filter p) = filter (all p) . cp}
```
map boxs . filter (all nodups) . cp .
map (cp . pruneRow) . boxs
```
=   {functor law of map}
```
map boxs . filter (all nodups) .
cp . map cp . map pruneRow . boxs
```
=   {definition of expand}
```
map boxs . filter (all nodups) .
expand . map pruneRow . boxs
```
=   {law of filter since boxs . boxs = id}
```
filter (all nodups . boxs) . map boxs .
expand . map pruneRow . boxs
```
=   {since map boxs . expand = expand . boxs}
```
filter (all nodups . boxs) . expand .
boxs . map pruneRow . boxs
```
=   {introducing pruneBy f = f . pruneRow . f}
```
filter (all nodups . boxs) . expand . pruneBy boxs
```

We have shown that

```
filter (all nodups . boxs) . expand
 = filter (all nodups . boxs) . expand . pruneBy boxs
```

where pruneBy f = f . map pruneRow . f. Repeating the same calculation for rows and columns, we obtain

```
filter valid . expand = filter valid . expand . prune
```

where

```
prune = pruneBy boxs . pruneBy cols . pruneBy rows
```

In conclusion, the previous definition of `solve` can now be replaced with a new one:

```
solve = filter valid . expand . prune . choices
```

In fact, rather than have just one `prune` we can have as many prunes as we like. This is sensible because after one round of pruning some choices may be resolved into singleton choices and another round of pruning may remove still more impossible choices.

So, let us define

```
many :: (Eq a) => (a -> a) -> a -> a
many f x = if x == y then x else many f y
           where y = f x
```

and redefine `solve` once again to read

```
solve = filter valid . expand . many prune . choices
```

The simplest Sudoku problems are solved just by repeatedly pruning the matrix of choices until only singleton choices are left.

5.4 Expanding a single cell

The result of `many prune . choices` is a matrix of choices that can be put into one of three classes:

1. A *complete* matrix in which every entry is a singleton choice. In this case `expand` will extract a single grid that can be checked for validity.

2. A matrix that contains the empty choice somewhere. In this case `expand` will produce the empty list.

3. A matrix that does not contain the empty choice but does contain some entry with two or more choices.

The problem is what to do in the third case. Rather than carry out full expansion, a more sensible idea is to make use of a partial expansion that installs the choices for just one of the entries, and to start the pruning process again on each result. The hope is that mixing pruning with single-cell expansions can lead to a solution more quickly. Our aim therefore is to construct a partial function

```
expand1 :: Matrix [Digit] -> [Matrix [Digit]]
```

that expands the choices for one cell only. This function will return well-defined
results only for incomplete matrices, and on such matrices is required to satisfy

```
expand = concat . map expand .  expand1
```

Actually this equality between two lists is too strong. We want to ensure that no
possible choice is lost by partial expansion, but do not really care about the precise
order in which the two sides deliver their results. So we will interpret the equation
as asserting the equality of the two sides up to some permutation of the answers.

Which cell should we perform expansion on? The simplest answer is to find the
first cell in the matrix with a non-singleton entry. Think of a matrix rows broken
up as follows:

```
rows = rows1 ++ [row] ++ rows2
row = row1 ++ [cs] ++ row2
```

The cell cs is a non-singleton list of choices in the middle of row, which in turn is
in the middle of the matrix rows.

Then we can define

```
expand1 :: Matrix [Digit] -> [Matrix [Digit]]
expand1 rows
  = [rows1 ++ [row1 ++ [c]:row2] ++ rows2 | c <- cs]
```

To break up the matrix in this way, we use the prelude function break:

```
break :: (a -> Bool) -> [a] -> ([a],[a])
break p = span (not . p)
```

The function span was defined in Section 4.8. For example,

```
ghci> break even [1,3,7,6,2,3,5]
([1,3,7],[6,2,3,5])
```

We also need the standard prelude function any, defined by

```
any :: (a -> Bool) -> [a] -> Bool
any p = or . map p
```

where or takes a list of booleans and returns True if any element is True, and
False otherwise:

```
or :: [Bool] -> Bool
or []     = False
or (x:xs) = x || or xs
```

Finally, the `single` test is defined (using don't care patterns) by

```
single :: [a] -> Bool
single [_] = True
single _   = False
```

Now we can define

```
expand1 :: Matrix [Digit] -> [Matrix [Digit]]
expand1 rows
  = [rows1 ++ [row1 ++ [c]:row2] ++ rows2 | c <- cs]
    where
    (rows1,row:rows2) = break (any (not . single)) rows
    (row1,cs:row2)    = break (not . single) row
```

The first `where` clause breaks a matrix into two lists of rows with the row at the head of the second list being one that contains a non-singleton choice. A second appeal to `break` then breaks this row into two lists, with the head of the second list being the first non-singleton element. If the matrix contains only singleton entries, then

```
break (any (not . single)) rows = [rows,[]]
```

and execution of `expand1` returns an error message.

The problem with this definition of `expand1` is that it can lead to wasted work. If the first non-singleton entry found in this way happens to be the empty list, then `expand1` will return the empty list, but if such a list is buried deep in the matrix, then `expand1` will do a lot of useless calculation trying to find a solution that isn't there. It is arguable that a better choice of cell on which to perform expansion is one with the *smallest* number of choices (not equal to 1 of course). A cell with no choices means that the puzzle is unsolvable, so identifying such a cell quickly is a good idea.

The change to `expand1` to implement this idea is as follows:

```
expand1 :: Matrix [Digit] -> [Matrix [Digit]]
expand1 rows
  = [rows1 ++ [row1 ++ [c]:row2] ++ rows2 | c <- cs]
    where
    (rows1,row:rows2) = break (any smallest) rows
    (row1,cs:row2)    = break smallest row
    smallest cs       = length cs == n
    n                 = minimum (counts rows)
```

The function `counts` is defined by

```
counts = filter (/= 1) . map length . concat
```

The value n is the smallest number of choices, not equal to 1, in any cell of the matrix of choices. We will leave the definition of `minimum` as an exercise. The value of n will be 0 if the matrix has an empty choice entry anywhere, and in this case `expand1` will return the empty list. On the other hand, if the matrix of choices contains only singleton choices, then n is the minimum of the empty list, which is the undefined value $\perp$. In this case `expand1` will also return $\perp$, so we had better ensure that `expand1` is applied only to incomplete matrices. A matrix is incomplete if it does not satisfy `complete`:

```
complete :: Matrix [Digit] -> Bool
complete = all (all single)
```

We can also usefully generalise `valid` to a test on matrices of choices. Suppose we define `safe` by

```
safe :: Matrix [Digit] -> Bool
safe m = all ok (rows cm) &&
         all ok (cols cm) &&
         all ok (boxs cm)
ok row = nodups [x | [x] <- row]
```

A matrix is safe if none of the singleton choices in any row, column or box contain duplicates. But a safe matrix may contain non-singleton choices. Pruning can turn a safe matrix into an unsafe one, but if a matrix is safe after pruning it has to be safe beforehand. In symbols, `safe . prune = safe`. A complete and safe matrix yields a solution to the Sudoku problem, and this solution can be extracted by a simplified version of `expand`:

```
extract :: Matrix [Digit] -> Grid
extract = map (map head)
```

Hence on a safe and complete matrix m we have

```
filter valid (expand m) = [extract m]
```

On a safe but incomplete matrix we have

```
  filter valid . expand
= filter valid . concat . map expand . expand1
```

up to permutation of each side. Since

```
filter p . concat = concat . map (filter p)
```

we obtain that `filter valid . expand` simplifies to

```
concat . map (filter p . expand) . expand1
```

And now we can insert a single prune to obtain

```
concat . map (filter p . expand . prune) . expand1
```

Hence, introducing

```
search = filter valid . expand . prune
```

we have, on safe but incomplete matrices, that

```
search = concat . map search . expand1 . prune
```

And now we can replace `solve` by a third version:

```
solve = search . choices
search cm
   | not (safe pm) = []
   | complete pm   = [extract pm]
   | otherwise     = concat (map search (expand1 pm))
   where pm = prune cm
```

This is our final simple Sudoku solver. We could replace prune in the last line by many prune. Sometimes many prunes work faster than one prune; sometimes not. Note that the very first safety test occurs immediately after one round of pruning on the installed choices; consequently flawed input is detected quickly.

5.5 Exercises

Exercise A

How would you add 1 to every element in a given matrix of integers? How would you sum the elements of a matrix? The function `zipWith (+)` adds two rows, but what function would add two matrices? How would you define matrix multiplication?

Exercise B

What are the dimensions of the matrix `[[],[]]`? Of the matrix `[]`?

The function `cols` (here renamed as `transpose`) was defined by

```
transpose :: [[a]] -> [[a]]
transpose [xs]      = [[x] | x <- xs]
transpose (xs:xss) = zipWith (:) xs (transpose xss)
```

Fill in the dots that would enable you to replace the first clause by

```
transpose []        = ...
```

The above definition of transpose proceeds row by row. Here is part of a definition that proceeds column by column:

```
transpose xss = map head xss:transpose (map tail xss)
```

Complete this definition.

Exercise C

Which of the following equations are true (no justification is necessary):

```
any p = not . all (not p)
any null = null . cp
```

Exercise D

Given a function sort :: (Ord a) => [a] -> [a] that sorts a list, construct a
definition of

```
nodups :: (Ord a) => [a] -> Bool
```

Exercise E

The function nub :: (Eq a) => [a] -> [a] removes duplicates from a list (a
version of this function is available in the library Data.List). Define nub. Assuming the order of the elements in the result is not important, define

```
nub :: (Ord a) => [a] -> [a]
```

so that the result is a more efficient function.

Exercise F

The functions takeWhile and dropWhile satisfy

```
span p xs = (takeWhile p xs,dropWhile p xs)
```

Give direct recursive definitions of takeWhile and dropWhile.

Assuming whiteSpace :: Char -> Bool is a test for whether a character is

white space (such as a space, a tab or a newline) or a visible character, construct a
definition of

```
words :: String -> [Word]
```

that breaks a string up into a list of words.

Exercise G

Define minimum :: Ord a => [a] -> a.

Exercise H

Why didn't we define solve by the following?

```
solve = search . choices
search m
  | not (safe m) = []
  | complete m   = [extract m]
  | otherwise    = process m
 where process = concat . map search . expand1 . prune
```

5.6 Answers

Answer to Exercise A

Adding 1 to every matrix element is defined by map (map (+1)).

Summing a matrix is defined by sum . map sum, where sum sums a list of numbers. Alternatively, we could use sum . concat.

Matrix addition is defined by zipWith (zipWith (+)).

For matrix multiplication we first define

```
scalarMult :: Num a => [a] -> [a] -> a
scalarMult xs ys = sum (zipwith (*) xs ys)
```

Then we have

```
matMult :: Num a => Matrix a -> Matrix a -> Matrix a
matMult ma mb = [map (scalarMult row) mbt | row <- ma]
                where mbt = transpose mb
```

Answer to Exercise B

The matrix $[[],[]]$ has dimensions 2×0. The matrix $[]$ has dimensions $0 \times n$ for every n. The transpose of such a matrix therefore has to have dimensions $n \times 0$ for every n. The only reasonable possibility is to let n be infinite:

```
transpose :: [[a]] -> [[a]]
transpose []       = repeat []
transpose (xs:xss) = zipWith (:) xs (transpose xss)
```

where `repeat` x gives an infinite list of repetitions of x. Note that

```
transpose [xs] = zipWith (:) xs (repeat [])
               = [[x] | x <- xs]
```

The alternative definition is

```
transpose ([]:xss) = []
transpose xss = map head xss:transpose (map tail xss)
```

The assumption in the first line is that if the first row is empty, then all the rows are empty and the transpose is the empty matrix.

Answer to Exercise C

Both the equations are true.

Answer to Exercise D

```
nodups :: (Ord a) => [a] -> Bool
nodups xs = and (zipWith (/=) ys (tail ys))
            where ys = sort xs
```

Answer to Exercise E

```
nub :: (Eq a) => [a] -> [a]
nub []     = []
nub (x:xs) = x:nub (filter (/= x) xs)

nub :: (Ord a) => [a] -> [a]
nub = remdups . sort

remdups []     = []
remdups (x:xs) = x:remdups (dropWhile (==x) xs)
```

The function `dropWhile` is defined in the next exercise.

Answer to Exercise F

```
takeWhile, dropWhile :: (a -> Bool) -> [a] -> [a]
takeWhile p [] = []
takeWhile p (x:xs)
          = if p x then x:takeWhile p xs else []
dropWhile p [] = []
dropWhile p (x:xs)
          = if p x then dropWhile p xs else x:xs
```

The definition of words is

```
words :: String -> [Word]
words xs | null ys   = []
         | otherwise = w:words zs
           where ys = dropWhile whiteSpace xs
                 (w,zs) = break whiteSpace ys
```

Answer to Exercise G

```
minimum :: Ord a => [a] -> a
minimum [x]     = x
minimum (x:xs) = x `min` minimum xs
```

Note that the minimum of the empty list is undefined.

Answer to Exercise H

The suggested definition of solve would return the undefined value if the matrix becomes complete after one round of pruning.

5.7 Chapter notes

The *Independent* newspaper no longer uses the rubric for Sudoku quoted at the start of the chapter. The presentation follows that in my book *Pearls of Functional Algorithm Design* (Cambridge, 2010). The site

```
haskell.org/haskellwiki/Sudoku
```

contains about 20 Haskell implementations of Sudoku, many of which use arrays and/or monads. We will meet arrays and monads in Chapter 10.

Chapter 6

Proofs

We have seen a lot of laws in the previous two chapters, though perhaps the word 'law' is a little inappropriate because it suggests something that is given to us from on high and which does not have to be proved. At least the word has the merit of being short. All of the laws we have encountered so far assert the equality of two functional expressions, possibly under subsidiary conditions; in other words, laws have been equations or *identities* between functions, and calculations have been point-free calculations (see Chapter 4, and the answer to Exercise K for more on the point-free style). Given suitable laws to work with, we can then use equational reasoning to prove other laws. Equational logic is a simple but powerful tool in functional programming because it can guide us to new and more efficient definitions of the functions and other values we have constructed. Efficiency is the subject of the following chapter. This one is about another aspect of equational reasoning, proof by induction. We will also show how to shorten proofs by introducing a number of *higher-order* functions that capture common patterns of computations. Instead of proving properties of similar functions over and over again, we can prove more general results about these higher-order functions, and appeal to them instead.

6.1 Induction over natural numbers

Consider the following definition of the exponential function:

```
exp :: Num a => a -> Nat -> a
exp x Zero     = 1
exp x (Succ n) = x * exp x n
```

In the old days we could have written

```
exp :: Num a => a -> Int -> a
exp x 0     = 1
exp x (n+1) = x * exp x n
```

but this precise form of definition using a (n+1)-pattern is no longer allowed in the current standard version of Haskell, Haskell 2010.

Anyway, we would expect that the equation

```
exp x (m+n) = exp x m * exp x n
```

is true for all m and n. After all, $x^{m+n} = x^m x^n$ is a true equation of mathematics. But how can we prove this law?

The answer, of course, is by *induction*. Every natural number is either Zero or of the form Succ n for some natural number n. That is exactly what the definition

```
data Nat = Zero | Succ Nat
```

of the data type Nat tells us. So to prove that $P(n)$ holds for all natural numbers n, we can prove

1. $P(0)$ holds;

2. For all natural numbers n, that $P(n+1)$ holds assuming that $P(n)$ does.

We have reverted to writing 0 for Zero and $n+1$ for Succ n, and we shall continue to do so. In the second proof we can assume $P(n)$ and use this assumption to prove $P(n+1)$.

As an example we prove that

```
exp x (m+n) = exp x m * exp x n
```

for all x, m and n by induction on m. We could also prove it by induction on n but that turns out to be more complicated. Here is the proof:

Case 0

```
    exp x (0 + n)              exp x 0 * exp x n
=   {since 0 + n = n}      =   {exp.1}
    exp x n                    1 * exp x n
                          =   {since 1 * x = x}
                               exp x n
```

Case m+1

```
   exp x ((m + 1) + n))              exp x (m+1) * exp x n
=  {arithmetic}                   =  {exp.2}
   exp x ((m + n) + 1               (x * exp x m) * exp x n
=  {exp.2}                        =  {since * is associative}
   x * exp x (m + n)                x * (exp x m * exp x n)
=  {induction}
   x * (exp x m * exp x n)
```

The above format will be used in all induction proofs. The proof breaks into two cases, the *base case* 0 and the *inductive case* $n + 1$. Each case is laid out in two columns, one for the left-hand side of the equation, and one for the right-hand side. (When there is not enough space for two columns, we display one after the other.) Each side is simplified until one can go no further, and the proof of each case is completed by observing that each side simplifies to the same result. The hints exp.1 and exp.2 refer to the first and second equations defining exp.

Finally, observe that the proof depends on three further laws, namely that

```
(m + 1) + n = (m + n) + 1
1 * x       = x
(x * y) * z = x * (y * z)
```

If we were recreating all of arithmetic from scratch – and that would be a tedious thing to do – we would also have to prove these laws. In fact, only the first can be proved because it is entirely about natural numbers and we have defined the operation of addition on natural numbers. The second two rely on the implementation of multiplication prescribed by Haskell for the various instances of the type class Num.

In fact, the associative law breaks down for floating-point numbers:

```
ghci> (9.9e10 * 0.5e-10) * 0.1e-10 :: Float
4.95e-11
ghci> 9.9e10 * (0.5e-10 * 0.1e-10) :: Float
4.9499998e-11
```

Recall that in scientific notation 9.9e10 means 9.9 * 10^10. So, although our proof was correct mathematically, one of the provisos in it wasn't, at least in Haskell.

6.2 Induction over lists

We have seen that every finite list is either the empty list `[]` or of the form `x:xs` where xs is a finite list. Hence, to prove that $P(xs)$ holds for all finite lists xs, we can prove:

1. $P([])$ holds;

2. For all x and for all finite lists xs, that $P(x:xs)$ holds assuming $P(xs)$ does.

As an example, recall the definition of concatenation (++):

```
[] ++ ys     = ys
(x:xs) ++ ys = x : (xs ++ ys)
```

We prove that ++ is associative:

```
(xs ++ ys) ++ zs = xs ++ (ys ++ zs)
```

for all finite lists xs and for all lists ys and zs (note that neither of the last two is required to be a finite list), by induction on xs:

Case []

```
    ([] ++ ys) ++ zs              [] ++ (ys ++ zs)
=   {++.1}                    =   {++.1}
    ys ++ zs                      ys ++ zs
```

Case x:xs

```
    ((x:xs) ++ ys) ++ zs            (x:xs) ++ (ys ++ zs)
=   {++.2}                      =   {++.2}
    (x:(xs ++ ys)) ++ zs           x:(xs ++ (ys ++ zs))
=   {++.2}                      =   {induction}
    x:((xs ++ ys) ++ zs)           x:((xs ++ ys) ++ zs)
```

As another example, given the definition

```
reverse []     = []
reverse (x:xs) = reverse xs ++ [x]
```

We prove that reverse is an involution:

```
reverse (reverse xs) = xs
```

for all finite lists xs. The base case is easy and the inductive case proceeds:

Case x:xs

```
   reverse (reverse (x:xs))
=  {reverse.2}
   reverse (reverse xs ++ [x])
=  {????}
   x:reverse (reverse xs)
=  {induction}
   x:xs
```

The right-hand column is omitted in this example, since it consists solely of x:xs.
But we got stuck in the proof halfway through. We need an auxiliary result, namely
that

```
   reverse (ys ++ [x]) = x:reverse ys
```

for all finite lists ys. This auxiliary result is also proved by induction:

Case []

```
   reverse ([] ++ [x])              x:reverse []
=  {++.1}                        =  {reverse.1}
   reverse [x]                      [x]
=  {reverse.2}
   reverse [] ++ [x]
=  {reverse.1 and ++.1}
   [x]
```

Case y:ys

```
   reverse ((y:ys) ++ [x])          x:reverse (y:ys)
=  {++.2}                        =  {reverse.2}
   reverse (y:(ys ++ [x]))          x:(reverse ys ++ [y])
=  {reverse.2}
   reverse (ys ++ [x]) ++ [y]
=  {induction}
   (x:reverse ys) ++ [y]
=  {++.2}
   x:(reverse ys ++ [y])
```

The auxiliary result holds, and therefore so does the main result.

Induction over partial lists

Every partial list is either the undefined list or of the form `x:xs` for some `x` and some partial list `xs`. Hence, to prove that $P(xs)$ holds for all partial lists xs we can prove that

1. $P(\texttt{undefined})$ holds;

2. $P(\texttt{x:xs})$ holds assuming $P(\texttt{xs})$ does, for all `x` and all partial lists `xs`.

As an example, we prove that

```
xs ++ ys = xs
```

for all partial lists `xs` and all lists `ys`:

Case `undefined`

```
    undefined ++ ys
=   {++.0}
    undefined
```

Case `x:xs`

```
    (x:xs) ++ ys
=   {++.2}
    x:(xs ++ ys)
=   {induction}
    x:xs
```

In each case the trivial right-hand column is omitted. The hint `(++).0` refers to the failing clause in the definition of `(++)`: since concatenation is defined by pattern matching on the left-hand argument, the result is undefined if the left-hand argument is.

Induction over infinite lists

Proving that something is true of all infinite lists requires a bit of background that we will elaborate on in a subsequent chapter. Basically an infinite list can be thought of as the limit of a sequence of partial lists. For example, [0..] is the limit of the sequence

```
undefined,   0:undefined,   0:1:undefined,   0:1:2:undefined,
```

and so on. A property P is called *chain complete* if whenever $xs_0, xs_1, \ldots$ is a sequence of partial lists with limit xs, and $P(xs_n)$ holds for all n, then $P(xs)$ also holds.

In other words, if P is a chain complete property that holds for all partial lists (and possibly all finite lists too), then it holds for all infinite lists.

Many properties are chain complete; for instance:

- All equations $e1 = e2$, where $e1$ and $e2$ are Haskell expressions involving universally quantified free variables, are chain complete.

- If P and Q are chain complete, then so is their conjunction $P \wedge Q$.

But inequalities $e1 \neq e2$ are not necessarily chain complete, and neither are properties involving existential quantification. For example, consider the assertion

```
drop n xs = undefined
```

for some integer n. This property is obviously true for all partial lists, and equally obviously not true for any infinite list.

Here is an example proof. Earlier we proved that

```
(xs ++ ys) ++ zs = xs ++ (ys ++ zs)
```

for all finite lists xs and for all lists ys and zs. We can extend this chain complete property to *all* lists xs by proving

Case undefined

```
   (undefined ++ ys) ++ zs            undefined ++ (ys ++ zs)
=  {++.0}                          =  {++.0}
   undefined ++ zs                    undefined
=  {++.0}
   undefined
```

Thus ++ is a truly associative operation on lists, independent of whether the lists are finite, partial or infinite.

But we have to be careful. Earlier we proved

```
reverse (reverse xs) = xs
```

for all finite lists xs. Can we extend this property to all lists by proving the following additional case?

Case undefined

```
    reverse (reverse undefined)
=   {reverse.0}
    undefined
```

That goes through but something is wrong: as a Haskell equation we have

```
reverse (reverse xs) = undefined
```

for all partial lists xs. What did we miss?

The answer is that in proving the involution property of reverse we made use of an auxiliary result:

```
reverse (ys ++ [x]) = x:reverse ys
```

for all finite lists ys. This result is not true for all lists, indeed not true for any partial list ys.

It follows that reverse . reverse is not the identity function on lists, A functional equation f = g over lists asserts that f xs = g xs for *all* lists xs, finite, partial and infinite. If the equation is true only for finite lists, we have to say so explicitly.

6.3 The function `foldr`

All the following functions have a common pattern:

```
sum []      = 0
sum (x:xs) = x + sum xs

concat []        = []
concat (xs:xss) =  xs ++ concat xss

filter p []      = []
filter p (x:xs) = if p x then x:filter p xs
                  else filter p xs
```

```
map f []     = []
map f (x:xs) = f x:map f xs
```

Similarly, the proofs by induction of the following laws all have a common pattern:

```
sum (xs ++ ys)       = sum xs + sum ys
concat (xss ++ yss) = concat xss ++ concat yss
filter p (xs ++ ys) = filter p xs ++ filter p ys
map f (xs ++ ys)     = map f xs ++ map f ys
```

Can we not ensure that the functions above are defined as instances of a more general function, and the laws above as instances of a more general law? That would save a lot of repetitive effort.

The function `foldr` (fold from the right) is defined by

```
foldr :: (a -> b -> b) -> b -> [a] -> b
foldr f e []     = e
foldr f e (x:xs) = f x (foldr f e xs)
```

To appreciate this definition, consider

```
foldr (@) e [x,y,z] = x @ (y @ (z @ e))
            [x,y,z] = x : (y : (z : []))
```

In other words, `foldr (@) e` applied to a list replaces the empty list by `e`, and (`:`) by (`@`) and evaluates the result. The parentheses group from the right, whence the name.

It follows at once that `foldr (:) []` is the identity function on lists. Furthermore,

```
sum       = foldr (+) 0
concat   = foldr (++) []
filter p = foldr (\x xs -> if p x then x:xs else xs) []
map f     = foldr ((:) . f) []
```

The following fact captures all the identities mentioned above:

```
foldr f e (xs ++ ys) = foldr f e xs @ foldr f e ys
```

for some operation (`@`) satisfying various properties. We prove this equation by induction on `xs`. Along the way, we discover what properties of `f`, `e` and (`@`) we need.

Case []

```
  foldr f e ([] ++ ys)         foldr f e [] @ foldr f e ys
= {++.1}                     = {foldr.1}
  foldr f e ys                   e @ foldr f e ys
```

Hence we need e @ x = x for all x.

Case x:xs

```
          foldr f e ((x:xs) ++ ys)
        = {++.2}
          foldr f e (x:(xs ++ ys)
        = {foldr.2}
          f x (foldr f e (xs ++ ys))
        = {induction}
          f x (foldr f e xs @ foldr f e ys)
```

The right-hand side in this case simplifies to

```
  f x (foldr f e xs) @ foldr f e ys
```

So, in summary, we require that

```
e @ x       = x
f x (y @ z) = f x y @ z
```

for all x, y and z. In particular the two requirements are met if f = (@) and (@) is associative with identity e. That immediately proves

```
sum (xs ++ ys)       = sum xs + sum ys
concat (xss ++ yss) = concat xss ++ concat yss
```

For the map law, we require that

```
[] ++ xs = xs
f x:(xs ++ ys) = (f x:ys) ++ ys
```

Both immediately follow from the definition of concatenation.

For the law of `filter` we require that

```
if p x then x:(ys ++ zs) else ys ++ zs
  = (if p x then x:ys else ys) ++ zs
```

This is immediate from the definitions of concatenation and conditional expressions.

Fusion

The most important property of `foldr` is the *fusion law*, which asserts that

```
f . foldr g a  =  foldr h b
```

provided certain properties of the ingredients hold. As two simple examples,

```
double . sum    = foldr ((+) . double) 0
length . concat = foldr ((+) . length) 0
```

In fact, many of the laws we have seen already are instances of the fusion law for `foldr`. In a word, the fusion law is a 'pre-packaged' form of induction over lists.

To find out what properties we need, we carry out an induction proof of the fusion law. The law is expressed as a functional equation, so we have to show that it holds for all finite and all partial lists:

Case `undefined`

```
    f (foldr g a undefined)           foldr h b undefined
=   {foldr.0}                     =   {foldr.0}
    f undefined                       undefined
```

So the first condition is that `f` is a strict function.

Case `[]`

```
    f (foldr g a [])                  foldr h b []
=   {foldr.1}                     =   {foldr.1}
    f a                               b
```

The second condition is that `f a = b`.

Case `x:xs`

```
    f (foldr g a (x:xs))              foldr h b (x:xs)
=   {foldr.2}                     =   {foldr.2}
    f (g x (foldr g a xs))            h x (foldr h b xs)
                                  =   {induction}
                                      h x (f (foldr g a xs))
```

The third condition is met by `f (g x y) = h x (f y)` for all x and y.

Let us apply the fusion law to show that

```
foldr f a . map g = foldr h a
```

Recall that `map g = foldr ((:) . g) []`. Looking at the conditions of the fusion law we have that

```
foldr f a undefined = undefined
foldr f a []         = a
```

So the first two fusion conditions are satisfied. The third one is

```
foldr f a (g x:xs) = h x (foldr f a xs)
```

The left-hand side simplifies to

```
f (g x) (foldr f a xs)
```

so we can define `h x y = f (g x) y`. More briefly, `h = f . g`. Hence we have the useful rule:

```
foldr f a . map g = foldr (f . g) a
```

In particular,

```
double . sum = sum . map double
             = foldr ((+) . double) 0

length . concat = sum . map length
                = foldr ((+) . length) 0
```

Other simple consequences of the fusion law are explored in the exercises.

A variant

Sometimes having the empty list around is a pain. For example, what is the minimum element in an empty list? For this reason, Haskell provides a variant on `foldr`, called `foldr1`, restricted to nonempty lists. The Haskell definition of this function is

```
foldr1 :: (a -> a -> a) -> [a] -> a
foldr1 f [x]    = x
foldr1 f (x:xs) = f x (foldr1 f xs)
```

So we can define

```
minimum, maximum :: Ord a => [a] -> a
minimum = foldr1 min
maximum = foldr1 max
```

and avoid two other explicit recursions. Actually the Haskell definition of `foldr1` is not as general as it should be, but we will leave that discussion to an exercise.

6.4 The function `foldl`

Recall that

```
foldr (@) e [w,x,y,z] = w @ (x @ (y @ (z @ e)))
```

Sometimes a more convenient pattern for the right-hand side is

```
(((e @ w) @ x) @ y) @ z
```

This pattern is encapsulated by a function `foldl` (fold from the left):

```
foldl :: (b -> a -> b) -> b -> [a] -> b
foldl f e []     = e
foldl f e (x:xs) = foldl f (f e x) xs
```

As an example, suppose we are given a string, such as 1234.567, representing a real number and we want to compute its integer part and fractional part. We could define

```
ipart :: String -> Integer
ipart xs = read (takeWhile (/= '.') xs) :: Integer

fpart :: String -> Float
fpart xs = read ('0':dropWhile (/= '.' xs) :: Float
```

This uses the function `read` of the type class `Read`. Note by the way that $.567$ is not a well-formed literal in Haskell. It is necessary to include at least one digit before and after the decimal point to ensure that the decimal point cannot be mistaken for functional composition. For example,

```
ghci> :t 3 . 4
3 . 4 :: (Num (b -> c), Num (a -> b)) => a -> c
```

As an alternative, we can define

```
parts :: String -> (Integer,Float)
parts ds = (ipart es,fpart fs)
           where (es,d:fs) = break (== '.') ds
ipart     = foldl shiftl 0 . map toDigit
            where shiftl n d = n*10 + d
fpart     = foldr shiftr 0 . map toDigit
            where shiftr d x = (d + x)/10
toDigit d = fromIntegral (fromEnum d - fromEnum '0')
```

We have

```
1234  = 1*1000 + 2*100 + 3*10 + 4
      = (((0*10 + 1)*10 + 2)*10 + 3)*10 + 4
0.567 = 5/10 + 6/100 + 7/1000
      = (5 + (6 + (7 + 0)/10)/10)/10
```

so use of foldl for the integer part and foldr for the fractional part are both indicated.

Here is another example. The function reverse was defined above by the equations

```
reverse []     = []
reverse (x:xs) = reverse xs ++ [x]
```

We are wiser now and would now write

```
reverse = foldr snoc []
          where snoc x xs = xs ++ [x]
```

But a little learning is a dangerous thing: both definitions of reverse are terrible because they take of the order of n^2 steps to reverse a list of length n. Much better is to define

```
reverse = foldl (flip (:)) []
```

where flip f x y = f y x. The new version reverses a list in linear time:

```
  foldl (flip (:)) [] [1,2,3]
= foldl (flip (:)) (1:[]) [2,3]
= foldl (flip (:)) (2:1:[]) [3]
= foldl (flip (:)) (3:2:1:[]) []
= 3:2:1:[]
```

That seems a bit of a trick, but there is a sound principle at work behind this new definition that we will take up in the following chapter.

As this example suggests, there are the following relationships between `foldr` and `foldl`: for all finite lists `xs` we have

```
foldl f e xs = foldr (flip f) e (reverse xs)
foldr f e xs = foldl (flip f) e (reverse xs)
```

Proofs are left as an exercise. Note the restriction to finite lists, even though both sides reduce to $\bot$ when `xs` is $\bot$. That means the proofs have to rely on a subsidiary result that is true only for finite lists.

Here is another relationship between the two folds:

```
foldl (@) e xs = foldr (<>) e xs
```

for all finite lists `xs`, provided that

```
(x <> y) @ z = x <> (y @ z)
e @ x        = x <> e
```

Again, the proof is left as an exercise. As one instructive application of this law, suppose `(<>) = (@)` and `(@)` is associative with identity `e`. Then the two provisos are satisfied and we can conclude that

```
foldr (@) e xs = foldl (@) e xs
```

for all finite lists `xs` whenever `(@)` is associative with identity `e`. In particular,

```
concat xss = foldr (++) [] xss = foldl (++) [] xss
```

for all finite lists `xss`. The two definitions are *not* the same if `xss` is an infinite list:

```
ghci> foldl (++) [] [[i] | i <- [1..]]
Interrupted.
ghci> foldr (++) [] [[i] | i <- [1..]]
[1,2,3,4,{Interrupted}
```

In response to the first expression, GHCi went into a long silence that was interrupted by pressing the 'Stop program execution' button. In response to the second, GHCi started printing an infinite list.

OK, so the definition in terms of `foldr` works on infinite lists, but the other one doesn't. But maybe the definition of `concat` in terms of `foldl` leads to a more efficient computation when all the lists are finite? To answer this question, observe that

```
foldr (++) [] [xs,ys,us,vs]
            = xs ++ (ys ++ (us ++ (vs ++ [])))
```

```
foldl (++) [] [xs,ys,us,vs]
        = (((([] ++ xs) ++ ys) ++ us) ++ vs)
```

Let all the component lists have length n. The first expression on the right takes $4n$ steps to perform all the concatenations, while the second takes $0 + n + (n + n) + (n + n + n) = 6n$ steps. Enough said, at least for now.

6.5 The function scanl

The function scanl f e applies foldl f e to each initial segment of a list. For example

```
ghci> scanl (+) 0 [1..10]
[0,1,3,6,10,15,21,28,36,45,55]
```

The expression computes the *running sums* of the first ten positive numbers:

```
    [0, 0+1, (0+1)+2, ((0+1)+2)+3, (((0+1)+2)+3)+4, ...]
```

The specification of scanl is

```
scanl :: (b -> a -> b) -> b -> [a] -> [b]
scanl f e = map (foldl f e) . inits

inits :: [a] -> [[a]]
inits []     = [[]]
inits (x:xs) = [] : map (x:) (inits xs)
```

For example

```
ghci> inits "barbara"
["","b","ba","bar","barb","barba","barbar","barbara"]
```

The function inits is in the library Data.List.

But this definition of scanl f involves evaluating f a total of

$$0 + 1 + 2 + \cdots + n = n(n+1)/2$$

times on a list of length n. Can we do better?

Yes, we can calculate a better definition by doing a kind of induction proof, except that we don't know what it is we are proving!

Case []

```
        scanl f e []
    =   {definition}
        map (foldl f e) (inits [])
    =   {inits.1}
        map (foldl f e) [[]]
    =   {map.1 and map.2}
        [foldl f e []]
    =   {foldl.1}
        [e]
```

Hence we have shown that scanl f e [] = [e]

Case x:xs

```
        scanl f e (x:xs)
    =   {definition}
        map (foldl f e) (inits (x:xs))
    =   {inits.2}
        map (foldl f e) ([]:map (x:) (inits xs))
    =   {map.1 and map.2}
        foldl f e []:map (foldl f e . (x:)) (inits xs)
    =   {foldl.1}
        e:map (foldl f e . (x:)) (inits xs)
    =   {claim: foldl f e . (x:) = foldl f (f e x)}
        e:map (foldl f (f e x)) (inits xs)
    =   {definition of scanl}
        e:scanl f (f e x)
```

The claim is an easy consequence of the definition of foldl. Hence, in summary, we have shown

```
scanl f e []     = [e]
scanl f e (x:xs) = e:scanl f (f e x) xs
```

This definition evaluates f only a linear number of times.

What we have just done is an example of optimising a function by *program calculation*. One of the exciting things about Haskell is that you can do this without fuss. There is no need to bring in a totally different logical language to reason about programs.

However, the prelude definition of scanl is a little different:

```
scanl f e xs = e : (case xs of
                      []   -> []
                      x:xs -> scanl f (f e x) xs)
```

Whereas for our version scanl f e undefined = undefined, the prelude version has

```
scanl f e undefined = e:undefined.
```

The reason is that the right-hand sides of the two clauses defining scanl are both lists that begin with e. We do not have to know anything about the left-hand sides to determine this fact, and laziness dictates that we don't ask.

The prelude version also uses a case expression. We won't go into details since such expressions are used rarely in this book. Haskell allows us many ways to say the same thing.

6.6 The maximum segment sum

Here is another example of program calculation. The *maximum segment sum* problem is a famous one and its history is described in J. Bentley's *Programming Pearls* (1987). Given is a sequence of integers and it is required to compute the maximum of the sums of all *segments* in the sequence. A segment is also called a *contiguous subsequence*. For example, the sequence

```
[-1,2,-3,5,-2,1,3,-2,-2,-3,6]
```

has maximum sum 7, the sum of the segment [5,-2,1,3]. On the other hand, the sequence [-1,-2,-3] has a maximum segment sum of zero, since the empty sequence is a segment of every list and its sum is zero. It follows that the maximum segment sum is always nonnegative.

Our problem is specified by

```
mss  :: [Int] -> Int
mss = maximum . map sum . segments
```

where `segments` returns a list of all segments of a list. This function can be defined in a number of ways, including

```
segments = concat . map inits . tails
```

where `tails` is dual to `inits` and returns all the tail segments of a list:

```
tails :: [a] -> [[a]]
tails []    = [[]]
tails (x:xs) = (x:xs):tails xs
```

The definition of `segments` describes the process of taking all the initial segments of all the tail segments. For example,

```
ghci> segments "abc"
["","a","ab","abc","","b","bc","","c",""]
```

The empty sequence appears four times in this list, once for every tail segment.

Direct evaluation of `mss` will take a number of steps proportional to n^3 on a list of length n. There are about n^2 segments, and summing each of them will take n steps, so in total it will take n^3 steps. It is not obvious that we can do better than cubic time for this problem.

However, let's see where some program calculation leads us. We can start by installing the definition of `segments`:

```
maximum . map sum . concat . map inits . tails
```

Searching for a law we can apply, we spot that

```
map f . concat = concat . map (map f)
```

applies to the subterm `map sum . concat`. That gives

```
maximum . concat . map (map sum) . map inits . tails
```

Now we can use the law `map f . map g = map (f . g)` to give

```
maximum . concat . map (map sum . inits) . tails
```

Oh, we can also use the law

```
maximum . concat = maximum . map maximum
```

can't we? No, not unless the argument to `concat` is a nonempty list of nonempty lists, because the maximum of the empty list is undefined. In the present example the rule is valid because both `inits` and `tails` return nonempty lists. That leads to

```
maximum . map (maximum . map sum . inits) . tails
```

The next step is to use the property of scanl described in the previous section, namely

```
map sum . inits =  scanl (+) 0
```

That leads to

```
maximum . map (maximum . scanl (+) 0) . tails
```

Already we have reduced a n^3 algorithm to a n^2 one, so we are making progress. But now we appear stuck since there is no law in our armoury that seems to help.

The next step obviously concerns maximum . scanl (+) 0. So, let's see what we can prove about

```
foldr1 max . scanl (+) 0
```

This looks like a fusion rule, but can scanl (+) 0 be expressed as a foldr? Well, we do have, for instance,

```
    scanl (+) 0 [x,y,z]
=   [0,0+x,(0+x)+y,((0+x)+y)+z]
=   [0,x,x+y,x+y+z]
=   0:map (x+) [0,y,y+z]
=   0:map (x+) (scanl (+) 0 [y,z])
```

This little calculation exploits the associativity of (+) and the fact that 0 is the identity element of (+). The result suggests, more generally, that

```
scanl (@) e = foldr f [e]
   where f x xs = e:map (x@) xs
```

provided that (@) is associative with identity e. Let us take this on trust and move on to the conditions under which

```
foldr1 (<>) . foldr f [e] = foldr h b
   where f x xs = e:map (x@) xs
```

It is immediate that foldr1 (<>) is strict and foldr1 (<>) [e] = e, so we have b = e. It remains to check the third proviso of the fusion rule: we require h to satisfy

```
foldr1 (<>) (e:map (x@) xs) = h x (foldr1 (<>) xs)
```

for all x and xs. The left-hand side simplifies to

```
e <> (foldr1 (<>) (map (x@) xs))
```

Taking the singleton case `xs = [y]`, we find that

```
h x y = e <> (x @ y)
```

That gives us our definition of h, but we still have to check that

```
foldr1 (<>) (e:map (x@) xs) = e <> (x @ foldr1 (<>) xs)
```

Simplifying both sides, this equation holds provided

```
foldr1 (<>) . map (x@) = (x@) . foldr1 (<>)
```

This final equation holds provided (@) *distributes* over (<>); that is

```
x @ (y <> z) = (x @ y) <> (x @ z)
```

The proof is left as an exercise.

Does addition distribute over (binary) maximum? Yes:

```
x + (y `max` z) = (x + y) `max` (x + z)
x + (y `min` z) = (x + y) `min` (x + z)
```

Back to the maximum segment sum. We have arrived at

```
maximum . map (foldr (@) 0) . tails
where x @ y = 0 `max` (x + y)
```

What we have left looks very like an instance of the `scanl` rule of the previous section, except that we have a `foldr` not a `foldl` and a `tails` not an `inits`. But a similar calculation to the one about `scanl` reveals

```
map (foldr f e) . tails = scanr f e
```

where

```
scanr :: (a -> b -> b) -> b -> [a] -> [b]
scanr f e []     = [e]
scanr f e (x:xs) = f x (head ys):ys
                   where ys = scanr f e xs
```

The function `scanr` is also defined in the standard prelude. In summary,

```
mss = maximum . scanr (@) 0
      where   x @ y = 0 `max` (x + y)
```

The result is a linear-time program for the maximum segment sum.

6.7 Exercises

Exercise A

In Chapter 3 we defined multiplication on natural numbers. The following definition is slightly different:

```
mult :: Nat -> Nat -> Nat
mult Zero y    = Zero
mult (Succ x) = mult x y + y
```

Prove that `mult (x+y) z = mult x z + mult y z`. You can use only the facts
that `x+0 = x` and that `(+)` is associative. That means a long think about which
variable x, y or z is the best one on which to do the induction.

Exercise B

Prove that

```
reverse (xs ++ ys) = reverse ys ++ reverse xs
```

for all finite lists `xs` and `ys`. You may assume that `(++)` is associative.

Exercise C

Recall our friends Eager Beaver and Lazy Susan from Exercise D in Chapter 2.
Susan happily used the expression `head . map f`, while Beaver would probably
prefer `f . head`. Wait a moment! Are these two expressions equal? Carry out an
induction proof to check.

Exercise D

Recall the cartesian product function `cp :: [[a]] -> [[a]]` from the previous
chapter. Give a definition of the form `cp = foldr f e` for suitable f and e. You
can use a list comprehension for the definition of f if you like.

The rest of this exercise concerns the proof of the identity

```
length . cp = product . map length
```

where `product` returns the result of multiplying a list of numbers.

1. Using the fusion theorem, express `length.cp` as an instance of `foldr`.

2. Express `map length` as an instance of `foldr`.

3. Using the fusion theorem again, express `product . map length` as an instance of `foldr`.

4. Check that the two results are identical. If they aren't, your definition of `cp` was wrong.

Exercise E

The first two arguments of `foldr` are replacements for the constructors

```
(:) :: a -> [a] -> [a]
[]  :: [a]
```

of lists. A fold function can be defined for any data type: just give replacements for the constructors of the data type. For example, consider

```
data Either a b = Left a | Right b
```

To define a fold for `Either` we have to give replacements for

```
Left  :: a -> Either a b
Right :: b -> Either a b
```

That leads to

```
foldE :: (a -> c) -> (b -> c) -> Either a b -> c
foldE f g (Left x)  = f x
foldE f g (Right x) = g x
```

The type `Either` is not a recursive data type and `foldE` is not a recursive function. In fact `foldE` is a standard prelude function, except that it is called `either` not `foldE`.

Now define fold functions for

```
data Nat = Zero | Succ Nat
data NEList a = One a | Cons a (NEList a)
```

The second declaration introduces nonempty lists.

What is wrong with the Haskell definition of `foldr1`?

Exercise F

Prove that

```
foldl f e xs = foldr (flip f) e (reverse xs)
```

for all finite lists `xs`. Also prove that

```
foldl (@) e xs = foldr (<>) e xs
```

for all finite lists xs, provided that

```
(x <> y) @ z = x <> (y @ z)
e @ x         = x <> e
```

Exercise G

Using

```
foldl f e (xs ++ ys) = foldl f (foldl f e xs) ys
foldr f e (xs ++ ys) = foldr f (foldr f e ys) xs
```

prove that

```
foldl f e . concat = foldl (foldl f) e
foldr f e . concat = foldr (flip (foldr f)) e
```

Exercise H

Mathematically speaking, what is the value of

```
sum (scanl (/) 1 [1..])   ?
```

Exercise I

Calculate the efficient definition of scanr from the specification

```
scan r f e = map (foldr f e) . tails
```

Exercise J

Consider the problem of computing

```
mss :: [Int] -> Int
mss = maximum . map sum . subseqs
```

where subseqs returns all the subsequences of a finite list, including the list itself:

```
subseqs :: [a] -> [[a]]
subseqs []     = [[]]
subseqs (x:xs) = xss ++ map (x:) xss
                where xss =  subseqs xs
```

Find a more efficient alternative for mss.

Exercise K

This question is in pieces.

1. The function `takePrefix` p applied to a list *xs* returns the longest initial segment of *xs* that satisfies *p*. Hence

    ```
    takePrefix :: ([a] -> Bool) -> [a] -> [a]
    ```

    What are the values of the following expressions?

    ```
    takePrefix nondec [1,3,7,6,8,9]
    takePrefix (all even) [2,4,7,8]
    ```

    Complete the right-hand side of

    ```
    takePrefix (all p) = ...
    ```

    Give a definition of `takePrefix` in terms of standard functions, including `inits`.

    We will return to `takePrefix` in the final part of this question.

2. The functions one and none are defined by the equations

    ```
    one  x = [x]
    none x = []
    ```

    Complete the right-hand side of the following identities:

    ```
    none . f      = ...
    map f . none = ...
    map f . one  = ...
    ```

3. Recall that `fork (f,g) x = (f x,g x)`. Complete the identities

    ```
    fst . fork (f,g) = ...
    snd . fork (f,g) = ...
    fork (f,g) . h   = ...
    ```

4. Define

    ```
    test p (f,g) x = if p x then f x else g x
    ```

    Complete the right-hand sides of

    ```
    test p (f,g) . h  = ...
    h . test p (f,g)  = ...
    ```

    The function `filter` can be defined by

```
filter p = concat . map (test p (one,none))
```

Using the identities above, together with other standard identities, prove using equational reasoning that

```
filter p = map fst . filter snd . map (fork (id,p))
```

(*Hint*: as always in calculations, start with the more complicated side.)

5. Recall the standard prelude functions `curry` and `uncurry` from the answer to Exercise K in Chapter 4:

```
curry :: ((a,b) -> c) -> a -> b -> c
curry f x y = f (x,y)

uncurry :: (a -> b -> c) -> (a,b) -> c
uncurry f (x,y) = f x y
```

Complete the right-hand side of

```
map (fork (f,g)) = uncurry zip . (??)
```

6. Returning to `takePrefix`, use equational reasoning to calculate an efficient program for the expression

```
takePrefix (p . foldl f e)
```

that requires only a linear number of applications of f.

6.8 Answers

Answer to Exercise A

The proof is by induction on y:

Case 0

```
    mult (x+0) z                      mult x z + mult 0 z
  = {since x + 0=x}                  = {mult.1}
    mult x z                           mult x z + 0
                                     = {since x + 0 = x}
                                       mult x z
```

Case y+1

```
   mult (x+(y+1)) z                    mult x z + mult (y+1) z
=   {as (+) is associative}         =   {mult.2}
   mult ((x+y)+1) z                    mult x z + (mult y z + z)
=   {mult.2}                         =   {since (+) is associative}
   mult (x+y) z + z                     (mult x z + mult y z) + z
=   {induction}
   (mult x z + mult y z) + z
```

Answer to Exercise B

The proof is by induction on *xs*:

Case []

```
    reverse ([]++ys)               reverse ys ++ reverse []
=    {++.1}                      =    {reverse.1}
    reverse ys                       reverse ys ++ []
                                =    {since xs ++ [] = xs}
                                    reverse ys
```

Case x:xs

```
        reverse ((x:xs)++ys)
    =    {++.2}
        reverse (x:(xs++ys))
    =    {reverse.2}
        reverse (xs++ys) ++ [x]
    =    {induction}
        (reverse ys ++ reverse xs) ++ [x]
```

and

```
        reverse ys ++ reverse (x:xs)
    =    {reverse.2}
        reverse ys ++ (reverse xs ++ [x])
    =    {since (++) is associative}
        (reverse ys ++ reverse xs) ++ [x]
```

Answer to Exercise C

We have to prove that

```
head (map f xs) = f (head xs)
```

for all lists *xs*, finite, partial or infinite. The case `undefined` and the inductive case `x:xs` are okay, but the case `[]` gives

```
head (map f []) = head [] = undefined
f (head [])     = f undefined
```

Hence the law holds only if `f` is a strict function. Eager Beaver is not bothered by this since he can only construct strict functions.

Answer to Exercise D

We have

```
cp = foldr op [[]]
  where op xs xss = [x:ys | x <- xs, ys <- xss]
```

1. `length . cp = foldr h b` provided `length` is strict (it is) and

```
length [[]] = b
length (op xs xss) = h xs (length xss)
```

The first equation gives b = 1 and as

```
length (op xs xss) = length xs * length xss
```

the second equation gives h = (*) . length.

2. `map length = foldr f []`, where `f xs ns = length xs:ns`. A shorter definition is `f = (:) . length`.

3. `product . map length = foldr h b` provided `product` is strict (it is) and

```
product [] = b
product (length xs:ns) = h xs (product ns)
```

The first equation gives b = 1, and as

```
product (length xs:ns) = length xs * product ns
```

the second equation gives h = (*) . length.

4. The two definitions of h and b are identical.

Answer to Exercise E

The definition of foldN is straightforward:

```
foldN :: (a -> a) -> a -> Nat -> a
foldN f e Zero     = e
foldN f e (Succ n) = f (foldN f e n)
```

In particular,

```
m+n = foldN Succ m n
m*n = foldN (+m) Zero n
m^n = foldN (*m) (Succ Zero) n
```

For nonempty lists, the definition of foldNE is:

```
foldNE :: (a -> b -> b) -> (a -> b) -> NEList a -> b
foldNE f g (One x)     = g x
foldNE f g (Cons x xs) = f x (foldNE f g xs)
```

To be a proper fold over nonempty lists, the correct definition of foldr1 should have been

```
foldr1 :: (a -> b -> b) -> (a -> b) -> [a] -> b
foldr1 f g [x]    = g x
foldr1 f g (x:xs) = f x (foldr1 f g xs)
```

The Haskell definition of foldr1 restricts g to be the identity function.

Answer to Exercise F

Write g = flip f for brevity. We prove that

```
foldl f e xs = foldr g e (reverse xs)
```

for all finite lists xs by induction:

Case []

```
    foldl f e []              foldl g e (reverse [])
  =  {foldl.1}              =  {reverse.1}
     e                          foldl g e []
                             =  {foldl.1}
                                e
```

Case x:xs

$$
\begin{aligned}
&\texttt{foldl f e (x:xs)} \\
={}& \{\texttt{foldl.2}\} \\
&\texttt{foldl f (f e x) xs} \\
={}& \{\text{induction}\} \\
&\texttt{foldr g (f e x) (reverse xs)}
\end{aligned}
$$

and

$$
\begin{aligned}
&\texttt{foldr g e (reverse (x:xs))} \\
={}& \{\texttt{reverse.2}\} \\
&\texttt{foldr g e (reverse xs ++ [x])} \\
={}& \{\text{claim: see below}\} \\
&\texttt{foldr g (foldr g e [x]) (reverse xs)} \\
={}& \{\text{since}\ \texttt{foldr (flip f) e [x] = f e x}\} \\
&\texttt{foldr g (f e x) (reverse xs)}
\end{aligned}
$$

The claim is that

    foldr f e (xs ++ ys) = foldr f (foldr f e ys) xs

We leave the proof to the reader. By the way, we have the companion result that

    foldl f e (xs ++ ys) = foldl f (foldl f e xs) ys

Again, the proof is left to you.

We prove

    foldl (@) e xs = foldr (<>) e xs

for all finite lists xs by induction. The base case is trivial. For the inductive case:

Case x:xs

$$
\begin{aligned}
&\texttt{foldl (@) e (x:xs)} \\
={}& \{\texttt{foldl.2}\} \\
&\texttt{foldl (@) (e @ x) xs} \\
={}& \{\text{given that}\ \texttt{e @ x = x <> e}\} \\
&\texttt{foldl (@) (x <> e) xs}
\end{aligned}
\qquad
\begin{aligned}
&\texttt{foldr (<>) e (x:xs)} \\
={}& \{\texttt{foldr.2}\} \\
&\texttt{x <> foldr (<>) e xs} \\
={}& \{\text{induction}\} \\
&\texttt{x <> foldl (@) e xs}
\end{aligned}
$$

The two sides have simplified to different results. We need another induction hypothesis:

```
foldl (@) (x <> y) xs = x <> foldl (@) y xs
```

The base case is trivial. For the inductive case

Case `z:zs`

$$
\begin{aligned}
& \text{foldl (@) (x <> y) (z:zs)} \\
= \ & \{\text{foldl.2}\} \\
& \text{foldl (@) ((x <> y) @ z) zs} \\
= \ & \{\text{since (x <> y) @ z = x <> (y @ z)}\} \\
& \text{foldl (@) (x <> (y @ z)) zs} \\
= \ & \{\text{induction}\} \\
& \text{x <> foldl (@) (y @ z) zs}
\end{aligned}
$$

and

$$
\begin{aligned}
& \text{x <> foldl (@) y (z:zs)} \\
= \ & \{\text{foldl.2}\} \\
& \text{x <> foldl (@) (y @ z) zs}
\end{aligned}
$$

Answer to Exercise G

The proofs are by induction. The base cases are easy and the inductive cases are

$$
\begin{aligned}
& \text{foldl f e (concat (xs:xss))} \\
= \ & \{\text{definition of concat}\} \\
& \text{foldl f e (xs ++ concat xss)} \\
= \ & \{\text{given property of foldl}\} \\
& \text{foldl f (foldl f e xs) (concat xss)} \\
= \ & \{\text{induction}\} \\
& \text{foldl (foldl f) (foldl f e xs) xss} \\
= \ & \{\text{definition of foldl}\} \\
& \text{foldl (foldl f) e (xs:xss)}
\end{aligned}
$$

and

```
      foldr f e (concat (xs:xss))
   =  {definition of concat}
      foldr f e (xs ++ concat xss)
   =  {given property of foldr}
      foldr f (foldr f e (concat xss)) xs
   =  {using flip}
      flip (foldr f) xs (foldr f e (concat xss))
   =  {induction}
      flip (foldr f) xs (foldr (flip (foldr f)) e xss)
   =  {definition of foldr}
      foldr (flip (foldr f)) e (xs:xss)
```

Answer to Exercise H

Mathematically speaking,

```
    sum (scanl (/) 1 [1..]) = e
```

since $\sum_{n=0}^{\infty} 1/n! = e$. Computationally speaking, replacing [1..] by a finite list [1..n] gives an approximation to e. For example,

```
ghci> sum (scanl (/) 1 [1..20])
2.7182818284590455
ghci> exp 1
2.718281828459045
```

The standard prelude function exp takes a number x and returns e^x. By the way, the prelude function log takes a number x and returns $\log_e x$. If you want logarithms in another base, use logBase whose type is

```
    logBase :: Floating a => a -> a -> a
```

Answer to Exercise I

We synthesise a more efficient definition by cases. The base case yields

```
    scanr f e [] = [e]
```

and the inductive case x:xs is:

```
        scanr f e (x:xs)
   =    {specification}
        map (foldr f e) (tails (x:xs))
   =    {tails.2}
        map (foldr f e) ((x:xs):tails xs)
   =    {definition of map}
        foldr f e (x:xs):map (foldr f e) (tails xs)
   =    {foldr.2 and specification}
        f x (foldr f e xs):scan f e xs
   =    {claim: foldr f e xs = head (scanr f e xs)}
        f x (head ys):ys where ys = scanr f e xs
```

Answer to Exercise J

Firstly,

```
    subseqs = foldr op [[]]
        where op x xss = xss ++ map (x:) xss
```

Appeal to the fusion law yields

```
    map sum . subseqs = foldr op [0]
        where op x xs = xs ++ map (x+) xs
```

A second appeal to fusion yields

```
    maximum . map sum . subseqs = foldr op 0
        where op x y = y `max` (x+y)
```

That will do nicely. Of course, sum . filter (>0) also does the job.

Answer to Exercise K

1. We have

```
        takePrefix nondec [1,3,7,6,8,9] = [1,3,7]
        takePrefix (all even) [2,4,7,8] = [2,4]
```

   The identity is

```
        takePrefix (all p) = takeWhile p
```

The specification is

```
takePrefix p = last . filter p . inits
```

2. We have

```
none . f      = none
map f . none = none
map f . one  = one . f
```

3. We have

```
fst . fork (f,g) = f
snd . fork (f,g) = g
fork (f,g) . h   = fork (f.h,g.h)
```

4. We have

```
test p (f,g) . h = test (p.h) (f . h, g . h)
h . test p (f,g) = test p (h . f, h . g)
```

The reasoning is:

```
    map fst . filter snd . map (fork (id,p))
=   {definition of filter}
    map fst . concat . map (test snd (one,none)) .
    map (fork (id,p))
=   {since map f . concat = concat . map (map f)}
    concat . map (map fst . test snd (one,none) .
    fork (id,p))
=   {second law of test; laws of one and none}
    concat . map (test snd (one . fst,none) .
    fork (id,p))
=   {first law of test; laws of fork}
    concat . map (test p (one . id, none . fork (id,p)))
=   {laws of id and none}
    concat . map (test p (one,none))
=   {definition of filter}
    filter p
```

5. We have

```
map (fork (f,g))  = uncurry zip . fork (map f,map g)
```

6. We have

```
        filter (p . foldl f e) . inits
    =   {derived law of filter}
        map fst . filter snd .
        map (fork (id, p . foldl f e)) . inits
    =   {law of zip}
        map fst . filter snd . uncurry zip .
        fork (id, map (p . foldl f e)) . inits
    =   {law of fork}
        map fst . filter snd . uncurry zip .
        fork (inits, map (p . foldl f e) . inits)
    =   {scan lemma}
        map fst . filter snd . uncurry zip .
        fork (inits, map p . scanl f e)
```

Hence

```
    takePrefix (p.foldl f e)
       = fst . last . filter snd . uncurry zip .
         fork (inits,map p . scanl f e)
```

6.9 Chapter notes

Gofer, an earlier version of Haskell designed by Mark Jones, was so named because it was GOod For Equational Reasoning. HUGS (The Haskell Users Gofer System) was an earlier alternative to GHCi, and used in the second edition of the book on which the current one is based, but is no longer maintained.

Many people have contributed to the understanding of the laws of functional programming, too many to list. The Haskellwiki page

```
haskell.org/haskellwiki/Equational_reasoning_examples
```

contains examples of equational reasoning and links to various discussions about the subject.

The fascinating history of the maximum segment sum problem is discussed in Jon Bentley's *Programming Pearls* (second edition) (Addison-Wesley, 2000).

Chapter 7

Efficiency

The question of efficiency has been an ever-present undercurrent in recent discussions, and the time has come to bring this important subject to the surface. The best way to achieve efficiency is, of course, to find a decent algorithm for the problem. That leads us into the larger topic of Algorithm Design, which is not the primary focus of this book. Nevertheless we will touch on some fundamental ideas later on. In the present chapter we concentrate on a more basic question: functional programming allows us to construct elegant expressions and definitions, but do we know what it costs to evaluate them? Alan Perlis, a US computer scientist, once inverted Oscar Wilde's definition of a cynic to assert that a functional programmer was someone who knew the value of everything and the cost of nothing.

7.1 Lazy evaluation

We said in Chapter 2 that, under lazy evaluation, an expression such as

```
sqr (sqr (3+4))
```

where sqr x = x*x, is reduced to its simplest possible form by applying reduction steps from the outside in. That means the definition of the function sqr is installed first, and its argument is evaluated only when needed. The following evaluation sequence follows this prescription, but is *not* lazy evaluation:

```
  sqr (sqr (3+4))
= sqr (3+4) * sqr (3+4)
= ((3+4)*(3+4)) * ((3+4)*(3+4))
= ...
= 2401
```

The ellipsis in the penultimate line hides no fewer than four evaluations of 3+4 and two of 7*7. Clearly the simple policy of substituting argument expressions into function expressions is a very inefficient way of carrying out reduction.

Instead, lazy evaluation guarantees that when the value of an argument is needed, it is evaluated *only once*. Under lazy evaluation, the reduction sequence would unfold basically as follows:

```
    sqr (sqr (3+4))
= let x = sqr (3+4) in x*x
= let y = 3+4 in
  let x = y*y in x*x
= let y = 7 in
  let x = y*y in x*x
= let x = 49 in x*x
= 2401
```

The expression 3+4 is evaluated only once (and so is 7*7). The names x and y have been *bound* to expressions using let, though in the implementation of Haskell these names are anonymous *pointers* to expressions. When an expression is reduced to a value, the pointer then points to the value and that value can then be *shared*.

Even then, the headline 'Under lazy evaluation arguments are evaluated only when needed and then only once!' doesn't tell the full story. Consider evaluation of sqr (head xs). In order to evaluate sqr we have to evaluate its argument, but in order to evaluate head xs we do not have to evaluate xs all the way, but only to the point where it becomes an expression of the form y:ys. Then head xs can return y and sqr (head xs) can return y*y. More generally, an expression is said to be in *head normal form* if it is a function (such as sqr) or if it takes the form of a data constructor (such as (:)) applied to its arguments. Every expression in normal form (i.e. in fully reduced form) is in head normal form but not vice versa. For example, (e1,e2) is in head normal form (because it is equivalent to (,) e1 e2, where (,) is the data constructor for pairs), but is in normal form only if both e1 and e2 are. Of course, for numbers or booleans there is no distinction between the two kinds of normal form.

'Under lazy evaluation arguments are evaluated only when needed and then only once, and then maybe only to head normal form' is not as catchy a headline as before, but it does tell a better story.

Next, consider the following two definitions of the inductive case of the function subseqs that returns all the subsequences of a list:

```
subseqs (x:xs) = subseqs xs ++ map (x:) (subseqs xs)
subseqs (x:xs) = xss ++ map (x:) xss
                 where xss = subseqs xs
```

In the first definition the expression subseqs xs appears twice on the right-hand side, so it is evaluated twice when the subsequences of a given list are required. In the second definition this duplication of effort has been recognised by the programmer and a where clause has been used to ensure that subseqs xs is evaluated only once (we could also have used a let expression).

The important point is that you, the programmer, are in control of which definition you want. It is quite possible for Haskell to recognise the double occurrence and to *abstract* it away using the equivalent of an internal let expression. This is a well-known technique called *common subexpression elimination*. But Haskell doesn't do this, and for a very good reason: it can cause a *space leak*. The second definition of subseqs (x:xs) has the following problem: the list subseqs xs is constructed only once, but it is retained in its entirety in memory because its value is used again, namely in the second expression map (x:) xss.

Look at it this way: the first definition takes longer because computation is duplicated; the second definition is faster (though still exponential) but can rapidly run out of available space. After all, there are 2^n subsequences of a list of length n. There is a fundamental dichotomy in programming we can never get away from: to avoid doing something twice you have to use up space to store the result of doing it once.

Here is a related example. Consider the following two definitions in a script:

```
foo1 n = sum (take n primes)
  where
  primes    = [x | x <- [2..], divisors x == [x]]
  divisors x = [d | d <- [2..x], x `mod` d == 0]


foo2 n = sum (take n primes)
primes    = [x | x <- [2..], divisors x == [x]]
divisors x = [d | d <- [2..x], x `mod` d == 0]
```

The programmer who wrote foo1 decided to structure their script by making the definitions of both primes and divisors local to the definition of foo1, presumably because neither definition was used elsewhere in the script. The programmer who wrote foo2 decided to allow these two subsidiary definitions to float to the status of a global or *top-level* definition. You might think that doesn't make any difference to the efficiency, but consider the following interaction with GHCi. (The command :set +s turns on some statistics which are printed after an expression is evaluated.)

```
ghci> :set +s
ghci> foo1 1000
3682913
(4.52 secs, 648420808 bytes)
ghci> foo1 1000
3682913
(4.52 secs, 648412468 bytes)
ghci> foo2 1000
3682913
(4.51 secs, 647565772 bytes)
ghci> foo2 1000
3682913
(0.02 secs, 1616096 bytes)
```

Why was the second evaluation of foo2 1000 so much faster than the first, while the two evaluations of foo1 1000 took the same time?

The answer is that in the definition of foo2 the first 1000 elements of the list primes is demanded, so after evaluation primes now points to a list in which the first 1000 primes appear explicitly. The second evaluation of foo 1000 does not require these primes to be computed again. Internally, the script has grown in size because primes now occupies at least 1000 units of space.

Programmer Three chooses to write foo in the following way:

```
foo3 = \n -> sum (take n primes)
  where
  primes     = [x | x <- [2..], divisors x == [x]]
  divisors x = [d | d <- [2..x], x `mod` d == 0]
```

This uses a lambda expression to express foo3 at the function level, but otherwise the definition is exactly the same as that of foo1. The alternative

```
foo3 = sum . flip take primes
```

also works but seems a little obscure. Now we have

```
ghci> foo3 1000
3682913
(3.49 secs, 501381112 bytes)
```

```
ghci> foo3 1000
3682913
(0.02 secs, 1612136 bytes)
```

Again, the second evaluation is much faster than the first. Why is that?

To see what is going on, we can rewrite the two functions in the form

```
foo1 n = let primes = ... in
             sum (take n primes)
foo3   = let primes = ... in
             \n -> sum (take n primes)
```

Now you can appreciate that in the first definition primes is re-evaluated every time foo1 1000 is called because it is bound to an application of foo1 not to the function itself. It is theoretically possible that the local definitions in the first definition depend on n, so any such definitions have to be re-evaluated for each n. In the second definition the local definitions are bound to the function itself (and can't possibly depend on any argument to the function); consequently, they are evaluated only once. Of course, after evaluating foo3 1000, the local definition of primes will be expanded to an explicit list of 1000 elements followed by a recipe for evaluating the rest.

7.2 Controlling space

Suppose we define sum by sum = foldl (+) 0. Under lazy evaluation the expression sum [1..1000] is reduced as follows

```
  sum [1..1000]
= foldl (+) 0 [1..1000]
= foldl (+) (0+1) [2..1000]
= foldl (+) ((0+1)+2) [3..1000]
= ...
= foldl (+) (..((0+1)+2)+ ... +1000) []
= (..((0+1)+2)+ ... +1000)
= ...
= 500500
```

It requires 1000 units of space just to build up the arithmetic expression that sums the first 1000 numbers before it pops to the surface and is finally evaluated.

Much better is to use a mixture of lazy and eager evaluation:

```
    sum [1..1000]
  = foldl (+) 0 [1..1000]
  = foldl (+) (0+1) [2..1000]
  = foldl (+) 1 [2..1000]
  = foldl (+) (1+2) [3..1000]
  = foldl (+) 3 [3..1000]
  = ...
  = foldl (+) 500500 []
  = 500500
```

While the list expression [1..1000] is evaluated lazily, the second argument of foldl, the accumulated sum, is evaluated eagerly. The result of interleaving lazy and eager evaluation steps is a sequence that uses a constant amount of space.

This suggests that it would be useful to have some way of controlling the reduction order. Such a method is provided by a primitive function seq with type

```
    seq :: a -> b -> b
```

Evaluation of x `seq` y proceeds by first evaluating x (to head normal form) and then returning the result of evaluating y. If evaluation of x does not terminate, then neither does x `seq` y. It's not possible to define seq in Haskell; instead Haskell provides it as a primitive function.

Now consider the following version foldl' of foldl that evaluates its second argument strictly:

```
    foldl' :: (b -> a -> b) -> b -> [a] -> b
    foldl' f e []     = e
    foldl' f e (x:xs) = y `seq` foldl' f y xs
                        where y = f e x
```

Haskell provides the function foldl' in the standard prelude (yes, with just this unimaginative name). Now we can define sum = foldl' (+) 0, with the consequence that evaluation proceeds in constant space. In fact, sum is another prelude function with essentially this definition.

Is it the case that foldl is now redundant and can be replaced by the new improved foldl'? The answer is in practice yes, but in theory no. It is possible to construct f, e and xs such that

$$\text{foldl } f \text{ e } xs \neq \text{foldl' } f \text{ e } xs$$

However, when f is strict (recall that f is strict if $f \perp = \perp$) the two expressions do return the same result. The exercises go into details.

Taking the mean

Armed with the above information, let's now consider a very instructive example: how to compute the average or *mean* of a list of numbers. Surely that is an easy problem, you might think, just divide the sum of the list by the length of the list:

```
mean :: [Float] -> Float
mean xs = sum xs / length xs
```

There are lots of things wrong with this definition, not the least of which is that the expression on the right is not well-formed! The function `length` in Haskell has type `[a] -> Int` and we can't divide a `Float` by an `Int` without performing an explicit conversion.

There is a function in the standard prelude that comes to our aid:

```
fromIntegral :: (Integral a, Num b) => a -> b
fromIntegral = fromInteger . toInteger
```

Recall from Chapter 3 the two conversion functions

```
toInteger   :: (Integral a) => a -> Integer
fromInteger :: (Num a) => Integer -> a
```

The first converts any integral type to an integer, and the second converts an integer to a number. Their composition converts an integral number, such as `Int`, to a more general kind of number, such as `Float`.

We can now rewrite `mean` to read

```
mean :: [Float] -> Float
mean xs = sum xs / fromIntegral (length xs)
```

The second thing wrong with this definition is that it silently ignores the case of the empty list. What is 0/0? Either we should identify the failing case with an explicit error message, or else adopt one common convention, which is to agree that the mean of the empty list should be zero:

```
mean [] = 0
mean xs = sum xs / fromIntegral (length xs)
```

Now we are ready to see what is *really* wrong with `mean`: it has a space leak. Evaluating `mean [1..1000]` will cause the list to be expanded and retained in memory after summing because there is a *second pointer* to it, namely in the computation of its length.

We can replace the two traversals of the list by one, using a strategy of program optimisation called *tupling*. The idea is simple enough in the present example: define sumlen by

```
sumlen :: [Float] -> (Float,Int)
sumlem xs = (sum xs,length xs)
```

and then calculate an alternative definition that avoids the two traversals. It is easy to carry out the calculation and we just state the result:

```
sumlen []     = (0,0)
sumlen (x:xs) = (s+x,n+1)  where (s,n) = sumlen xs
```

The pattern of the definition of sumlen should be familiar by now. An alternative definition is

```
sumlen = foldr f (0,0)  where f x (s,n) = (s+x,n+1)
```

Even better, we can replace foldr f by foldl g, where

```
g (s,n) x = (s+x,n+1)
```

The justification of this step is the law in the previous chapter that said

```
foldr f e xs = foldl g e xs
```

for all finite lists xs, provided

```
f x (g y z) = g (f x y) z
f x e = g e x
```

The verification of these two conditions is left as an exercise.

And that means we can use foldl':

```
sumlen = foldl' g (0,0)  where g (s,n) x = (s+x,n+1)
```

Now we can replace our heavily criticised definition of mean by

```
mean [] = 0
mean xs = s / fromIntegral n
          where (s,n) = sumlen xs
```

Surely we have now achieved our goal of a constant-space computation for mean?

Unfortunately not. The problem is with sumlen and it is a little tricky to spot. Expanding the definition out a little, we find

```
foldl' f (s,n) (x:xs) = y `seq` foldl' f y xs
                  where y = (s+x,n+1)
```

Ah, but y `seq` z reduces y to head normal form and the expression (s+x,n+1) is already in head normal form. Its two components are not evaluated until the end of the computation. That means we have to dig deeper with our seqs and rewrite sumlen in the following way:

```
sumlen = foldl' f (0,0)
  where f (s,n) x = s `seq` n `seq` (s+x,n+1)
```

Finally, everything in the garden is rosy and we have a computation that runs in constant space.

Two more application operators

Function application is the only operation not denoted by any visible sign. However, Haskell provides two more application operators, ($) and ($!):

```
infixr 0 $,$!
($),($!) :: (a -> b) -> a -> b
f $ x  = f x
f $! x = x `seq` f x
```

The only difference between f x and f $! x is that in the second expression the argument x is evaluated *before* f is applied. The only difference between f x and f $ x is that ($) (and also ($!)) is declared to have the lowest binding power of 0 and to associate to the right in expressions. That is exactly what the *fixity* declaration in the first line provides. Why do we want that?

The answer is that we can now write, for example

```
process1 $ process2 $ process3 input
```

instead of having to write either of

```
process1 (process2 (process3 x))
(process1 . process2 . process3) x
```

It is undeniable that ($) can be quite useful on occasions, especially when submitting expressions for evaluation with GHCi, so it's worth mentioning its existence. And the strict application operator ($!) is useful for the reasons discussed above.

7.3 Controlling time

We have seen that having an 'eager' button on our dashboard is a very simple way of controlling the space involved in driving a computation, but what about time? Unfortunately there is no analogous button for speeding up computations; instead we have to understand some of the things that can unintentionally slow down a computation. The Haskell platform comes with documentation on GHC, which contains useful advice on how to make your program run more quickly. The documentation makes three key points:

- Make use of GHC's *profiling* tools. There is no substitute for finding out where your program's time and space is really being used up. We will not discuss profiling in this book, but it is important to mention that such tools are available.

- The best way to improve a program's performance is to use a better algorithm. We mentioned this point at the beginning of the chapter.

- It is far better to use library functions that have been Seriously Tuned by Someone Else, than to craft your own. You might be able to write a better sorting algorithm than the one provided in `Data.List`, but it will take you longer than just writing `import Data.List (sort)`. This is particularly true when you use GHCi because GHCi loads *compiled* versions of the functions in its standard libraries. Compiled functions typically run about an order of magnitude faster than interpreted ones.

Much of the detailed advice in the GHC documentation is beyond the scope of this book, but two tips can be explained here. Firstly, the management of lazy evaluation involves more overheads than eager evaluation, so that if you know that a function's value will be needed, it is better to push the eager button. As the documentation says: 'Strict functions are your dear friends'.

The second piece of advice is about types. Firstly, `Int` arithmetic is faster than `Integer` arithmetic because Haskell has to perform more work in handling potentially very large numbers. So, use `Int` rather than `Integer` whenever it is safe to do so. Secondly, there is less housekeeping work for Haskell if you tailor the type of your function to the instance you want. For example, consider the type of `foo1`, defined in Section 7.1. There we did not provide a type signature for `foo1` (or indeed for any of the other related functions) and that was a mistake. It turns out that

```
foo1 :: Integral a => Int -> a
```

If we are really interested in the sum of the first *n* prime numbers, it is better to declare the type of foo1 to be (say)

```
foo1 :: Int -> Integer
```

With this more specialised definition Haskell does not have to carry around a dictionary of the methods and instances of the type class Integral, and that lightens the load.

These pieces of advice can help shave off constant amounts of time and do not affect *asymptotic* time complexity, the order of magnitude of the timing function. But sometimes we can write code that is inadvertently less efficient asymptotically than we intended. Here is an instructive example. Consider the cartesian product function cp discussed in Chapter 5:

```
cp []        = [[]]
cp (xs:xss) = [x:ys | x <- xs, ys <- cp xss]
```

Pretty and clear enough you would think, but compare it with

```
cp' = foldr op [[]]
    where op xs yss = [x:ys | x <- xs, ys <- yss]
```

The first version is a direct recursive definition, while the second uses foldr to encapsulate the pattern of the recursion. The two 'algorithms' are the same, aren't they? Well,

```
ghci> sum $ map sum $ cp [[1..10] | j <- [1..6]]
33000000
(12.11 secs, 815874256 bytes)
ghci> sum $ map sum $ cp' [[1..10] | j <- [1..6]]
33000000
(4.54 secs, 369640332 bytes)
```

The expression sum $ map sum is there just to force complete evaluation of the cartesian product. Why is the first computation three times slower than the second?

To answer this question, look at the translation that eliminates the list comprehension in the first definition:

```
cp [] = [[]]
cp (xs:xss) = concat (map f xs)
        where f x = [x:ys | ys <- cp xss]
```

Now we can see that cp xss is evaluated *each time* f is applied to elements of xs. That means, in the examples above, that cp is evaluated many more times in the first example than in the second. We cannot be more precise at this point, but will be below when we develop a little calculus for estimating running times. But the issue should be clear enough: the simple recursive definition of cp has led us inadvertently into a situation in which more evaluations are carried out than we intended.

One other way to get a more efficient cartesian product is to just write

```
cp []       = [[]]
cp (xs:xss) = [x:ys | x <- xs, ys <- yss]
                where yss = cp xss
```

This definition has exactly the same efficiency as the one in terms of foldr. The lesson here is that innocent-looking list comprehensions can hide the fact that some expressions, though only written once, are evaluated multiple times.

7.4 Analysing time

Given the definition of a function f we will write $T(\mathtt{f})(n)$ to denote an asymptotic estimate of the number of reduction steps required to evaluate f on an argument of 'size' n in the worst case. Moreover, for reasons explained in a moment, we will assume eager, not lazy, evaluation as the reduction strategy involved in defining T.

The definition of T requires some amplification. Firstly, $T(\mathtt{f})$ refers to the complexity of a given *definition* of f. Time complexity is a property of an expression, not of the value of that expression.

Secondly, the number of reduction steps does not correspond exactly to the elapsed time between submitting an expression for evaluation and waiting for the answer. No account is taken of the time to find the next subexpression to be reduced in a possibly large and complicated expression. For this reason the statistics facility of GHCi does not count reduction steps, but produces a measure of elapsed time.

Thirdly, we do not formalise the notion of size, since different measures are appropriate in different situations. For example, the cost of evaluating xs++ys is best measured in terms of (m, n), a pair describing the lengths of the two lists. In the case of concat xss we could take the length of concat xss as a measure of size, but if xss is a list of length m consisting of lists all of length n, then (m, n) might be a more suitable measure.

The fourth and crucial remark is that $T(\mathtt{f})(n)$ is determined under an *eager* evaluation model of reduction. The reason is simply that estimating the number of

reduction steps under lazy evaluation is difficult. To illustrate, consider the definition `minimum` = `head` . `sort`. Under eager evaluation, the time to evaluate the
minimum on a list of length n under this definition is given by

$$T(\texttt{minimum})(n) = T(\texttt{sort})(n) + T(\texttt{head})(n).$$

In other words we first have to completely sort a list of length n and then take the
head of the result (presumably a constant-time operation). This equation does not
hold under lazy evaluation, since the number of reduction steps required to find the
head of `sort` `xs` requires only that `sort` `xs` be reduced to head normal form. How
long that takes depends on the precise algorithm used for `sort`. Timing analysis
under eager reduction is simpler because it is *compositional*. Since lazy evaluation
never requires more reduction steps than eager evaluation, any upper bound for
$T(\texttt{f})(n)$ will also be an upper bound under lazy evaluation. Furthermore, in many
cases of interest, a lower bound will also be a lower bound under lazy evaluation.

In order to give some examples of timing analyses we have to introduce a little
order notation. So far, we have used the awkward phrase 'taking a number of steps
proportional to' whenever efficiency is discussed. It is time to replace it by something shorter. Given two functions f and g on the natural numbers, we say that f
is of order g, and write $f = \Theta(g)$ if there are positive constants C_1 and C_2 and a
natural number n_0 such that $C_1 g(n) \leq f(n) \leq C_2 g(n)$ for all $n > n_0$. In other words,
f is bounded above and below by some constant times g for all sufficiently large
arguments.

The notation is abused to the extent that one conventionally writes, for example,
$f(n) = \Theta(n^2)$ rather than the more correct $f = \Theta(\lambda n.n^2)$. Similarly, one writes
$f(n) = \Theta(n)$ rather than $f = \Theta(id)$. The main use of Θ-notation is to hide constants;
for example, we can write

$$\sum_{j=1}^{n} j = \Theta(n^2) \quad \text{and} \quad \sum_{j=1}^{n} j^2 = \Theta(n^3)$$

without bothering about the exact constants involved. When $\Theta(g)$ appears in a
formula it stands for some unnamed function f satisfying $f = \Theta(g)$. In particular,
$\Theta(1)$ denotes an anonymous constant.

With that behind us, we give three examples of how to analyse the running time of
a computation. Consider first the following two definitions of `concat`:

```
concat xss  = foldr (++) [] xss
concat' xss = foldl (++) [] xss
```

The two definitions are equivalent provided `xss` is a finite list. Suppose `xss` is a list of length m of lists all of length n. Then the first definition gives

$$T(\texttt{concat})(m,n) = T(\texttt{foldr (++) []})(m,n),$$
$$T(\texttt{foldr (++) []})(0,n) = \Theta(1),$$
$$T(\texttt{foldr (++) []})(m{+}1,n) = T(\texttt{++})(n,mn) +$$
$$T(\texttt{foldr (++) []})(m,n).$$

The estimate $T(\texttt{++})(n,mn)$ arises because a list of length n is concatenated with a list of length mn. Since $T(\texttt{++})(n,m) = \Theta(n)$, we obtain

$$T(\texttt{foldr (++) []})(m,n) = \sum_{k=0}^{m} \Theta(n) = \Theta(mn).$$

For the second definition of $\texttt{concat}$ we have

$$T(\texttt{concat'})(m,n) = T(\texttt{foldl (++)})(0,m,n),$$
$$T(\texttt{foldl (++)})(k,0,n) = O(1),$$
$$T(\texttt{foldl (++)})(k,m{+}1,n) = T(\texttt{++})(k,n) +$$
$$T(\texttt{foldl (++)})(k{+}n,m,n).$$

The additional argument k refers to the length of the accumulated list in the second argument of $\texttt{foldl}$. This time we obtain

$$T(\texttt{foldl (++)})(k,m,n) = \sum_{j=0}^{m-1} \Theta(k+jn) = \Theta(k+m^2n).$$

Hence $T(\texttt{concat'})(m,n) = \Theta(m^2n)$. The conclusion, which was anticipated in the previous chapter, is that using $\texttt{foldr}$ rather than $\texttt{foldl}$ in the definition of $\texttt{concat}$ leads to an asymptotically faster program.

For the second example let us time the two programs for $\texttt{subseqs}$ discussed in Section 7.1, where we had either of the following two possibilities:

```
subseqs (x:xs)  = subseqs xs ++ map (x:) (subseqs xs)
subseqs' (x:xs) = xss ++ map (x:) xss
                  where xss = subseqs' xs
```

Bearing in mind that (i) if $\texttt{xs}$ has length n, then $\texttt{subseqs xs}$ has length 2^n; and (ii) the time for both the concatenation and for applying $\texttt{map (x:)}$ is therefore $\Theta(2^n)$, the two timing analyses give

$$T(\texttt{subseqs})(n{+}1) = 2T(\texttt{subseqs})(n) + \Theta(2^n),$$
$$T(\texttt{subseqs'})(n{+}1) = T(\texttt{subseqs'})(n) + \Theta(2^n)$$

together with $T(\texttt{subseqs})(0) = \Theta(1)$. We will just state the two solutions (which can be proved by a simple induction argument):

$$T(\texttt{subseqs})(n) = \Theta(n2^n),$$
$$T(\texttt{subseqs'})(n) = \Theta(2^n).$$

The latter is therefore asymptotically faster than the former by a logarithmic factor.

For the third example, let us time the two programs for cp discussed at the beginning of this section. The first one was

```
cp []       = [[]]
cp (xs:xss) = [x:ys | x <- xs, ys <- cp xss]
```

Suppose once again that xss is a list of length m of lists all of length n. Then the length of cp xss is n^m. Then we have

$$T(\texttt{cp})(0,n) = \Theta(1),$$
$$T(\texttt{cp})(m+1,n) = nT(\texttt{cp})(m,n) + \Theta(n^m).$$

because it takes $\Theta(n^m)$ steps to apply (x:) to every subsequence. The solution is

$$T(\texttt{cp})(m,n) = \Theta(mn^m).$$

On the other hand, the definition of cp in terms for `foldr` gives

$$T(\texttt{cp})(0,n) = \Theta(1),$$
$$T(\texttt{cp})(m+1,n) = T(\texttt{cp})(m,n) + \Theta(n^m).$$

with solution $T(\texttt{cp})(m,n) = \Theta(n^m)$. The second version is therefore asymptotically faster, again by a logarithmic factor.

7.5 Accumulating parameters

Sometimes we can improve the running time of a computation by adding an extra argument, called an *accumulating parameter*, to a function. The canonical example is the function `reverse`:

```
reverse []     = []
reverse (x:xs) = reverse xs ++ [x]
```

With this definition we have $T(\texttt{reverse})(n) = \Theta(n^2)$. In search of a linear-time program, suppose we define

```
revcat :: [a] -> [a] -> [a]
revcat xs ys = reverse xs ++ ys
```

It is clear that `reverse xs = revcat xs []`, so if we can obtain an efficient version of `revcat` we can obtain an efficient version of `reverse`. To this end we calculate a recursive definition of `revcat`. The base case `revcat [] ys = ys` is left as an exercise, and the inductive case is as follows:

$$
\begin{array}{ll}
 & \texttt{revcat (x:xs) ys} \\
= & \{\text{definition of revcat}\} \\
 & \texttt{reverse (x:xs) ++ ys} \\
= & \{\text{definition of reverse}\} \\
 & \texttt{(reverse xs ++ [x]) ++ ys} \\
= & \{\text{associativity of (++)}\} \\
 & \texttt{reverse xs ++ ([x] ++ ys)} \\
= & \{\text{definition of (:)}\} \\
 & \texttt{reverse xs ++ (x:ys)} \\
= & \{\text{definition of revcat}\} \\
 & \texttt{revcat xs (x:ys)}
\end{array}
$$

Hence

```
revcat [] ys     = ys
revcat (x:xs) ys = revcat xs (x:ys)
```

As to the running time, $T(\texttt{revcat})(m,n) = \Theta(m)$. In particular,

$$T(\texttt{reverse}(n) = T(\texttt{revcat}(n,0) = \Theta(n)$$

That gives a linear-time computation for reversing a list.

Here is another example. The function `length` is defined by

```
length :: [a] -> Int
length []     = 0
length (x:xs) = length xs + 1
```

We have $T(\texttt{length})(n) = \Theta(n)$, so there is no time advantage in calculating another definition. Nevertheless, define `lenplus` by

```
lenplus :: [a] -> Int -> Int
lenplus xs n = length xs + n
```

If we go through exactly the same calculation for `lenplus` as we did for `revcat`, we arrive at

```
lenplus []     n = n
lenplus (x:xs) n = lenplus xs (1+n)
```

The reason the calculation goes through is that `(+)`, like `(++)`, is an associative operation. The advantage of defining

```
length xs = lenplus xs 0 = foldl (\n x -> 1+n) 0 xs
```

is that, by using `foldl'` in place of `foldl`, the length of a list can be computed in constant space. That indeed is how `length` is defined in Haskell's prelude.

As the really astute reader might have spotted, there is actually no need to go through the calculations above. Both the examples are, in fact, instances of a law already described in the previous chapter, namely that

```
foldr (<>) e xs = foldl (@) e xs
```

for all finite lists xs provided

$$x <> (y @ z) = (x <> y) @ z$$
$$x <> e = e @ x$$

The two instances are:

```
foldr (\x n -> n+1) 0 xs = foldl (\n x -> 1+n) 0 xs
foldr (\x xs -> xs++[x]) [] xs
                 = foldl (\xs x -> [x]++xs) [] xs
```

We leave the detailed verification of these equations as an exercise.

For a final demonstration of the accumulating parameter technique we move from lists to trees. Consider the data declaration

```
data GenTree a = Node a [GenTree a]
```

An element of this type is a tree consisting of a node with a label and a list of subtrees. Such trees arise in problems that can be formulated in terms of positions and moves. The label of a node specifies the current position, and the number of subtrees corresponds to the number of possible moves in the current position. Each subtree has a label that specifies the result of making the move, and its subtrees describe the moves that can be made from the new position. And so on.

Here is a function for computing the list of labels in a tree:

```
labels :: GenTree a -> [a]
labels (Node x ts) = x:concat (map labels ts)
```

The method is simple enough: compute the labels of each subtree, concatenate the results, and stick the label of the tree at the front of the final list.

Let us analyse the running time of this program on a tree t. To keep things simple, suppose that t is a *perfect* k-ary tree of height h. What that means is that if $h = 1$ then t has no subtrees, while if $h > 1$ then t has exactly k subtrees, each with height $h-1$. The number $s(h,k)$ of labels in such a tree satisfies

$$s(1,t) = 1,$$
$$s(h+1,k) = 1 + ks(h,k),$$

with solution $s(h,k) = \Theta(k^h)$. Now we have

$$T(\texttt{labels})(1,k) = \Theta(1),$$
$$T(\texttt{labels})(h+1,k) = \Theta(1) + T(\texttt{concat})(k,s) + T(\texttt{map labels})(h,k),$$

where $s = s(h,k)$. The term $T(\texttt{map labels})(h,k)$ estimates the running time of applying map labels to a list of length k of trees all of height h. In general, given a list of length k consisting of elements each of size n, we have

$$T(\texttt{map f})(k,n) = kT(\texttt{f})(n) + \Theta(k).$$

Furthermore $T(\texttt{concat})(k,s) = \Theta(ks) = \Theta(k^{h+1})$. Hence

$$T(\texttt{labels})(h+1,k) = \Theta(k^{h+1}) + kT(\texttt{labels})(h,k)$$

since $\Theta(1) + \Theta(k) = \Theta(k)$. The solution is given by

$$T(\texttt{labels})(h,k) = \Theta(hk^h) = \Theta(s \log s).$$

In words, computing the labels of a tree using the definition above takes time that is asymptotically greater than the size of the tree by a logarithmic factor.

Let us now see what an accumulating parameter can do. Define labcat by

```
labcat :: [GenTree a] -> [a] -> [a]
labcat ts xs = concat (map labels ts) ++ xs
```

As well as adding in a list xs we have also generalised the first argument from a tree to a list of trees. We have labels t = labcat [t] [], so any improvement on labcat leads to a corresponding improvement on labels.

We now synthesise an alternative definition for labcat. For the base case we obtain

```
labcat [] xs = xs
```

For the inductive case we reason:

```
  labcat (Node x us:vs) xs
=   {definition}
  concat (map labels (Node x us:vs)) ++ xs
=   {definitions}
  labels (Node x us) ++ concat (map labels vs) ++ xs
=   {definition}
  x:concat (map labels us) ++ concat (map labels vs) ++ xs
=   {definition of labcat}
  x:concat (map labels us) ++ labcat vs xs
=   {definition of labcat (again)}
  labcat us (labcat vs xs)
```

The result of this calculation is the following program for `labels`:

```
labels t = labcat [t] []
labcat [] xs             = xs
labcat (Node x us:vs) = x:labcat us (labcat vs xs)
```

For the timing analysis, let $T(\texttt{labcat})(h,k,n)$ estimate the running time of

```
  labcat ts xs
```

when `ts` is a list of length n of trees, each of which is a perfect k-ary tree of height h (the size of `xs` is ignored since it doesn't affect the estimate). Then

$$T(\texttt{labcat})(h,k,0) = \Theta(1),$$
$$T(\texttt{labcat})(1,k,n+1) = \Theta(1) + T(\texttt{labcat})(1,k,n)),$$
$$T(\texttt{labcat})(h+1,k,n+1) = \Theta(1) + T(\texttt{labcat})(h,k,k) +$$
$$T(\texttt{labcat})(h+1,k,n).$$

Solving the first two equations gives $T(\texttt{labcat})(1,k,n) = \Theta(n)$. An induction argument now shows $T(\texttt{labcat})(h,k,n) = \Theta(k^h n)$. Hence

$$T(\texttt{labels})(h,k) = T(\texttt{labcat})(h,k,1) = \Theta(k^h) = \Theta(s).$$

That means we can compute the labels of a tree in time proportional to the size of the tree, a logarithmic improvement over our first version.

7.6 Tupling

We met the idea of tupling two functions in the discussion of the function mean. Tupling is sort of dual to the method of accumulating parameters: we generalise a function not by including an extra argument but by including an extra result.

The canonical example of the power of tupling is the Fibonacci function:

```
fib :: Int -> Integer
fib 0 = 0
fib 1 = 1
fib n = fib (n-1) + fib (n-2)
```

The time to evaluate fib by these three equations is given by

$$T(\texttt{fib})(0) = \Theta(1),$$
$$T(\texttt{fib})(1) = \Theta(1),$$
$$T(\texttt{fib})(n) = T(\texttt{fib})(n-1) + T(\texttt{fib})(n-2) + \Theta(1).$$

The timing function therefore satisfies equations very like that of fib itself. In fact $T(\texttt{fib})(n) = \Theta(\phi^n)$, where ϕ is the golden ratio $\phi = (1+\sqrt{5})/2$. That means that the running time to compute fib on an input n is exponential in n.

Now consider the function fib2 defined by

```
fib2 n = (fib n,fib (n+1))
```

Clearly fib n = fst (fib2 n). Synthesis of a direct recursive definition of fib2 yields

```
fib2 0 = (0,1)
fib2 n = (b,a+b)  where (a,b) = fib2 (n-1)
```

This program takes linear time. In this example the tupling strategy leads to a dramatic increase in efficiency, from exponential time to linear time.

It's great fun to formulate general laws that encapsulate gains in efficiency. One such law concerns the computation of

```
(foldr f a xs, foldr g b xs)
```

As expressed above, the two applications of foldr involve two traversals of the list xs. There is a modest time advantage, and possibly a greater space advantage, in formulating a version that traverses the list only once. In fact

```
(foldr f a xs, foldr g b xs) = foldr h (a,b) xs
```

where

```
h x (y,z) = (f x y,g x z)
```

The result can be proved by induction and we leave details as an easy exercise.

As one more example, we again move from lists to trees. But this time we have a different kind of tree, a *leaf-labelled binary tree*:

```
data BinTree a = Leaf a | Fork (BinTree a) (BinTree a)
```

In contrast to a `GenTree` discussed above, a `BinTree` is either a leaf, with an associated label, or a fork of two subtrees.

Suppose we wanted to build such a tree with a given list as the labels. More precisely, we want to define a function `build` satisfying

```
labels (build xs) = xs
```

for all finite nonempty lists `xs`, where `labels` returns the labels of a binary tree:

```
labels :: BinTree a -> [a]
labels (Leaf x)   = [x]
labels (Fork u v) = labels u ++ labels v
```

We are attuned now to possible optimisations, and the definition of `labels` suggest that it could be improved with an accumulating parameter. So it can, but that is not our primary interest here, and we leave the optimisation as an exercise.

One way to build a tree is to arrange that half the list goes into the left subtree, and the other half into the right subtree:

```
build :: [a] -> BinTree a
build [x] = Leaf x
build xs  = Fork (build ys) (build zs)
            where (ys,zs) = halve xs
```

The function `halve` made an appearance in Section 4.8:

```
halve xs = (take m xs,drop m xs)
           where m = length xs `div` 2
```

Thus `halve` splits a list into two approximately equal halves. The definition of `halve` involves a traversal of the list to find its length, and two further (partial) traversals to compute the two components. It is therefore a prime candidate for applying the tupling strategy to get something better. But as with `labels` we are going to ignore that particular optimisation for now. And we are also going to ignore the proof that this definition of build meets its specification. That's three calculations we are leaving as exercises in order to concentrate on a fourth.

Let's time build:

$$T(\text{build})(1) = \Theta(1),$$
$$T(\text{build})(n) = T(\text{build})(m) + T(\text{build})(n-m) + \Theta(n)$$
$$\textbf{where } m = n \operatorname{div} 2$$

It takes $\Theta(n)$ steps to halve a list of length n, and then we recursively build two subtrees from lists of length m and $n - m$, respectively. The solution is

$$T(\text{build})(n) = \Theta(n \log n).$$

In words, building a tree by the above method takes longer than the length of the list by a logarithmic factor.

Having established this fact, let us define build2 by

```
build2 :: Int -> [a] -> (BinTree a,[a])
build2 n xs = (build (take n xs),drop n xs)
```

This builds a tree from the first n elements, but also returns the list that is left. We have

```
build xs = fst (build2 (length xs) xs)
```

so our original function can be determined from the tupled version.

Our aim now is to construct a direct recursive definition of build2. First of all, it is clear that

```
build2 1 xs = (Leaf (head xs),tail xs)
```

For the recursive case we start with

```
build2 n xs = (Fork (build (take m (take n xs)))
                     (build (drop m (take n xs))),
               drop n xs)   where m = n `div` 2
```

This equation is obtained by substituting in the recursive case of build. It suggests that the next step is to use some properties of take and drop. Here they are: if m <= n then

```
take m . take n = take m
drop m . take n = take (n-m) . drop m
```

That leads to

```
build2 n xs = (Fork (build (take m xs))
                    (build (take (n-m) (drop m xs))),
              drop n xs)  where m = n `div` 2
```

Using the definition of build2 we can rewrite the above as follows:

```
build2 n xs = (Fork u v, drop n xs)
              where (u,xs')  = build2 m xs
                    (v,xs'') = build2 (n-m) xs'
                    m        = n `div` 2
```

But as a final step, observe that

```
xs'' = drop (n-m) xs'
     = drop (n-m) (drop m xs)
     = drop n xs
```

Hence we can rewrite build2 once again to read

```
build2 1 xs = (Leaf (head xs),tail xs)
build2 n xs = (Fork u v, xs'')
              where (u,xs')  = build2 m xs
                    (v,xs'') = build2 (n-m) xs'
                    m        = n `div` 2
```

Timing this program yields

$$T(\text{build2})(1) = \Theta(1),$$
$$T(\text{build2})(n) = T(\text{build2})(m) + T(\text{build2})(n-m) + \Theta(1).$$

with solution $T(\text{build2})(n) = \Theta(n)$. Using build2 as a subsidiary function has therefore improved the running time of build by a logarithmic factor.

7.7 Sorting

Sorting is a big topic and one can spend many happy hours tinkering with different algorithms. Knuth devotes about 400 pages to the subject in Volume 3 of his series *The Art of Computer Programming*. Even then some of his conclusions have to be reformulated when sorting is considered in a purely functional setting. Here we briefly consider two sorting algorithms, keeping an eye out for possible optimisations.

Mergesort

The sorting method called *Mergesort* made an appearance in Section 4.8:

```
sort :: (Ord a) => [a] -> [a]
sort []  = []
sort [x] = [x]
sort xs  = merge (sort ys) (sort zs)
           where (ys,zs) = halve xs
halve xs = (take m xs,drop m xs)
           where m = length xs `div` 2
```

In fact there are a number of variants for sorting by merging, and the standard prelude function `sort` uses a different variant than the one above.

As we said above, the definition of `halve` looks fairly inefficient in that it involves multiple traversals of its argument. One way to improve matters is to make use of the standard prelude function `splitAt`, whose specification is

```
splitAt :: Int -> [a] -> ([a],[a])
splitAt n xs = (take n xs,drop n xs)
```

The prelude version of this function is the result of a tupling transformation:

```
splitAt 0 xs     = ([],xs)
splitAt n []     = ([],[])
splitAt n (x:xs) = (x:ys,zs)
                   where (ys,zs) = splitAt (n-1) xs
```

It is easy enough to calculate this definition using the two facts that

```
take n (x:xs) = x:take (n-1) xs
drop n (x:xs) = drop (n-1) xs
```

provided $0 < n$. Now we have

```
halve xs = splitAt (length xs `div` 2) xs
```

There are still two traversals here of course.

Another way to improve `sort` is to define

```
sort2 n xs = (sort (take n xs),drop n xs)
```

We have `sort xs = fst (sort2 (length xs) xs)`, so our original sorting function can be retrieved from the general one. An almost exactly similar calculation to the one in the previous section leads to

```
sort2 0 xs = ([],xs)
sort2 1 xs = ([head xs],tail xs)
sort2 n xs = (merge ys zs, xs'')
             where (ys,xs')  = sort2 m xs
                   (zs,xs'') = sort2 (n-m) xs'
                   m         = n `div` 2
```

With this definition there are no length calculations and no multiple traversals of xs.

Another way to optimise halve is to realise that no human would split up a list in this way if forced to do so by hand. If asked to divide a list into two, you and I would surely just deal out the elements into two piles:

```
halve []       = ([],[])
halve [x]      = ([x],[])
halve (x:y:xs) = (x:ys,y:zs)
                 where (ys,zs) = halve xs
```

Of course, this definition returns a different result than the previous one, but the order of the elements in the two lists does not matter if the result is to be sorted; what is important is that the elements are all there.

That is a total of three ways to improve the performance of sort. However, it turns out that none of them makes that much difference to the total running time. A few per cent perhaps, but nothing substantial. Furthermore, if we are using GHCi as our functional evaluator, none of the versions compares in performance to the library function sort because that function is given to us in a compiled form, and compiled versions of functions are usually about ten times faster. We can always compile our functions using GHC of course.

Quicksort

Our second sorting algorithm is a famous one called *Quicksort*. It can be expressed in just two lines of Haskell:

```
sort :: (Ord a) => [a] -> [a]
sort []     = []
sort (x:xs) = sort [y | y <- xs, y < x] ++ [x] ++
              sort [y | y <- xs, x <= y]
```

That's very pretty and a testament to the expressive power of Haskell. But the prettiness comes at a cost: the program can be very inefficient in its use of space. The situation is the same as with the program for `mean` seen earlier.

Before plunging into ways the code can be optimised, let's compute $T(\text{sort})$. Suppose we want to sort a list of length $n+1$. The first list comprehension can return a list of any length k from 0 to n. The length of the result of the second list comprehension is therefore $n-k$. Since our timing function is an estimate of the worst-case running time, we have to take the maximum of these possibilities:

$$T(\text{sort})(n+1)$$
$$= \max\,[T(\text{sort})(k) + T(\text{sort})(n-k) \mid k \leftarrow [0\mathbin{..}n]] + \Theta(n).$$

The $\Theta(n)$ term accounts for both the time to evaluate the two list comprehensions and the time to perform the concatenations. Note, by the way, the use of a list comprehension in a mathematical expression rather than a Haskell one. If list comprehensions are useful notations in programming, they are useful in mathematics too.

Although not immediately obvious, the worst case occurs when $k = 0$ or $k = n$. Hence

$$T(\text{sort})(0) = \Theta(1),$$
$$T(\text{sort})(n+1) = T(\text{sort})(n) + \Theta(n),$$

with solution $T(\text{sort})(n) = \Theta(n^2)$. Thus Quicksort is a quadratic algorithm in the worst case. This fact is intrinsic to the algorithm and has nothing to do with the Haskell expression of it. Quicksort achieved its fame for two other reasons, neither of which hold in a purely functional setting. Firstly, when Quicksort is implemented in terms of arrays rather than lists, the partitioning phase can be performed *in place* without using any additional space. Secondly, the *average case* performance of Quicksort, under reasonable assumptions about the input, is $\Theta(n \log n)$ with a smallish constant of proportionality. In a functional setting this constant is not so small and there are better ways to sort than Quicksort.

With this warning, let us now see what we can do to optimise the algorithm without changing it in any essential way (i.e. to a completely different sorting algorithm). To avoid the two traversals of the list in the partitioning process, define

```
partition p xs = (filter p xs, filter (not . p) xs)
```

This is another example of tupling two definitions to save on a traversal. Since `filter p` can be expressed as an instance of `foldr` we can appeal to the tupling law of `foldr` to arrive at

```
partition p = foldr op ([],[])
  where op x (ys,zs) | p x       = (x:ys,zs)
                     | otherwise = (ys,x:zs)
```

Now we can write

```
sort []     = []
sort (x:xs) = sort ys ++ [x] ++ sort zs
              where (ys,zs) = partition (<x) xs
```

But this program still contains a space leak. To see why, let us write the recursive case in the equivalent form

```
sort (x:xs) = sort (fst p) ++ [x] ++ sort (snd p)
              where p = partition (<x) xs
```

Suppose $x:xs$ has length $n+1$ and is in strictly decreasing order, so x is the largest element in the list and p is a pair of lists of length n and 0, respectively. Evaluation of p is triggered by displaying the results of the first recursive call, but the n units of space occupied by the first component of p cannot be reclaimed because there is another reference to p in the second recursive call. Between these two calls further pairs of lists are generated and retained. All in all, the total space required to evaluate sort on a strictly decreasing list of length $n+1$ is $\Theta(n^2)$ units. In practice this means that evaluation of sort on some large inputs can abort owing to lack of sufficient space.

The solution is to force evaluation of partition and, equally importantly, to bind ys and zs to the components of the pair, not to p itself.

One way of bringing about a happy outcome is to introduce two accumulating parameters. Define sortp by

```
sortp x xs us vs = sort (us ++ ys) ++ [x] ++
                   sort (vs ++ zs)
                   where (ys,zs) = partition (<x) xs
```

Then we have

```
sort (x:xs) = sortp x xs [] []
```

We now synthesise a direct recursive definition of sortp. The base case is

```
sortp x [] us vs = sort us ++ [x] ++ sort vs
```

For the recursive case y:xs let us assume that y < x. Then

```
     sortp x (y:xs) us vs
  =  {definition of sortp with (ys,zs) = partition (<x) xs}
     sort (us ++ y:ys) ++ [x] ++ sort (vs ++ zs)
  =  {claim (see below)}
     sort (y:us ++ ys) ++ [x] ++ sort (vs ++ zs)
  =  {definition of sortp}
     sortp x (y:us) vs
```

The claim is that if as is any permutation of bs then sort as and sort bs return the same result. The claim is intuitively obvious: sorting a list depends only on the elements in the input not on their order. A formal proof is omitted.

Carrying out a similar calculation in the case that x <= y and making sortp local to the definition of sort, we arrive at the final program

```
sort []     = []
sort (x:xs) = sortp xs [] []
   where
   sortp [] us vs      = sort us ++ [x] ++ sort vs
   sortp (y:xs) us vs = if y < x
                           then sortp xs (y:us) vs
                           else sortp xs us (y:vs)
```

Not quite as pretty as before, but at least the result has $\Theta(n)$ space complexity.

7.8 Exercises

Exercise A

One simple definition of sort is

```
sort []     = []
sort (x:xs) = insert x (sort xs)
insert x [] = [x]
insert x (y:ys)
        = if x <= y then x:y:ys else y:insert x ys
```

This method is called *insertion sort*. Reduce sort [3,4,2,1] to head normal form under lazy evaluation. Now answer the following questions: (i) How long, as a function of n, does it take to compute head . sort when applied to a list of length n? (ii) How long does it take under eager evaluation? (iii) Does insertion sort, evaluated lazily, carry out exactly the same sequence of comparisons as the following *selection sort* algorithm?

```
sort [] = []
sort xs = y:sort ys   where (y,ys) = select xs

select [x]      = (x,[])
select (x:xs) | x <= y      = (x,y:ys)
              | otherwise = (y,x:ys)
              where (y,ys) = select xs
```

Exercise B

Write down a definition of length that evaluates in constant space. Write a second definition of length that evaluates in constant space but does not make use of the primitive seq (either directly or indirectly).

Exercise C

Construct f, e and xs so that

$$\text{foldl f e xs} \neq \text{foldl' f e xs}$$

Exercise D

Would

```
cp []       = [[]]
cp (xs:xss) = [x:ys | ys <- cp xss, x <- xs]
```

be an alternative way of defining the function cp that is as efficient as the definition in terms of foldr? Yes, No or Maybe?

Time for a calculation. Use the fusion law of foldr to calculate an efficient alternative to

```
fcp = filter nondec . cp
```

See Section 4.7 for a definition of nondec.

Exercise E

Suppose

$$T(1) = \Theta(1),$$
$$T(n) = T(n \operatorname{div} 2) + T(n - n \operatorname{div} 2) + \Theta(n)$$

for $2 \leq n$. Prove that $T(2^k) = \Theta(k 2^k)$. Hence prove $T(n) = \Theta(n \log n)$.

Exercise F

Prove that

```
foldr (\x n -> n+1) 0 xs = foldl (\n x -> 1+n) 0 xs
foldr (\x xs -> xs++[x]) [] xs
                    = foldl (\xs x -> [x]++xs) [] xs
```

Exercise G

Prove that if `h x (y,z) = (f x y,g x z)`, then

```
(foldr f a xs,foldr g b xs) = foldr h (a,b) xs
```

for all finite lists `xs`. A tricky question: does the result hold for *all* lists `xs`?

Now find a definition of `h` such that

```
(foldl f a xs,foldl g b xs) = foldl h (a,b) xs
```

Exercise H

Recall that

```
partition p xs = (filter p xs, filter (not . p) xs)
```

Express the two components of the result as instances of `foldr`. Hence use the result of the previous exercise to calculate another definition of `partition`.

Define

```
part p xs us vs = (filter p xs ++ us,
                   filter (not . p) xs ++ vs)
```

Calculate another definition of `partition` that uses `part` as a local definition.

Exercise I

Recall that

```
labels :: BinTree a -> [a]
labels (Leaf x)   = [x]
labels (Fork u v) = labels u ++ labels v
```

Compute $T(\text{labels})(n)$, where n is the number of leaves in the tree. Now use the accumulating parameter technique to find a faster way of computing labels.

Prove that labels (build xs) = xs for all finite nonempty lists xs.

Exercise J

Define select k = (!!k) . sort, where sort is the original Quicksort. Thus select k selects the kth smallest element of a nonempty finite list of elements, the 0th smallest being the smallest element, the 1st smallest being the next smallest element, and so on. Calculate a more efficient definition of select and estimate its running time.

7.9 Answers

Answer to Exercise A

```
  sort [3,4,1,2]
= insert 3 (sort [4,1,2])
= ...
= insert 3 (insert 4 (insert 1 (insert 2 [])))
= insert 3 (insert 4 (insert 1 (2:[])))
= insert 3 (insert 4 (1:2:[]))
= insert 3 (1:insert 4 (2:[]))
= 1:insert 3 (insert 4 (2:[]))
```

It takes $\Theta(n)$ steps to compute head . sort on a list of length n. Under eager evaluation it takes about n^2 steps. As to part (iii), the answer is yes. You may think we have defined sorting by insertion, but under lazy evaluation it turns out to be selection sort. The lesson here is that, under lazy evaluation, you don't always get what you think you are getting.

Answer to Exercise B

For the first part, the following does the job:

```
length = foldl' (\n x -> n+1) 0
```

For the second part, one solution is

```
length              = length2 0
length2 n []        = n
length2 n (x:xs) = if n==0 then length2 1 xs
                   else length2 (n+1) xs
```

The test n==0 forces evaluation of the first argument.

Answer to Exercise C

Take f n x = if x==0 then undefined else 0. Then

```
foldl  f 0 [0,2]  = 0
foldl' f 0 [0,2] = undefined
```

Answer to Exercise D

The answer is: maybe! Although the given version of cp is efficient, it returns the component lists in a different order than any of the definitions in the text. That probably doesn't matter if we are only interested in the *set* of results, but it might affect the running time and result of any program that searched cp to find some list satisfying a given property.

According to the fusion rule we have to find a function g so that

```
filter nondec (f xs yss) = g xs (filter nondec yss)
```

where f xs yss = [x:ys | x <- xs, ys <- yss]. Then we would have

```
filter nondec . cp
 = filter nondec . foldr f [[]]
 = foldr g [[]]
```

Now

```
nondec (x:ys) = null ys || (x <= head ys && nondec ys)
```

That leads to

```
g xs [[]] = [[x] | x <- xs]
g xs yss  = [x:ys | x <- xs, ys <- yss, x <= head ys]
```

Answer to Exercise E

For the first part, we have

$$T(2^k) = 2T(2^{k-1}) + \Theta(2^k).$$

By induction we can show $T(2^k) = \sum_{i=0} k\Theta(2^k)$. The induction step is

$$T(2^k) = 2\sum_{i=0}^{k-1}\Theta(2^{k-1}) + \Theta(2^k)$$

$$= \sum_{i=0}^{k-1}\Theta(2^k) + \Theta(2^k)$$

$$= \sum_{i=0}^{k}\Theta(2^k).$$

Hence $T(2^k) = \Theta(k2^k)$. Now suppose $2^k \leq n < 2^{k+1}$, so

$$\Theta(k2^k) = T(2^k) \leq T(n) \leq T(2^{k+1}) = \Theta((k+1)2^{k+1}) = \Theta(k2^k).$$

Hence $T(n) = \Theta(k2^k) = \Theta(n\log n)$.

Answer to Exercise F

Define x <> n = n+1 and n @ x = 1+n. We have

```
(x <> n) @ y = 1+(n+1) = (1+n)+1 = x <> (n @ y)
```

The second proof is similar.

Answer to Exercise G

The induction step is

```
  (foldr f a (x:xs),foldr g b (x:xs)
= (f x (foldr f a xs),g x (foldr g b xs))
= h x (foldr f a xs,foldr g b xs)
= h x (foldr h (a,b) xs
= foldr h (a,b) (x:xs)
```

The answer to the tricky question is No. The values $(\bot, \bot)$ and $\bot$ are different in Haskell. For example, suppose we define foo (x,y) = 1. Then

```
foo undefined = undefined
foo (undefined,undefined) = 1
```

For the last part, the definition of h is that

```
h (y,z) x = (f y x,g z x)
```

Answer to Exercise H

We have filter p = foldr (op p) [], where

```
op p x xs = if p x then x:xs else xs
```

Now

```
(op p x ys,op (not . p) x zs)
= if p x then (x:ys,zs) else (ys,x:zs)
```

Hence

```
partition p xs = foldr f ([],[]) xs
  where f x (ys,zs) = if p x
                      then (x:ys,zs)
                      else (ys,x:zs)
```

For the last part we obtain

```
partition p xs = part p xs [] []
part p [] ys zs = (ys,zs)
part p (x:xs) ys zs = if p x
                      then part p xs (x:ys) zs
                      else part p xs ys (z:zs)
```

Answer to Exercise I

Remember that T estimates the *worst case* running time. The worst case for `labels` arises when every right subtree of the tree is a leaf. Then we have

$$T(\texttt{labels})(n) = T(\texttt{labels})(n-1) + \Theta(n),$$

where $\Theta(n)$ accounts for the time to concatenate a list of length $n-1$ with a list of length 1. Hence

$$T(\texttt{labels})(n) = \sigma_{j=0}^{n}\Theta(n) = \Theta(n^2).$$

The accumulating parameter method yields

```
labels t              = labels2 t []
labels2 (Leaf x) xs   = x:xs
labels2 (Fork u v) xs = labels2 u (labels2 v xs)
```

and $T(\texttt{labels2})(n) = \Theta(n)$. This improves the running time of `labels` from quadratic to linear time.

The induction step in the proof that `labels (build xs) = xs` is to assume the hypothesis for all lists strictly shorter than xs:

```
      labels (build xs)
```

= {assume xs has length at least two
and let (ys,zs) = halve xs}

```
      labels (Fork (build ys) (build zs))
```

= {definition of labels}

```
      labels (build ys) ++ labels (build zs)
```

= {induction, since ys and zs are strictly shorter than xs}

```
      ys ++ zs
```

= {definition of halve xs}

```
      xs
```

The induction here is *general induction*: in order to prove $P(xs)$ for all finite lists xs it is sufficient to prove that: (i) $P([])$; and (ii) $P(xs)$ holds under the assumption that P holds for all lists of length strictly less than xs.

Answer to Exercise J

One key property is that

```
(xs ++ [x] ++ ys)!!k | k < n    = xs!!k
                     | k==n      = x
                     | k > n     = ys!!(n-k)
                     where n = length xs
```

The other key property is that sorting a list does not change the length of the list. Hence

```
select k []      = error "list too short"
select k (x:xs) | k < n      = select k ys
                | k==n       = x
                | otherwise = select (n-k) zs
                where ys = [y | y <- xs, y < x]
                      zs = [z | z <- xs, x <= z]
                      n  = length ys
```

The worst-case running time for a list of length n occurs when $k = 0$ and the length of ys is $n-1$, i.e. when x:xs is in strictly decreasing order. Thus

$$T(\texttt{select})(0,n) = T(\texttt{select})(0,n-1) + \Theta(n),$$

with solution $T(\texttt{select})(0,n) = \Theta(n^2)$. But, assuming a reasonable distribution in which each permutation of the sorted result is equally likely as input, we have $T(\texttt{select})(k, n) = \Theta(n)$.

7.10 Chapter notes

There are many books on algorithm design, but two that concentrate on functional programming are *Algorithms: A Functional Programming Approach* (second edition) (Addison-Wesley, 1999) by Fethi Rabbi and Guy Lapalme, and my own *Pearls of Functional Algorithm Design* (Cambridge, 2010).

Information about profiling tools comes with the documentation on the Haskell Platform. The source book on sorting is Don Knuth's *The Art of Computer Programming, Volume 3: Sorting and Searching* (second edition) (Addison-Wesley, 1998).

Chapter 8

Pretty-printing

This chapter is devoted to an example of how to build a small library in Haskell. A library is an organised collection of types and functions made available to users for carrying out some task. The task we have chosen to discuss is *pretty-printing*, the idea of taking a piece of text and laying it out over a number of lines in such a way as to make the content easier to view and understand. We will ignore many of the devices for improving the readability of a piece of text, devices such as a change of colour or size of font. Instead we concentrate only on where to put the line breaks and how to indent the contents of a line. The library won't help you to lay out bits of mathematics, but it can help in presenting tree-shaped information, or in displaying lists of words as paragraphs.

8.1 Setting the scene

Let's begin with the problem of displaying conditional expressions. In this book we have used three ways of displaying such expressions:

```
if p then expr1 else expr2

if p then expr1
else expr2

if p
then expr1
else expr2
```

These three layouts, which occupy one, two or three lines, respectively, are considered acceptable, but the following two are not:

```
if p then
expr1 else expr2

if p
then expr1 else expr2
```

The decision as to what is or is not acceptable is down to me, the author. You may disagree with my choices (some do), and a flexible library should provide you with the ability to make your own reasonable choices. In any case, two basic questions have to be answered. Firstly, how can we describe the acceptable alternatives while rejecting the unacceptable ones? Secondly, how do we choose between the acceptable alternatives?

A quick answer to the second question is that the choice depends on the permitted line width. For instance we might choose a layout with the fewest lines, subject to the condition that each line fits within the allotted line width. Much more on this later.

As to the first question, one answer is just to write out all the acceptable alternatives. That's going to involve a lot of writing. A better alternative is to provide the user with a suitable *layout description language*. As a rough and ready guide we might write something like

```
if p <0> then expr1 (<0> + <1>) else expr2 +
if p <1> then expr1 <1> else expr2
```

where <0> means a single space, <1> means a line break and + means 'or'. The expression above yields our three layouts described earlier. However, the danger with providing the user with an unfettered choice of alternatives is that it becomes difficult to make a decision about the best layout without exploring every possible alternative, and that could take a long time.

Another possibility is to allow only restricted choice by forcing the user to describe layouts in terms of certain functions and operations provided by the library. For example, consider the description

```
group (group (if p <1> then expr1) <> <1> else expr2)
```

where group augments a set of layouts with one additional layout in which every <1> is replaced by <0>, thereby flattening the layout to just one line, and (<>) means concatenation lifted to sets of alternatives. For example,

```
group (if p <1> then expr1)
   = {if p <0> then expr1, if p <1> then expr1}
```

```
group (if p <1> then expr1) <> <1> else expr2
  = {if p <0> then expr1 <1> else expr2,
     if p <1> then expr1 <1> else expr2}
group (group (if p <1> then expr1) <> <1> else expr2)
  = {if p <0> then expr1 <0> else expr2,
     if p <0> then expr1 <1> else expr2,
     if p <1> then expr1 <1> else expr2}
```

Thus our set of three acceptable layouts is captured by the above description which contains two occurrences of group.

There is another aspect to the problem of displaying conditional expressions. What if expr1 or expr2 are themselves conditional expressions? Here we might want to allow a layout like

```
if p
then if q
     then expr1
     else expr2
else expr3
```

The point is that we should allow for *indentation* in our description language. Indentation means putting in a suitable number of spaces after each line break. This idea can be captured by providing a function nest so that nest i x is a layout in which *each* line break in layout x is followed by i spaces.

8.2 Documents

For the sake of a name let us agree to call a *document* some entity that represents the set of possible layouts of a piece of text. Documents are given as elements of the type Doc whose definition is left for later on. On the other hand, a layout is simply a string:

```
type Layout = String
```

We are deliberately being cagey about what a document actually is because we want to consider two representations of Doc. For now we concentrate on the operations on documents that our library might provide.

The first operation is a function

```
pretty :: Int -> Doc -> Layout
```

that takes a given line width and a document, and returns the best layout. How to define this function efficiently is really the main concern of the chapter.

The second operation is a function

```
layouts :: Doc -> [Layout]
```

that returns the set of possible layouts as a list. Why should we want such a function when we have `pretty`? Well, it takes a little experimentation to find the definitions that describe the layouts we regard as acceptable. The way to experiment is to formulate an initial definition and then rework it after inspecting all the resulting layouts on a small number of examples. That way we can see whether some layouts should be excluded or others added. So, whatever our final representation of documents turns out to be, we should provide `layouts` as a sensible diagnostic tool for the user.

The remaining operations deal with constructing documents. First up is the operation of concatenating two documents to give a new one:

```
(<>) :: Doc -> Doc -> Doc
```

Document concatenation should surely be an associative operation so we require of any implementation of (<>) that

```
(x <> y) <> z = x <> (y <> z)
```

for all documents x, y and z.

Whenever there is an associative operation there is usually an identity element, so we also provide an empty document

```
nil :: Doc
```

We require nil <> x = x and x <> nil = x for all documents x.

The next operation is a function

```
text :: String -> Doc
```

that takes a string not containing newlines into a document. To provide for documents containing more than one line, we can provide another basic document

```
line :: Doc
```

For example,

```
text "Hello" <> line <> text "World!"
```

is a document with a single layout that consists of two lines. You might think that `line` is unnecessary because we could always allow newline characters in text strings, but to indent a document we would then have to inspect the contents of every `text`. Far better is to have an explicit newline document; that way we know where line breaks are.

Next, the function

```
nest :: Int -> Doc -> Doc
```

provides a way of nesting documents: `nest i` indents a document by inserting `i` spaces *after* every newline. Note the emphasis: indentation is not done at the beginning of a document unless it begins with a newline. The reason for this choice is explained below.

Finally, to complete a library of eight operations, we have the function

```
group :: Doc -> Doc
```

This is the function that produces multiple layouts. The function `group` takes a document and adds an extra layout, one that consists of a single line of text with no line breaks.

We have named eight operations and given informal descriptions of what they are intended to mean, but can we be more precise about their properties and the relationships between them? An even more fundamental question is whether these operations are sufficiently flexible to allow for a reasonable class of layouts.

Let's first concentrate on what equational laws we might want. Finding such laws can boost our confidence that we have in hand an adequate and smoothly integrated box of tools, and that there isn't some crucial gadget we have missed. Such laws can also influence the meanings of operations and guide implementations. We have already asserted that (`<>`) should be associative with identity element `nil`, but what else should we require?

Well, for `text` we want the following properties:

```
text (s ++ t) = text s <> text t
text ""       = nil
```

In mathematical language this asserts that `text` is a *homomorphism* from string concatenation to document concatenation. An impressive (and possibly intimidating) name for something quite simple. Note that the associativity of string concatenation implies the associativity of document concatenation, at least for `text` documents.

For `nest` we require the following equations to hold:

```
nest i (x <> y)   = nest i x <> nest i y
nest i nil        = nil
nest i (text s)   = text s
nest i line       = line <> text (replicate i ' ')
nest i (nest j x) = nest (i+j) x
nest 0 x          = x
nest i (group x)  = group (nest i x)
```

All very reasonable (except possibly for the last), and we could give some of them mathematical names (`nest i` distributes through concatenation, `nest` is a homomorphism from numerical addition to functional composition and `nest i` commutes with `group`). The third law fails if `nest` were to indent from the beginning of a document; and it would also fail if we allowed text strings to contain newline characters. The last law holds because grouping adds a layout with no line breaks, and nesting has no effect on such a layout. See Exercise D for a more precise argument.

Turning to the properties of `layouts`, we require that

```
layouts (x <> y)   = layouts x <++> layouts y
layouts nil        = [""]
layouts (text s)   = [s]
layouts line       = ["\n"]
layouts (nest i x) = map (nestl i) (layouts x)
layouts (group x)  = layouts (flatten x) ++ layouts x
```

The operation (`<++>`) is lifted concatenation:

```
xss <++> yss = [xs ++ ys | xs <- xss, ys <- yss]
```

The function `nestl :: Int -> Layout -> Layout` is defined by

```
nestl i    = concat (map indent i)
indent i c = if c=='\n' then c:replicate i ' ' else [c]
```

Finally, `flatten :: Doc -> Doc` is the function that converts a document into one with a single layout in which each newline and its associated indentation is replaced by a single space. This function is not provided in the public interface of our documents library, though it will be needed internally. It is a missing gadget in the sense that we need it to complete the description of the algebraic laws.

We require that `flatten` should satisfy the following conditions:

```
flatten (x <> y)    = flatten x <> flatten y
flatten nil         = nil
flatten (text s)    = text s
flatten line        = text " "
flatten (nest i x)  = flatten x
flatten (group x)   = flatten x
```

That makes 24 laws in total (one for <>, two each for nil and text, seven for nest and six each for layouts and flatten). Many of the laws look like constructive Haskell definitions of functions over a data type in which nil, text and so on are constructors. More on this is in Section 8.6.

The eight operations certainly seem reasonable enough, but do they give us sufficient flexibility to describe the layouts we might want? The proof of the pudding is in the eating, so in a moment we will pause to consider three examples. Before doing so, some implementation of documents, however quick and dirty, will be needed to test the examples.

8.3 A direct implementation

One obvious choice of representation is to identify a document with its list of layouts:

```
type Doc = [Layout]
```

Such a representation is called a *shallow embedding*. With a shallow embedding, the library functions are implemented directly in terms of the values of interest (here, layouts). Later on we will abandon this representation in favour of a more structured alternative, but it is the obvious one to try first.

Here are the definitions of the operations above (we will leave pretty until later):

```
layouts    = id
x <> y     = x <++> y
nil        = [""]
line       = ["\n"]
text s     = [s]
nest i     = map (nestl i)
group x    = flatten x ++ x
flatten x  = [flattenl (head x)]
```

We have already defined nestl, and flattenl is defined by

```
flattenl :: Layout -> Layout
flattenl [] = []
flattenl (c:cs)
    | c=='\n'   = ' ':flattenl (dropWhile (== ' ') cs)
    | otherwise = c:flattenl cs
```

Do the 24 laws hold for this implementation? Well, let's go through them. Lifted concatentation <++> is associative with [[]] as identity element, so the first three laws are okay. The two laws of text are easy to check, and the six laws of layouts are immediate. All but two laws of nest are routine. The remaining two, namely

```
nest i . nest j = nest (i+j)
nest i . group  = group . nest i
```

involve a bit of work (see Exercises C and D). That leaves the laws of flatten. Three are easy, and one can show

```
flatten . nest i = flatten
flatten . group  = flatten
```

with a bit of work (see Exercises E and F). But the stumbling block is the law

```
flatten (x <> y) = flatten x <> flatten y
```

This one is false. Take x = line and y = text " hello". Then

```
flatten (x <> y) = ["hello"]
flatten x <> flatten y = ["  hello"]
```

and the two results are different. The reason is that flatten removes the effect of nesting, but does not remove spaces after newlines if they are present in an un-nested document. On the other hand, flattenl removes spaces after every newline in the document.

Rather than try to fix up this deficiency, we can accept the less than perfect implementation and move on. One can show that all layouts of a document flatten to the same string (see the Answer to Exercise E). The shallow embedding also possesses another property that we will exploit in the definition of pretty. To see what it is, consider the function shape that returns the shape of a layout:

```
shape :: Layout -> [Int]
shape = map length . lines
```

The prelude function lines breaks up a string on newline characters, returning a list of strings without newlines. Thus the shape of a layout is the list of lengths of the lines that make up the layout. The crucial property of layouts is that the list of shapes of the layouts of a document is in lexicographically decreasing order. For example, one of the documents described in the following section has 13 possible layouts whose shapes are given by

```
[[94],[50,43],[50,28,19],[50,15,17,19],[10,39,43],
[10,39,28,19],[10,39,15,17,19],[10,28,15,43],
[10,28,15,28,19],[10,28,15,15,17,19],[10,13,19,15,43],
[10,13,19,15,28,19],[10,13,19,15,15,17,19]]
```

This list is in decreasing lexicographic order. The reason the property holds is that `layouts (group x)` puts the flattened layout at the head of the list of layouts of document x, and a flattened layout consists of a single line. Exercise G goes into more details.

·

8.4 Examples

Our first example deals with laying out conditional expressions. For present purposes a conditional expression can be represented as an element of the data type CExpr, where

```
data CExpr = Expr String | If String CExpr CExpr
```

Here is a function `cexpr` that specifies the acceptable layouts described earlier:

```
cexpr :: CExpr -> Doc
cexpr (Expr p) = text p
cexpr (If p x y)
        = group (group (text "if " <> text p <>
                        line <> text "then " <>
                        nest 5 (cexpr x)) <>
                 line <> text "else " <>
                 nest 5 (cexpr y))
```

This definition is similar to our previous version, except for the nesting of the subexpressions.

For example, two of the 13 possible layouts for one particular expression are as follows:

```
if wealthy
then if happy then lucky you else tough
else if in love then content else miserable
```

```
if wealthy
then if happy
     then lucky you
     else tough
else if in love
     then content
     else miserable
```

You can see from the last expression why we have chosen an indentation of five spaces. The 13 possible layouts for this particular conditional expression have the shapes displayed in the previous section.

The second example concerns how to lay out general trees, trees with an arbitrary number of subtrees:

```
data GenTree a = Node a [GenTree a]
```

Here is an example tree, laid out in two different ways:

```
Node 1
  [Node 2
     [Node 7 [],
      Node 8 []],
   Node 3
     [Node 9
        [Node 10 [],
         Node 11 []]],
   Node 4 [],
   Node 5
     [Node 6 []]]

Node 1
  [Node 2 [Node 7 [], Node 8 []],
   Node 3 [Node 9 [Node 10 [], Node 11 []]],
   Node 4 [],
   Node 5 [Node 6 []]]
```

The function gtree that produced these trees (coincidentally, also among a total of 13 different ways) was defined as follows:

```
gtree :: Show a => GenTree a -> Doc
gtree (Node x [])
    = text ("Node " ++ show x ++ " []")
```

```
gtree (Node x ts)
   =  text ("Node " ++ show x) <>
      group (nest 2 (line <> bracket ts))
```

The first clause says that a tree with no subtrees is always displayed on a single line; the second clause says that a tree with at least one subtree is displayed either on a single line or has its subtrees each displayed on a new line with an indentation of two units. The function `bracket` is defined by

```
bracket :: Show a => [GenTree a] -> Doc
bracket ts = text "[" <> nest 1 (gtrees ts) <> text "]"

gtrees [t]    = gtree t
gtrees (t:ts) = gtree t <> text "," <> line <> gtrees ts
```

To be honest, it took a little time and experimentation to find the definitions above (for which the function `layouts` proved indispensable), and the result is certainly not the only way to lay out trees.

Finally, here is a way of laying out a piece of text (a string of characters containing spaces and newlines, not a document `text`) as a single paragraph:

```
para :: String -> Doc
para = cvt . map text . words

cvt [] = nil
cvt (x:xs)
    = x <> foldr (<>) nil [group (line <> x) | x <- xs]
```

First, the words of the text are computed using the standard library function `words`, a function we have encountered a number of times before. Then each word is converted into a document using `text`. Finally, each word, apart from the first, is laid out either on the same line or on a new line. If there are $n+1$ words in the text, and so n inter-word spaces, the code above describes 2^n possible layouts. We certainly don't want to examine all these layouts in computing one that will fit within a given line width.

8.5 The best layout

As we said above, the best layout depends on the maximum permitted line width. That's a simple decision, but not the only one. In general a pretty layout of a nested document will consist of a ribbon of text snaking across the page, and it is arguable that the width of the ribbon should also play a part in determining the best layout. After all, is the best layout on an infinitely wide page one in which everything is placed on one line? However, for simplicity we will ignore this very reasonable refinement and take only the line width as the deciding factor.

There is also another decision to be made. Suppose we choose the best layout, according to some criterion, among those layouts all of whose lines fit within the given line width. That's fine if there is at least one such layout, but what if there isn't? The two options are either to abandon the formatting process with a suitable error message, or else to do the best we can, accepting that the width may be exceeded.

Psychologically and practically the second option seems the better one, so let us explore what it entails. We can start by comparing the first lines, ℓ_1 and ℓ_2, of two layouts. We can decide that line ℓ_1 is better than ℓ_2 if: (i) both lines fit into width w and ℓ_1 is longer than ℓ_2; (ii) ℓ_1 fits w but ℓ_2 doesn't; or (iii) neither fits w and ℓ_1 is shorter than ℓ_2. The decision is a reasonable one because it should be capable of being implemented by a *greedy* strategy: fill up the first line as much as possible without exceeding the line width; and if that is not possible, stop as soon as the width is exceeded.

The comparison test above doesn't determine what should happen if the two lines have the same length. But it is a consequence of the fact that all layouts flatten to the same string that two first lines with the same length will be the *same* line. Consequently, the first line is fixed and the comparison can pass to the second pair of lines. And so on.

The second property about decreasing shapes can be used to simplify the comparison test slightly because if layout lx precedes layout ly in the list of layouts, then the first line of lx is known to be at least as long as the first line of ly. And if the two lines are equally long, then the same statement is true of the second lines. And so on.

Given our shallow embedding of documents, here is a simple implementation of the function `pretty` that finds the best layout:

```
pretty :: Int -> Doc -> Layout
pretty w = fst . foldr1 choose . map augment
  where
  augment lx = (lx,shape lx)
  choose alx aly
    = if better (snd alx) (snd aly) then alx else aly
  better [] ks            = True
```

```
better js []            = False
better (j:js) (k:ks) | j == k    = better js ks
                     | otherwise = (j <= w)
```

Each layout is augmented with shape information to guide the choice of layout, which is then determined by a simple search. The test `better` implements the comparison operation described above. Finally, shape information is discarded.

This definition of `pretty` is hopelessly inefficient because every layout is computed and examined. If there are n possible choices of whether to have a line break or not, there are 2^n layouts to be examined and pretty-printing will be very slow indeed. For example,

```
ghci> putStrLn $ pretty 30 $ para pg
This is a fairly short
paragraph with just twenty-two
words. The problem is that
pretty-printing it takes time,
in fact 31.32 seconds.
(31.32 secs, 17650013284 bytes)
```

Ouch! What is worse, pretty-printing a longer paragraph will cause GHCi to crash with an 'out of memory' message. An exponential time and space algorithm is not acceptable.

What is wanted is an algorithm for `pretty` that can decide on which first line to choose without looking ahead more than w characters. The algorithm should also be efficient, taking linear time in the size of the document being pretty-printed. Ideally the running time should be independent of w, but a running time that does depend on w is acceptable if a faster one means a much more complicated program.

8.6 A term representation

The problem with identifying a document with its list of possible layouts is that useful structure is lost. Rather than bring all the alternatives to the top level as a list, we really want to bury them as deep as possible. For example, consider the following two expressions for a document:

```
A<0>B<0>D + A<0>B<1>D + A<1>C<0>E + A<1>C<1>E
A(<0>B(<0>D + <1>D) + <1>C(<0>E + <1>E))
```

As before, <0> denotes a single space and <1> a single line break. The five letters denote five nonempty texts. Since all four alternatives have to flatten to the same document, we require that B<0>D = C<0>E. In the first expression (which is essentially what is given by representing a document by its list of layouts) we have four layouts to compare. In the second expression we can shortcut some of the comparisons. For example, if we know that the common prefix A cannot fit in the given width, the first two layouts can be thrown away without further comparisons. Even better, if we choose between alternatives from the innermost to the outermost, we can base the comparison test on just the first lines of layouts. For instance, if we choose the better of C<0>E and C<1>E first, then that choice is not changed by subsequent choices.

The way to maintain the structure of documents is to represent a document as a tree:

```
data Doc = Nil
         | Line
         | Text String
         | Nest Int Doc
         | Group Doc
         | Doc :<>: Doc
```

Note the use of an infix constructor in the last line. Haskell allows infix operators as constructors, but they have to begin with a colon. They do not have to end with a colon as well, but it seems more attractive if they do. This tree is called an *abstract syntax tree*; each operation of the library is represented by its own constructor. An implementation in terms of abstract syntax trees is known as a *deep embedding*.

We will *not* provide the user with the details of the data type Doc, just its name. To explain why not, it is useful to insert a short digression about Haskell data types. In Haskell the effect of a `data` declaration is to introduce a new data type by describing how its values are constructed. Each value is named by an expression built only from the constructors of the data type, in other words a *term*. Moreover, different terms denote different values (provided there are no strictness flags). We can define functions on the data type by pattern matching on the constructors. There is therefore no need to state what the operations on the data type are – we can just define them. Types in which the values are described, but the operations are not, are called *concrete* types.

The situation is exactly the reverse with *abstract* data types. Here the operations are named, but not how the values are constructed, at least not publicly. For example, Float is an abstract data type; we are given the names of the primitive arithmetic and comparison operations, and also a way of displaying floating-point numbers, but it is not stated how such numbers are actually represented. We cannot define functions on these numbers by pattern matching, but only in terms of the given operations. What can and should be stated publicly are intended meanings and the algebraic properties of the operations. However, Haskell provides no means for such descriptions beyond informal comments.

As it stands, Doc is a concrete type. But in our understanding of this type, different terms do not denote different values. For instance, we intend each constructor to be a replacement for the corresponding operation. Thus

```
nil       = Nil
line      = Line
text s    = Text s
nest i x  = Nest i x
group x   = Group x
x <> y    = x :<>: y
```

We also want to keep the algebraic properties of these operations, so equations such as

```
(x :<>: y) :<>: z = x :<>: (y :<>: z)
Nest i (Nest j x) = Nest (i+j) x
```

should hold. But of course they do not. The solution is to use the module structure to hide the constructors of Doc from the user and insist only that the laws are 'observably' true. For instance we require

```
layouts ((x :<>: y) :<>: z) = layouts (x :<>: (y :<>: z))
```

The only way we can observe documents is through layouts; from the user's point of view if two documents produce the same layouts, then they are essentially the same document.

Let's get back to programming. Here is one definition of layouts. It is just the laws of layouts that we saw earlier, but now expressed as a proper Haskell definition:

```
layouts :: Doc -> [Layout]
layouts (x :<>: y) = layouts x <++> layouts y
layouts Nil        = [""]
layouts Line       = ["\n"]
layouts (Text s)   = [s]
layouts (Nest i x) = map (nestl i) (layouts x)
layouts (Group x)  = layouts (flatten x) ++ layouts x
```

The function `flatten` is similarly defined by

```
flatten :: Doc -> Doc
flatten (x :<>: y) = flatten x :<>: flatten y
flatten Nil        = Nil
flatten Line       = Text " "
flatten (Text s)   = Text s
flatten (Nest i x) = flatten x
flatten (Group x)  = flatten x
```

With these definitions, our 24 laws are either true by definition, or are observably true in the sense above.

The definition of `layouts` is simple enough, but it is unnecessarily inefficient. There are two separate reasons why this is so. First, consider the function `egotist` defined by

```
egotist :: Int -> Doc
egotist n | n==0     = nil
          | otherwise = egotist (n-1) <> text "me"
```

The document `egotist n` is a very boring one, and its sole layout consists of a string of n repetitions of me. By the way, we could have expressed the definition using `Nil`, `(:<>:)` and `Text` but, as we have said, we are not going to make these constructors public. As it stands, the definition of `egotist` could have been made by a user of the library. Anyway, back to the main point, which is that the association of the `(<>)` operations is to the left, and it takes $\Theta(n^2)$ steps to compute its layout(s). The `(++)` operations pile up to the left. The situation is entirely analogous to the fact that `concat` defined in terms of `foldl` is an order of magnitude less efficient than one defined in terms of `foldr`.

The second source of inefficiency concerns nesting. For example, consider the function `egoist` defined by

```
egoist :: Int -> Doc
egoist n | n==0     = nil
         | otherwise = nest 1 (text "me" <> egoist (n-1))
```

There are no line breaks in sight, so `egoist n` describes the same boring document as `egotist n`. But although the concatenation associates to the right, it still takes quadratic time to construct the layout. Each nesting operation is carried out by running through the entire document. Try it and see.

The way to solve the first problem is to delay concatenation, representing a con-catenated document by a list of its component documents. The way to solve the second problem is to delay nesting, representing a nested document by a pair con-sisting of an indentation to be applied only when necessary and the document it is to be applied to. Combining both solutions, we represent a document by a list of indentation-document pairs. Specifically, consider the function toDoc defined by

```
toDoc :: [(Int,Doc)] -> Doc
toDoc ids = foldr (:<>:) Nil [Nest i x | (i,x) <- ids]
```

We can now calculate a definition of a function layr such that

```
layr = layouts . toDoc
```

and then define a new version of layouts based on layr. We leave the details as an exercise, but here is the result:

```
layouts x = layr [(0,x)]
layr []                  = [""]
layr ((i,x :<>: y):ids) = layr ((i,x):(i,y):ids)
layr ((i,Nil):ids)       = layr ids
layr ((i,Line):ids)      = ['\n':replicate i ' ' ++ ls
                           | ls <- layr ids]
layr ((i,Text s):ids)   = [s ++ ls | ls <- layr ids]
layr ((i,Nest j x):ids) = layr ((i+j,x):ids)
layr ((i,Group x):ids)  = layr ((i,flatten x):ids) ++
                          layr ((i,x):ids)
```

This definition takes linear time for each layout. Exactly the same template is used for the function pretty, which chooses a single best layout:

```
pretty w x = best w [(0,x)]
  where
  best r []                  = ""
  best r ((i,x :<>: y):ids) = best r ((i,x):(i,y):ids)
  best r ((i,Nil):ids)       = best r ids
  best r ((i,Line):ids)      = '\n':replicate i ' ' ++
                               best (w-i) ids
  best r ((i,Text s):ids)   = s ++ best (r-length s) ids
  best r ((i,Nest j x):ids) = best r ((i+j,x):ids)
  best r ((i,Group x):ids)  = better r
                              (best r ((i,flatten x):ids))
                              (best r ((i,x):ids))
```

The first argument of best is the remaining space available on the current line. This function is made local to the definition of pretty to avoid having to carry around the maximum line width w as an additional argument.

That leaves us with the problem of computing better r lx ly. Here we can make use of the fact that the first line of lx is guaranteed to be at least as long as the first line of ly. Thus it suffices to compare the length of the first line of lx with r. If the former fits within the latter, we choose lx; otherwise we choose ly. We therefore define

```
better r lx ly = if fits r lx then lx else ly
```

But we don't want to compute the length of the whole of the first line of lx since that looks ahead too far. Instead, we take a more miserly approach:

```
fits r _  | r<0 = False
fits r []       = True
fits r (c:cs)   = if c == '\n' then True
                  else fits (r-1) cs
```

For exactly the same reason it is essential that the second and third arguments to better are computed lazily, that is, the two layouts are evaluated just enough to determine which is the better one, and no further.

Let's revisit our troublesome paragraph:

```
ghci> putStrLn $ pretty 30 $ para pg
This is a fairly short
paragraph with just twenty-two
words. The problem is that
pretty-printing it takes time,
in fact 31.32 seconds.
(0.00 secs, 1602992 bytes)
```

Much better. Exercise L discusses what we can say about the running time of pretty.

The final task is to put our small library together as a module. Here is the main declaration:

```
module Pretty
    (Doc, Layout,
     nil, line, text,
     nest, (<>), group,
     layouts, pretty, layout) where
```

The module name is `Pretty` and the file containing the above declaration and the definitions of the library functions has to be saved in a file called `Pretty.lhs`.

The module exports 11 entities. Firstly, there is the name `Doc` of the abstract type of documents. The constructors of this type are not exported. (By the way, if we did want to export all the constructors we can write `Doc ()` in the export list, and if we wanted just, say, `Nil` and `Text`, we can write `Doc (Nil, Text)`.) Secondly, there is the name `Layout` which is just a synonym for `String`. The next eight constants and functions are the ones we have defined above. The final function `layout` is used for printing a layout:

```
layout :: Layout -> IO ()
layout = putStrLn
```

And that's it. Of course, in a really useful library a number of additional combinators could be provided. For example, we could provide

```
(<+>),(<|>) :: Doc -> Doc -> Doc
x <+> y = x <> text " " <> y
x <|> y = x <> line <> y

spread,stack :: [Doc] -> Doc
spread = foldr (<+>) nil
stack  = foldr (<|>) nil
```

No doubt the reader can think of many others.

8.7 Exercises

Exercise A

A picky user of the library wants just three layouts for a certain document:

```
A B C        A B        A
             C          B C
```

Can the user do it with the given functions?

Exercise B

The layouts of a document are given as a list. But are they all different? Either prove that they are or give a counterexample.

By the way, is it obvious from the laws that each document has a nonempty set of layouts?

Exercise C

The next four exercises refer to the shallow embedding of Section 8.3. Prove, by equational reasoning, that

```
nest i . nest j  = nest (i + j)
```

You will need a subsidiary result about `nestl`, which you don't have to prove.

Exercise D

Continuing on from the previous question, prove that

```
nest i (group x) = group (nest i x)
```

by equational reasoning (at the point level). Again, you will need a subsidiary result.

Exercise E

Continuing on, prove that `flatten . group = flatten`. You will need a subsidiary result.

Exercise F

The final law is `flatten . nest i = flatten`. And, yes, you will need yet another subsidiary result.

Exercise G

We said in the text that the prelude function `lines` breaks up a string on newline characters. In fact, `lines` treats a newline as a terminator character, so both `lines "hello"` and `lines "hello\n"` return the same result. It is arguable that a better definition treats newlines as *separator* characters, so there is always one more line than there are newlines. Define a function `lines` that has this behaviour. We will need the new definition below.

Now, the proof that `map shape` applied to the layouts of a document returns a lexicographically decreasing sequence of list of integers can be structured into the following steps. First, define

```
msl   = map shape . layouts
shape = map length . lines
```

where `lines` refers to the revised version above. We have to prove that `msl` returns a decreasing sequence on every document. To this end, we can define functions `nesty` and `groupy` so that

```
nesty i . msl = msl . nest i
groupy . msl  = msl . group
```

and an operation `<+>` so that

```
msl x <+> msl y = msl (x <> y)
```

(It is this equation that requires the revised definition of `lines`.) The proof is then completed by showing that if `xs` and `ys` are decreasing, then so are `nesty i xs` and `groupy xs` and `xs <+> ys`. All this exercise asks though is that you construct definitions of `nesty`, `groupy` and `<+>`.

Exercise H

Write a function `doc :: Doc -> Doc` that describes how to lay out elements of `Doc` where `Doc` is the abstract syntax tree representation in Section 8.6.

Exercise I

Consider a function `prettybad` that chooses a best layout from the list `layouts` by taking the first layout all of whose lines fit within the given width, and the last layout if this is not possible. Does `prettybad` always compute the same layout as `pretty`? (Hint: think about paragraphs.)

Exercise J

Using the algebraic properties of the constructors of `Doc`, calculate the efficient version of `layouts`.

Exercise K

We have designed `pretty w` to be *optimal*, meaning that it chooses line breaks to avoid overflowing lines if at all possible. We also have that `pretty w` is *bounded*, meaning that it can make the choice about the next line break without looking at more than the next `w` characters of the input. Given that, what do you expect GHCi's response would be to the commands

```
layout $ pretty 5 $ para pg
layout $ pretty 10 $ cexpr ce
```

where

```
pg = "Hello World!" ++ undefined
ce = If "happy" (Expr "great") undefined
```

Exercise L

We cannot relate the cost of `pretty w x` to the size of x without saying what the size of a document is. Here is a reasonable measure:

```
size :: Doc -> Int
size Nil         = 1
size Line        = 1
size (Text s)    = 1
size (Nest i x)  = 1 + size x
size (x :<>: y)  = 1 + size x + size y
size (Group x)   = 1 + size x
```

Under this definition both the documents

```
nest 20 (line <> text "!")
nest 40 (line <> text "!")
```

have size two. But it takes twice as long to produce the second layout, so the cost of `pretty` cannot be linear in the document size.

Instead of having `pretty` produce the final layout, a string, we can interpose an additional data type of layouts:

```
data Layout = Empty
            | String String Layout
            | Break Int Layout
```

and define `layout :: Layout -> String` by

```
layout Empty      = ""
layout (String s x) = s ++ layout x
layout (Break i x)  = '\n':replicate i ' ' ++ layout x
```

We have

```
pretty w = layout . prettyl w
```

where the new function `prettyl` produces a Layout rather than a string. Define `prettyl`.

A fairer question to ask is whether `prettyl w x` takes linear time in the size of x. Does it?

8.8 Answers

Answer to Exercise A

No. There is no way of allowing both A<0>B<1>C and A<1>B<0>C without also having both of A<0>B<0>C and A<1>B<1>C. These four are given by the expression

```
group (A <> line <> B) <> group (line <> C)
```

Answer to Exercise B

The layouts of a document are not necessarily all different. For example

```
layouts (group (text "hello")) = ["hello","hello"]
```

Yes, it is obvious that each document has a nonempty set of layouts. Look at the laws of layouts. The basic documents have a nonempty list of layouts and this property is preserved by the other operations.

Answer to Exercise C

The calculation is:

$$
\begin{array}{ll}
& \texttt{nest i . nest j} \\
= & \{\text{definition of } \texttt{nest}\} \\
& \texttt{map (nestl i) . map (nestl j)} \\
= & \{\text{functor law of } \texttt{map}\} \\
& \texttt{map (nestl i . nestl j)} \\
= & \{\text{claim}\} \\
& \texttt{map (nestl (i+j))} \\
= & \{\text{definition of } \texttt{nest}\} \\
& \texttt{nest (i+j)}
\end{array}
$$

The claim is that nestl i . nestl j = nestl (i+j), which follows – after a short calculation – from

```
indent (i+j) = concat . map (indent i) . indent j
```

We omit the proof.

Answer to Exercise D

We reason:

```
      nest i (group x)
   =   {definition of group}
      nest i (flatten x ++ x)
   =   {since nest i = map (nestl i)}
      nest i (flatten x) ++ nest i x
   =   {claim}
      flatten (nest i x) ++ nest i x
   =   {definition of group}
      group (nest i x)
```

The claim follows from

```
   nest i . flatten
 =   {since there are no newlines in flatten x}
   flatten
 =   {since flatten . nest i = flatten (Exercise F)}
   flatten . nest i
```

Answer to Exercise E

We reason:

```
      flatten . group
   =   {definition of flatten and group}
      one . flattenl . flattenl . head
   =   {claim}
      one . flattenl . head
   =   {definition of flatten}
      flatten
```

The claim is that flattenl is *idempotent*:

```
   flattenl . flattenl = flattenl
```

This follows because flattenl returns a layout with no newlines.

By the way, it is the idempotence of `flatten1` that ensures all layouts of a document flatten to the same string. The only function that introduces multiple layouts is group, whose definition is

```
group x = flatten x ++ x
```

We have therefore to show that flattening the first element of this list gives the same string as flattening the second element. Thus we need to show

```
flatten1 . head . flatten = flatten1 . head
```

This follows at once from the definition of `flatten` and the idempotence of the function `flatten1`.

Answer to Exercise F

We reason:

```
    flatten . nest i
=   {definitions}
    one . flatten1 . head . map (nestl i)
=   {since head . map f = f . head}
    one . flatten1 . nestl i . head
=   {claim}
    one . flatten1 . head
=   {definition of flatten}
    flatten
```

The claim is that `flatten1 . nestl i = flatten1`.

Answer to Exercise G

We can define

```
lines xs = if null zs then [ys]
             else ys:lines (tail zs)
             where (ys,zs) = break (=='\n') xs
```

The function groupy is defined by

```
groupy :: [[Int]] -> [[Int]]
groupy (xs:xss) = [sum xs + length xs - 1]:xs:xss
```

The function nesty is defined by

```
nesty :: :: Int -> [[Int]] -> [[Int]]
nesty i = map (add i)
          where add i (x:xs) = x:[i+x | x <- xs]
```

The function (<+>) is defined by

```
(<+>) :: [[Int]] -> [[Int]] -> [[Int]]
xss <+> yss = [glue xs ys | xs <- xss, ys <- yss]
  where glue xs ys = init xs ++ [last xs + head ys] ++
                     tail ys
```

Answer to Exercise H

One possibility, which no doubt can be improved on:

```
doc :: Doc -> Doc
doc Nil        = text "Nil"
doc Line       = text "Line"
doc (Text s)   = text ("Text " ++ show s)
doc (Nest i x) = text ("Nest " ++ show i) <>
                 group (nest 2 (line <> paren (doc x)))
doc (x :<>: y) = doc x <> text " :<>:" <>
                 group (line <> nest 3 (doc y))
doc (Group x)  = text "Group " <>
                 group (nest 2 (line <> paren (doc x)))

paren x = text "(" <> nest 1 x <> text ")"
```

Answer to Exercise I

No. Consider a paragraph whose longest word is one character longer than the line width. In this case, prettybad will lay out each word on a single line, while pretty will still fill lines with groups of words provided they fit. For example:

```
ghci> putStrLn $ pretty 11 $ para pg4
A lost and
lonely
hippopotamus
went into a
bar.
```

Answer to Exercise J

First we show `layouts x = layr [(0,x)]`:

> ```
> layr [(0,x)]
> ```
> = {definition of `layr`}
> ```
> layouts (toDoc [(0,x)])
> ```
> = {definition of `toDoc`}
> ```
> layouts (Nest 0 x :<>: Nil)
> ```
> = {laws of Doc}
> ```
> layouts x
> ```

It remains to give a recursive definition of `layr`. We will just give two clauses:

> ```
> toDoc ((i,Nest j x):ids)
> ```
> = {definition of `toDoc`}
> ```
> Nest i (Nest j x) :<>: toDoc ids
> ```
> = {laws}
> ```
> Nest (i+j) x :<>: toDoc ids
> ```
> = {definition of `toDoc`}
> ```
> toDoc ((i+j x):ids)
> ```

Hence `layr ((i,Nest j x):ids) = layr ((i+j x):ids)`. Next:

> ```
> toDoc ((i,x:<>:y):ids)
> ```
> = {definition of `toDoc`}
> ```
> Nest i (x :<>: y) <> toDoc ids
> ```
> = {laws}
> ```
> Nest i x :<>: Nest i y :<>: toDoc ids
> ```
> = {definition of `toDoc`}
> ```
> toDoc ((i,x):(i,y):ids)
> ```

Hence `layr ((i,x:<>:y):ids) = layr ((i,x):(i,y):ids)`.

Answer to Exercise K

```
ghci> layout $ pretty 5 $ para pg
Hello
World1*** Exception: Prelude.undefined
```

```
ghci> layout $ pretty 10 $ cexpr ce
if happy
then great
else *** Exception: Prelude.undefined
```

Answer to Exercise L

The definition is

```
prettyl :: Int -> Doc -> Layout
prettyl w x = best w [(0,x)]
 where
 best r []              = Empty
 best r ((i,Nil):ids)   = best r ids
 best r ((i,Line):ids)  = Break i (best (w-i) ids)
 best r ((i,Text s):ids) = String s (best (r-length s) ids)
 best r ((i,Nest j x):ids) = best r ((i+j,x):ids)
 best r ((i,x :<>: y):ids) = best r ((i,x):(i,y):ids)
 best r ((i,Group x):ids) = better r
                              (best r ((i,flatten x):ids))
                              (best r ((i,x):ids))
```

where better is changed to read

```
    better r lx ly = if fits r (layout lx) then lx else ly
```

The number of steps required to evaluate better r is proportional to r and thus at most w.

Now, prettyl takes linear time if best does. The second argument of best is a list of indentation-document pairs, and we can define the size of this list by

```
    isize ids = sum [size x | (i,x) <- ids]
```

For each of the inner five clauses in the definition of best, the size decreases by 1. For instance

```
    isize ((i,x :<>: y):ids)
    = size (x :<> y) + isize ids
    = 1 + size x + size y + isize ids
    = 1 + isize ((i,x):(i,y):ids)
```

It follows that if we let $T(s)$ denote the running time of best r on an input of size s, then $T(0) = \Theta(1)$ from the first clause of best, and $T(s+1) = \Theta(1) + T(s)$ for each of the five inner clauses, and

$$T(s+1) = \Theta(w) + maximum\ [T(k)+T(s-k)|k \leftarrow [1\mathbin{..}s-1]]$$

for the last clause. And now we can deduce that $T(s) = \Theta(ws)$.

In conclusion, our algorithm for `pretty` is linear, though not independently of w.

8.9 Chapter notes

We referred to pretty-printing as a library, but another name for it is an *embedded domain specific language* (EDSL). It is a language for pretty-printing documents embedded in the host language Haskell. Many people believe that the growing success of Haskell is due to its ability to host a variety of EDSLs without fuss.

The detailed material in this chapter has been based closely on work by Philip Wadler, see 'A prettier printer', Chapter 11 in *The Fun of Programming* in *Cornerstones of Computing Series* (Palgrave MacMillan, 2003). The main difference is that Wadler used an explicit alternation operator in the term representation of `Doc` (though it was hidden from the user) rather than the constructor `Group`. Jeremy Gibbons suggested that the latter was a better fit with the idea of a deep embedding.

An earlier functional pretty-printing library based on a different set of combinators was described by John Hughes, 'The design of a pretty-printer library', in Johan Jeuring and Erik Meijer, editors, *Advanced Functional Programming*, volume 925 of *LNCS*, Springer, 1995. Hughes' library was later reworked by Simon Peyton Jones and installed as a Haskell library

```
Text.PrettyPrint.HughesPJ
```

Another pretty-printing library, in an imperative rather than functional style, was constructed 30 years ago by Derek Oppen, 'Pretty-printing'. *ACM Transactions on Programming Languages and Systems* 2(4), 465–483, 1980 and is widely used as the basis of pretty-printing facilities in a number of languages. More recently, efficient pretty-printing algorithms in a functional style have been described by Olaf Chitil, 'Pretty printing with lazy dequeues', *ACM Transactions on Programming Languages and Systems* 27(1),163–184, 2005, and by Olaf Chitil and Doaitse Swierstra, 'Linear, bounded, functional pretty-printing', *Journal of Functional Programming* 19(1), 1–16, 2009. These algorithms are considerably more complicated than the one described in the text.

Chapter 9

Infinite lists

We have already met infinite lists in Chapter 4 and even given an induction principle for reasoning about them in Chapter 6. But we haven't really appreciated what can be done with them. In this chapter we want to explain in more detail exactly what an infinite list is, and how they can be represented by *cyclic* structures. We also describe another useful method for reasoning about infinite lists, and discuss a number of intriguing examples in which infinite and cyclic lists can be used to good effect.

9.1 Review

Recall that [m..] denotes the infinite list of all integers from m onwards:

```
ghci> [1..]
[1,2,3,4,5,6,7,{Interrupted}
ghci> zip [1..] "hallo"
[(1,'h'),(2,'a'),(3,'l'),(4,'l'),(5,'o')]
```

It would take forever to print [1..], so we interrupt the first computation. The second example illustrates a simple but typical use of infinite lists in finite computations.

In Haskell, the arithmetic expression [m..] is translated into enumFrom m, where enumFrom is a method in the Enum class, and defined by

```
enumFrom :: Integer -> [Integer]
enumFrom m = m:enumFrom (m+1)
```

Thus [m..] is defined as an instance of a recursively defined function. The computation makes progress because (:) is non-strict in its second argument.

It is important to bear in mind that infinite lists in computing do not have the same properties as infinite sets do in mathematics. For example, in set theory

$$\{x \mid x \in \{1,2,3,\ldots\}, x^2 < 10\}$$

denotes the set $\{1,2,3\}$, but

```
ghci> [x | x <- [1..], x*x < 10]
[1,2,3
```

After printing the first three values the computer gets stuck in an infinite loop looking for the next number after 3 whose square is less than 10. The value of the expression above is the partial list 1:2:3:undefined.

It is possible to have an infinite list of infinite lists. For example,

```
multiples = [map (n*) [1..] | n <- [2..]]
```

defines an infinite list of infinite lists of numbers, the first three being

```
[2,4,6,8,...]   [3,6,9,12,...]   [4,8,12,16,...]
```

Suppose we ask whether the above list of lists can be merged back into a single list, namely [2..]. We can certainly merge two infinite lists:

```
merge :: Ord a => [a] -> [a] -> [a]
merge (x:xs) (y:ys) | x<y  = x:merge xs (y:ys)
                    | x==y = x:merge xs ys
                    | x>y  = y:merge (x:xs) ys
```

This version of merge removes duplicates: if the two arguments are in strictly increasing order, so is the result. Note the absence of any clauses of merge mentioning the empty list. Now it seems that, if we define

```
mergeAll = foldr1 merge
```

then mergeAll multiples will return the infinite list [2..]. But it doesn't. What happens is that the computer gets stuck in an infinite loop attempting to compute the first element of the result, namely

```
minimum (map head multiples)
```

It is simply not possible to compute the minimum element in an infinite list. Instead we have to make use of the fact that map head multiples is in strictly increasing order, and define

```
mergeAll = foldr1 xmerge
xmerge (x:xs) ys = x:merge xs ys
```

With this definition, `mergeAll multiples` does indeed return `[2..]`.

Finally, recall the induction principle described in Chapter 6 for proving facts about infinite lists. Provided P is a chain-complete assertion, we can prove that $P(\text{xs})$ holds for all infinite lists xs by showing that: (i) $P(\text{undefined})$ holds; and (ii) $P(\text{xs})$ implies $P(\text{x:xs})$ for all x and xs. Using this principle, we proved in Chapter 6 that xs++ys = xs for all infinite lists xs. But it's not immediately clear how induction can be used to prove, for example,

```
map fact [0..] = scanl (*) 1 [1..]
```

The obvious result to prove is

```
map fact [0..n] = scanl (*) 1 [1..n]
```

for all n, but can one then assert the first identity holds?

9.2 Cyclic lists

Data structures, like functions, can be defined recursively. For instance

```
ones :: [Int]
ones = 1:ones
```

This is an example of a *cyclic* list, a list whose definition is recursive. Contrast this definition with ones = repeat 1, where

```
repeat x = x:repeat x
```

This definition of ones creates an infinite, not a cyclic list. We could define

```
repeat x = xs   where xs = x:xs
```

Now the function repeat is defined in terms of a cyclic list. The second definition (call it repeat2) is faster to evaluate than the first (call it repeat1) because there is less overhead:

```
ghci> last $ take 10000000 $ repeat1 1
1
(2.95 secs, 800443676 bytes)
ghci> last $ take 10000000 $ repeat2 1
1
```

(0.11 secs, 280465164 bytes)

As another example, consider the following three definitions of the standard prelude function `iterate`:

```
iterate1 f x = x:iterate1 f (f x)
iterate2 f x = xs  where xs = x:map f xs
iterate3 f x = x:map f (iterate3 f x)
```

All three functions have type `(a -> a) -> a -> [a]` and produce an infinite list of the iterates of `f` applied to `x`. The three functions are equal, but the induction principle reviewed earlier doesn't seem to be applicable in proving this assertion because there is no obvious argument on which to perform the induction. More on this later. The first definition is the one used in the standard prelude, but it does not create a cyclic list. The second definition does, and the third is obtained from the second by eliminating the `where` clause. Assuming `f x` can be computed in constant time, the first definition takes $\Theta(n)$ steps to compute the first n elements of the result, but the third takes $\Theta(n^2)$ steps:

```
  iterate3 (2*) 1
= 1:map (2*) (iterate3 (2*1))
= 1:2:map (2*) (map (2*) (iterate3 (2*1)))
= 1:2:4:map (2*) (map (2*) (map (2*) (iterate3 (2*1))))
```

Evaluating the nth element requires n applications of `(2*)`, so it takes $\Theta(n^2)$ to produce the first n elements.

That leaves the second definition. Does it take linear or quadratic time? The evaluation of `iterate2 (2*) 1` proceeds as follows:

```
  xs         where xs = 1:map (2*) xs
= 1:ys       where ys = map (2*) (1:ys)
= 1:2:zs     where zs = map (2*) (2:zs)
= 1:2:4:ts where ts = map (2*) (4:ts)
```

Each element of the result is produced in constant time, so `iterate2 (2*) 1` takes $\Theta(n)$ steps to produce n elements.

Let us now develop a cyclic list to generate an infinite list of all the primes. To start with we define

```
primes     = [2..] \\ composites
composites = mergeAll multiples
multiples  = [map (n*) [n..] | n <- [2..]]
```

where (\\) subtracts one strictly increasing list from another:

```
(x:xs) \\ (y:ys) | x<y   = x:(xs \\ (y:ys))
                 | x==y  = xs \\ ys
                 | x>y   = (x:xs) \\ ys
```

Here, `multiples` consists of the list of all multiples of 2 from 4 onwards, all multiples of 3 from 9 onwards, all multiples of 4 from 16 onwards, and so on. Merging the list gives the infinite list of all the composite numbers, and taking its complement with respect to [2..] gives the primes. We saw the definition of `mergeAll` in the previous section.

So far, so good. But the algorithm can be made many times faster by observing that too many multiples are being merged. For instance, having constructed the multiples of 2 there is no need to construct the multiples of 4, or of 6, and so on. What we really would like to do is just to construct the multiples of the primes. That leads to the idea of 'tying the recursive knot' and defining

```
primes = [2..] \\ composites
  where
  composites = mergeAll [map (p*) [p..] | p <- primes]
```

What we have here is a cyclic definition of `primes`. It looks great, but does it work? Unfortunately, it doesn't: `primes` produces the undefined list. In order to determine the first element of `primes` the computation requires the first element of `composites`, which in turn requires the first element of `primes`. The computation gets stuck in an infinite loop. To solve the problem we have to pump-prime (!) the computation by giving the computation the first prime explicitly. We have to rewrite the definition as

```
primes = 2:([3..] \\ composites)
  where
  composites = mergeAll [map (p*) [p..] | p <- primes]
```

But this still doesn't produce the primes! The reason is a subtle one and is quite hard to spot. It has to do with the definition

```
mergeAll = foldr1 xmerge
```

The culprit is the function `foldr1`. Recall the Haskell definition:

```
foldr1 :: (a -> a -> a) -> [a] -> a
foldr1 f [x]    = x
foldr1 f (x:xs) = f x (foldr1 xs)
```

The order of the two defining equations is significant. In particular,

```
foldr1 f (x:undefined) = undefined
```

because the list argument is first matched against `x:[]`, causing the result to be undefined. That means

```
mergeAll [map (p*) [p..] | p <- 2:undefined] = undefined
```

What we wanted was

```
mergeAll [map (p*) [p..] | p <- 2:undefined] = 4:undefined
```

To effect this change we have to define `mergeAll` differently:

```
mergeAll (xs:xss) = xmerge xs (mergeAll xss)
```

Now we have

```
  mergeAll [map (p*) [p..] | p <- 2:undefined]
= xmerge (map (2*) [2..]) undefined
= xmerge (4:map (2*) [3..]) undefined
= 4:merge (map (2*) [3..]) undefined
= 4:undefined
```

This version of `mergeAll` behaves differently on finite lists from the previous one. Why?

With this final change we claim that `primes` does indeed get into gear and produces the primes. But how can the claim be proved? To answer this question we need to know something about the semantics of recursively defined functions and other values in Haskell, and how infinite lists are defined as limits of their partial approximations.

9.3 Infinite lists as limits

In mathematics, certain values are defined as *limits* of infinite sequences of approximations of simpler values. For example, the irrational number

$$\pi = 3.14159265358979323846\cdots$$

can be defined as the limit of the infinite sequence of rational approximations

$$3, \ 3.1, \ 3.14, \ 3.141, \ 3.1415, \ \ldots$$

The first element of the sequence, 3, is a fairly crude approximation to π. The next element, 3.1, is a little better; 3.14 is better still, and so on.

Similarly, an infinite list can also be regarded as the limit of a sequence of approximations. For example, the infinite list $[1..]$ is the limit of the infinite sequence of partial lists

$$\bot, \; 1:\bot, \; 1:2:\bot, \; 1:2:3:\bot, \; \ldots$$

Again, the sequence consists of better and better approximations to the intended limit. The first term, $\bot$, is the undefined element, and thus a very crude approximation: it tells us nothing about the limit. The next term, $1:\bot$, is a slightly better approximation: it tells us that the limit is a list whose first element is 1, but says nothing about the rest of the list. The following term, $1:2:\bot$, is a little better still, and so on. Each successively better approximation is derived by replacing $\bot$ with a more defined value, and thus gives more information about the limit.

Here is another sequence of approximations whose limit is $[1..]$:

$$\bot, \; 1:2:\bot, \; 1:2:3:4:\bot, \; 1:2:3:4:5:6:\bot, \; \ldots$$

This sequence is a subsequence of the one above but it converges to the same limit.

Here is a sequence of approximations that does not converge to a limit:

$$\bot, \; 1:\bot, \; 2:1:\bot, \; 3:2:1:\bot, \; \ldots$$

The problem with this sequence is that it gives conflicting information: the second term says that the limit begins with 1. However, the third term says that the limit begins with 2, and the fourth term says that it begins with 3, and so on. No approximation tells us anything about the intended limit and the sequence does not converge.

It should not be thought that the limit of a sequence of lists is necessarily infinite. For example, the sequence

$$\bot, \; 1:\bot, \; 1:[], \; 1:[], \; \ldots$$

in which every element after the first two is $[1]$, is a perfectly valid sequence with limit $[1]$. Similarly,

$$\bot, \; 1:\bot, \; 1:2:\bot, \; 1:2:\bot, \; \ldots$$

is a sequence with limit $1:2:\bot$. Finite and partial lists are limits of sequences possessing only a finite number of distinct elements.

The way to formalise the property that an infinite sequence of partial lists converges to a limit is to introduce the notion of an *approximation ordering* $\sqsubseteq$ on the elements of each type. The assertion $x \sqsubseteq y$ means that x is an approximation to y. The ordering $\sqsubseteq$ will be reflexive ($x \sqsubseteq x$), transitive ($x \sqsubseteq y$ and $y \sqsubseteq z$ implies $x \sqsubseteq z$), and anti-symmetric ($x \sqsubseteq y$ and $y \sqsubseteq x$ implies $x = y$). However, it is not the case that every pair of elements have to be comparable by $\sqsubseteq$. Thus $\sqsubseteq$ is what is known as a *partial* ordering. Note that $\sqsubseteq$ is a mathematical operator (like $=$), and not a Haskell operator returning boolean results.

The approximation ordering for numbers, booleans, characters and any other enumerated type, is defined by

$$x \sqsubseteq y \equiv (x = \bot) \vee (x = y).$$

The first clause says that $\bot$ is an approximation to everything. In other words, $\bot$ is the *bottom* element of the ordering. This explains why $\bot$ is pronounced 'bottom'. The value $\bot$ is the bottom element of $\sqsubseteq$ for every type. The above ordering is *flat*. With a flat ordering one either knows everything there is to know about a value, or one knows absolutely nothing.

The approximation ordering on the type (a, b) is defined by $\bot \sqsubseteq (x, y)$ and

$$(x, y) \sqsubseteq (x', y') \equiv (x \sqsubseteq x') \wedge (y \sqsubseteq y').$$

The occurrences of $\sqsubseteq$ on the right refer to the orderings on the types a and b, respectively. The ordering $\sqsubseteq$ on (a, b) is not flat, even when the component orderings are. For example, in (Bool, Bool) we have the following chain of distinct elements:

$$\bot \sqsubseteq (\bot, \bot) \sqsubseteq (\bot, \text{False}) \sqsubseteq (\text{True}, \text{False}).$$

Note that in Haskell the pair $(\bot, \bot)$ is distinct from $\bot$:

```
ghci> let f (a,b) = 1
ghci> f (undefined,undefined)
1
ghci> f undefined
*** Exception: Prelude.undefined
```

The ordering $\sqsubseteq$ on [a] is defined by $\bot \sqsubseteq xs$ and $(x:xs) \not\sqsubseteq []$ and

$$[] \sqsubseteq xs \equiv xs = [],$$
$$(x:xs) \sqsubseteq (y:ys) \equiv (x \sqsubseteq y) \wedge (xs \sqsubseteq ys).$$

These equations should be read as an inductive definition of a mathematical assertion, not as a Haskell definition. The second condition says that [] approximates only itself, and the third condition says that (x:xs) is an approximation to (y:ys) if and only if x is an approximation to y and xs is an approximation to ys. The first occurrence of $\sqsubseteq$ on the right-hand side refers to the approximation ordering on the type a.

As two examples, we have

$$[1, \bot, 3] \sqsubseteq [1, 2, 3] \quad \text{and} \quad 1 : 2 : \bot \sqsubseteq [1, 2, 3].$$

However, $1 : 2 : \bot$ and $[1, \bot, 3]$ are not related by $\sqsubseteq$.

The approximation ordering for each type T is assumed to have another property in addition to those described above: each *chain* of approximations $x_0 \sqsubseteq x_1 \sqsubseteq \ldots$ has to possess a limit which is also a member of T. The limit, which we denote by $\lim_{n \to \infty} x_n$, is defined by two conditions:

1. $x_n \sqsubseteq \lim_{n \to \infty} x_n$ for all n. This condition states that the limit is an *upper bound* on the sequence of approximations.

2. If $x_n \sqsubseteq y$ for all n, then $\lim_{n \to \infty} x_n \sqsubseteq y$. This condition states that the limit is the *least* upper bound.

The definition of the limit of a chain of approximations applies to every type. Partial orderings possessing this property are called *complete*, and every Haskell type is a complete partial ordering (CPO for short). In particular, the property, introduced in Chapter 6, of a mathematical assertion P being chain complete can now be formalised as

$$(\forall n : P(x_n)) \Rightarrow P(\lim_{n \to \infty} x_n).$$

In words, P holds in the limit if it holds for each approximation to the limit.

For lists there is a useful Haskell function approx, which produces approximations to a given list. The definition is

```
approx :: Integer -> [a] -> [a]
approx n []     | n>0 = []
approx n (x:xs) | n>0 = x:approx (n-1) xs
```

The definition of approx is very similar to that of take except that, by case exhaustion, we have approx 0 xs = undefined for all xs. For example,

```
approx 0 [1] = undefined
approx 1 [1] = 1:undefined
approx 2 [1] = 1:[]
```

The crucial property of approx is that

$$\lim_{n \to \infty} \text{approx } n \text{ xs} = \text{xs}$$

for all lists xs, finite, partial or infinite. The proof, an induction on xs, is left as an exercise.

It follows that if approx n xs = approx n ys for all natural numbers n, then xs = ys. Thus we can prove that

```
iterate f x = x:map f (iterate f x)
```

by showing

```
approx n (iterate f x) = approx n (x:map f (iterate f x))
```

for all natural numbers n. And, of course, we can use induction over the natural numbers to establish this fact. The details are left as an easy exercise.

As another example, consider the value primes defined in the previous section. Suppose we define

```
prs n = approx n primes
```

We would like to show that prs $n = p_1 : p_2 : \cdots p_n :\perp$, where p_j is the jth prime. We claim that

```
prs n = approx n (2:([3..] \\ crs n))
crs n = mergeAll [map (p*) [p..] | p <- prs n]
```

Given this, it is sufficient to show that crs $n = c_1 : c_2 : \cdots c_m :\perp$, where c_j is the jth composite number (so $c_1 = 4$) and $m = p_n^2$. Then the proof is completed by using the fact that $p_{n+1} < p_n^2$, which is a non-trivial result in Number Theory. Details are in the exercises.

Computable functions and recursive definitions

One can describe many functions in mathematics, but only some of them are computable. There are two properties of computable functions not shared by arbitrary functions. Firstly, a computable function f is *monotonic* with respect to the approximation ordering. In symbols,

$$x \sqsubseteq y \Rightarrow f(x) \sqsubseteq f(y)$$

for all x and y. Roughly speaking, monotonicity states that the more information you supply about the argument, the more information you get as a result. Secondly, a computable function f is *continuous*, which means that

$$f\left(\lim_{n \to \infty} x_n\right) = \lim_{n \to \infty} f(x_n)$$

for all chains of approximations $x_0 \sqsubseteq x_1 \sqsubseteq \ldots$. Roughly speaking, continuity states that there are no surprises on passing to the limit.

Continuity appears similar to chain completeness but differs in two respects. One is that the chain completeness of P does not imply the converse property that if P is false for all approximations, then P is false for the limit. In other words, it does not imply that $\neg P$ is chain complete. Secondly, P is a mathematical assertion, not a Haskell function returning a boolean value.

Although we won't prove it, every monotonic and continuous function f has a *least fixed point*. A fixed point of a function f is a value x such that $f(x) = x$. And x is a least fixed point if $x \sqsubseteq y$ for any other fixed point y. The least fixed point of a monotonic and continuous function f is given by $\lim_{n \to \infty} x_n$ where $x_0 = \bot$ and $x_{n+1} = f(x_n)$. In functional programming, recursive definitions are interpreted as least fixed points.

Here are three examples. Consider the definition ones = 1:ones. This definition asserts that ones is a fixed point of the function (1:). Haskell interprets it as the least fixed point, so ones $= \lim_{n \to \infty}$ ones$_n$, where ones$_0 = \bot$ and ones$_{n+1} =$ 1:ones$_n$. It is easy to see that ones$_n$ is the partial list consisting of n ones, so the limit is indeed an infinite list of ones.

Second, consider the factorial function

```
fact n = if n==0 then 1 else n*fact (n-1)
```

We can rewrite this definition in the equivalent form

```
fact = (\f n -> if n==0 then 1 else n*f(n-1)) fact
```

Again, this definition asserts that fact is a fixed point of a function. Here we have

$$\text{fact}_0 \ n = \bot$$
$$\text{fact}_1 \ n = \text{if } n{==}0 \text{ then } 1 \text{ else } \bot$$
$$\text{fact}_2 \ n = \text{if } n{<=}1 \text{ then } 1 \text{ else } \bot$$

and so on. The value of fact$_k$ n is the factorial of n if n is less than k, and $\bot$ otherwise.

Finally, consider the list primes once again. Here we have

$$\text{primes}_0 \quad = \quad \bot$$
$$\text{primes}_{n+1} \quad = \quad 2{:}([3..] \ \backslash\backslash$$
$$\text{mergeAll [map (p*) [p..] | p <- primes}_n])$$

It is not the case that $primes_n = approx\ n\ primes$. In fact,

$$primes_1 = 2 : \perp$$
$$primes_2 = 2 : 3 : \perp$$
$$primes_3 = 2 : 3 : 5 : 7 : \perp$$
$$primes_4 = 2 : 3 : 5 : 7 : \cdots : 47 : \perp$$

The partial list $primes_2$ produces all the primes less than 4, $primes_3$ all the primes less than 9, and $primes_4$ all the primes less than 49. And so on.

9.4 Paper–rock–scissors

Our next example of infinite lists is entertaining as well as instructive. Not only does it introduce the idea of using potentially infinite lists to model a sequence of interactions between processes, it also provides another concrete illustration of the necessity for formal analysis.

The paper–rock–scissors game is a familiar one to children, though it is known by different names in different places. The game is played by two people facing one another. Behind their backs, each player forms a hand in the shape of either a rock (a clenched fist), a piece of paper (a flat palm) or a pair of scissors (two fingers extended). At a given instant, both players bring their hidden hand forward. The winner is determined by the rule 'paper wraps rock, rock blunts scissors, and scissors cut paper'. Thus, if player 1 produces a rock and player 2 produces a pair of scissors, then player 1 wins because rock blunts scissors. If both players produce the same object, then the game is a tie and neither wins. The game continues in this fashion for a fixed number of rounds agreed in advance.

Our objective in this section is to write a program to play and score the game. We begin by introducing the types

```
data Move  = Paper | Rock | Scissors
type Round = (Move,Move)
```

To score a round we define

```
score :: Round -> (Int,Int)
score (x,y) | x `beats` y  = (1,0)
            | y `beats` x  = (0,1)
            | otherwise    = (0,0)
```

where

```
Paper `beats` Rock       = True
Rock `beats` Scissors    = True
Scissors `beats` Paper   = True
_ `beats` _              = False
```

Each player in the game will be represented by a certain strategy. For instance, one simple strategy is, after the first round, always to produce what the opposing player showed in the previous round. This strategy will be called copy. Another strategy, which we will call smart, is to determine a move by analysing the number of times the opponent has produced each of the three possible objects, and calculating an appropriate response based on probabilities.

We will consider the details of particular strategies, and how they can be represented, in a moment. For now, suppose the type Strategy is given in some way. The function

```
rounds :: (Strategy,Strategy) -> [Round]
```

takes a pair of strategies and returns the infinite list of rounds that ensue when each player follows his or her assigned strategy. The function

```
match :: Int -> (Strategy,Strategy) -> (Int,Int)
match n = total . map score . take n . rounds
   where total rs = (sum (map fst rs),sum (map snd rs))
```

determines the total score after playing a given number of rounds.

The instructive aspect of the game is how to represent strategies. We are going to consider two ways, calling them Strategy1 and Strategy2. The obvious idea is to take

```
type Strategy1 = [Move] -> Move
```

Here, a strategy is a function which takes the (finite) list of moves made by the opponent so far and returns an appropriate move for the subsequent round. For efficiency in processing lists, we suppose that the list of moves is given in reverse order, with the last move first.

For example, the copy1 strategy is implemented by

```
copy1 :: Strategy1
copy1 ms = if null ms then Rock else head ms
```

The first move is an arbitrary choice of Rock, The second strategy smart1 is implemented by

```
smart1 :: Strategy1
smart1 ms = if null ms then Rock
            else pick (foldr count (0,0,0) ms)

count :: Move -> (Int,Int,Int) -> (Int,Int,Int)
count Paper   (p,r,s) = (p+1,r,s)
count Rock    (p,r,s) = (p,r+1,s)
count Scissors (p,r,s) = (p,r,s+1)

pick :: (Int,Int,Int) -> Move
pick (p,r,s)
     | m < p       = Scissors
     | m < p+r     = Paper
     | otherwise   = Rock
     where m = rand (p+r+s)
```

This strategy counts the number of times each move has been made, and uses the results to pick a move. The value of `rand` applied to n is some integer m in the range $0 \leq m < n$. (Note that `rand` is never applied to the same integer.) Thus the choice of move depends on whether m falls in one of the three ranges

$$0 \leq m < p \quad \text{or} \quad p \leq m < p+r \quad \text{or} \quad p+r \leq m < p+r+s.$$

For example, if p is large, then `Scissors` will be chosen with high probability (because scissors cuts paper); and if r is large, then `Paper` will be chosen with high probability (because paper wraps rock); and so on.

To define `rand` we can make use of two functions in the library `System.Random`:

```
rand :: Int -> Int
rand n = fst $ randomR (0,n-1) (mkStdGen n)
```

The function `mkStdGen` takes an integer and returns a random number generator, likely to be different for different integers. The choice of argument to `mkStdGen` is arbitrary, and we have simply chosen n. The function `randomR` takes a range (a,b) and a random number generator, and returns a pseudo-random integer r in the range $a \leq r \leq b$ and a new random number generator.

We can now define `rounds1`:

```
rounds1 :: (Strategy1,Strategy1) -> [Round]
rounds1 (p1,p2)
          = map head $ tail $ iterate (extend (p1,p2)) []
    extend (p1,p2) rs = (p1 (map snd rs),p2 (map fst rs)):rs
```

The function extend adds a new pair of moves to the front of the list of existing rounds, and rounds1 generates the infinite list of rounds by repeatedly applying extend to the initially empty list. It is more efficient to add something to the front of a list than to the end, which is why we keep the list of moves in reverse order.

Nevertheless rounds1 is inefficient. Suppose a strategy takes time proportional to the length of its input to compute the next move. It follows that extend takes $\Theta(n)$ steps to update a game of n rounds with a new round. Therefore, it takes $\Theta(N^2)$ steps to compute a game of N rounds.

For comparison, let's consider another way we might reasonably represent strategies. This time we take

```
type Strategy2 = [Move] -> [Move]
```

In the new representation, a strategy is a function that takes the potentially infinite list of moves made by the opponent and returns the potentially infinite list of replies. For example, the copy strategy is now implemented by

```
copy2 :: Strategy2
copy2 ms = Rock:ms
```

This strategy returns Rock the first time, and thereafter returns just the move made by the opponent in the previous round. The smart strategy is reprogrammed as

```
smart2 :: Strategy2
smart2 ms = Rock:map pick (stats ms)
 where stats = tail . scanl (flip count) (0,0,0)
```

The function stats computes the running counts of the three possible moves. This strategy, like copy2, is also efficient in that it produces each successive output with constant delay.

With this new model of strategies we can redefine the function rounds:

```
rounds2 :: (Strategy2,Strategy2) -> [Round]
rounds2 (p1,p2) = zip xs ys
                   where xs = p1 ys
                         ys = p2 xs
```

Here, xs is the list of replies computed by the first player in response to the list ys which, in turn, is the list of replies made by the second player in response to the list of moves xs. Thus rounds2 is defined by two cyclic lists and we are obliged to show that it does indeed generate an infinite list of well-defined moves. More on this below. If the two players do encapsulate legitimate strategies, then rounds2 computes the first n moves of the game in $\Theta(n)$ steps, assuming that both players compute each new move with constant delay. Thus the second method for modelling strategies leads to a more efficient program than the earlier one.

Unfortunately, there is a crucial flaw with the second representation of strategies: it offers no protection against someone who cheats! Consider the strategy

```
cheat ms = map trump ms
```

```
trump Paper    = Scissors
trump Rock     = Paper
trump Scissors = Rock
```

The first reply of cheat is the move guaranteed to beat the opponent's first move; similarly for subsequent moves. To see that cheat cannot be prevented from subverting the game, consider a match in which it is played against copy2, and let xs = cheat ys and ys = copy2 xs. The lists xs and ys are the limits of the two chains $\{xs_n \mid 0 \leq n\}$ and $\{ys_n \mid 0 \leq n\}$, where $xs_0 = \bot$ and $xs_{n+1} = \text{cheat } ys_n$, and $ys_0 = \bot$ and $ys_{n+1} = \text{copy2 } xs_n$. Now, we have

$$
\begin{array}{lclcl}
xs_1 & = & \text{cheat } \bot & = & \bot \\
ys_1 & = & \text{copy2 } \bot & = & \text{Rock: } \bot \\
xs_2 & = & \text{cheat (Rock: } \bot) & = & \text{Paper: } \bot \\
ys_2 & = & \text{copy2 } \bot & = & \text{Rock: } \bot \\
xs_3 & = & \text{cheat (Rock: } \bot) & = & \text{Paper: } \bot \\
ys_3 & = & \text{copy2 (Paper: } \bot) & = & \text{Rock:Paper: } \bot
\end{array}
$$

Continuing in this way, we see that the limits of these sequences are indeed infinite lists of well-defined moves. Moreover, cheat always triumphs. Another cheating strategy is given by

```
devious :: Int -> Strategy2
devious n ms = take n (copy2 ms) ++ cheat (drop n ms)
```

This strategy behaves like copy for n moves then starts to cheat.

Can we find a way to protect against cheats? To answer this question, we need to take a closer look at what constitutes an honest strategy. Informally speaking, a strategy is honest if its first move is computed in the absence of any information about the opponent's first move, the second move is computed without any information about the opponent's second move, and so on. Moreover, each of these moves should be well-defined, given that the opponent's moves are well-defined. More precisely, let $wdf(n, ms)$ denote the assertion that the first n elements in the (possibly partial) list of moves *ms* are well-defined. Then a strategy *f* is *honest* if

$$wdf(n, ms) \Rightarrow wdf(n+1, f(ms))$$

for all *n* and *ms*. It is easy to show that `copy2` is honest. On the other hand, `cheat` is not honest because $wdf(0, \bot)$ is true but $wdf(1, \text{cheat } \bot)$ is false. The strategy dozy, where

```
dozy ms = repeat undefined
```

is also dishonest according to this definition although it doesn't actually cheat.

Having identified the source of criminal or lackadaisical behaviour, can we ensure that only honest strategies are admitted to the game? The answer is a qualified yes: although it is not possible for a mechanical evaluator to recognise cheating (in the same way that it is not possible to recognise $\bot$, or strategies that do not return well-defined moves), it is possible to define a function `police` so that if p is an honest player and `ms` is an infinite sequence of well-defined moves, then `police p ms = p ms`. On the other hand, if p is dishonest at some point, then the game ends at that point in $\bot$. Operationally speaking, `police` works by forcing p to return the first (well-defined!) element of its output before it gives p the first element of its input. Similarly for the other elements. The definition is

```
police p ms = ms'  where ms' = p (synch ms ms')
synch (x:xs) (y:ys) = (y `seq` x):synch xs ys
```

Recall from Chapter 7 that x `seq` y evaluates x before returning the value of y. The proof that this implementation meets its specification is rather involved, so we are not going into details. It follows from the above analysis that to prevent cheating we must rewrite the definition of `rounds2` to read

```
rounds2 (p1,p2) = zip xs ys
                  where xs = police p1 ys
                        ys = police p2 xs
```

9.5 Stream-based interaction

In the paper–rock–scissors game we modelled interaction by a function that took an infinite list of moves and returned a similar list. The same idea can be used to provide a simple model of input–output interaction. It's called *stream-based* interaction because infinite lists are also called streams. Haskell provides a function

```
interact :: ([Char] -> [Char]) -> IO ()
```

for interacting with the world. The argument to `interact` is a function that takes
a potentially infinite list of characters from the standard input channel, and returns
a potentially infinite list of characters to be typed on the standard output channel.

For example,

```
ghci> import Data.Char
ghci> interact (map toUpper)
hello world!
HELLO WORLD!
Goodbye, cruel world!
GOODBYE, CRUEL WORLD!
{Interrupted}
```

We imported the library `Data.Char` to make `toUpper` available, and then created
an interaction that capitalised each letter. Each time a line of input was typed (and
echoed) the interaction produced the same line in capital letters. The process continues until we interrupt it.

We can also design an interactive program that terminates. For example,

```
interact (map toUpper . takeWhile (/= '.'))
```

will interact as above but terminate as soon as a line containing a period is typed:

```
ghci> interact (map toUpper . takeWhile (/= '.'))
Goodbye. Forever
GOODBYE
```

Finally, here is a stand-alone program that takes a literate Haskell file as input
and returns a file in which all nonempty lines not beginning with > are removed.
The remaining lines are modified by removing the > character, so the result is a
legitimate `.hs` file (a Haskell script not using the literate style):

```
main    = interact replace
replace = unlines . map cleanup . filter code . lines
code xs = null xs || head xs == '>'
cleanup xs = if null xs then [] else tail xs
```

The program is the computation associated with the identifier `main`, and there always has to be a definition associated with this name if we want to compile a program. The function `lines` splits a text into lines, and `unlines` reassembles the text
by putting a single newline between lines. If we store the program in `lhs2hs.lhs`,
we can compile it and then run it:

```
$ ghc lhs2hs.lhs
$ lhs2hs <myscript.lhs >myscript.hs
```

In the second line, the input is taken from `myscript.lhs` and the output is directed to `myscript.hs`.

Stream-based interaction was the main method for interacting with the outside world in early versions of Haskell. However, the model presented above is too simple for most practical purposes. In a serious application one wants to do other things than reading and printing characters to a screen. For example, one also wants to open and read files, to write to or delete files, and in general to interact with all the mechanisms that are available in the world outside the confines of a functional programming language. Interaction takes place in time, and the order in which events occur has to be managed correctly by the programmer. In the stream-based approach, this ordering of events is represented by the order of the elements in a list; in other words, it is represented in the data and not reflected primarily in the way the program is composed. In the following chapter we will consider another approach to interaction, indeed, a general method for writing programs that have to control an orderly sequence of events. In this approach, the order is made explicit in the way the program is composed.

9.6 Doubly-linked lists

We end with another application of cyclic lists. Imagine reading a book consisting of a nonempty list of pages. To navigate around the book we need some way of moving on to the next page and moving back to the previous page. Other navigation tools would be useful, but we'll stick with these two. Here is an interactive session with a particularly boring book book consisting of three pages:

```
ghci> start book
"Page 1"
ghci> next it
"Page 2"
ghci> prev it
"Page 1"
ghci> next it
"Page 2"
ghci> next it
"Page 3"
```

In GHCi the variable it is bound to the expression just typed at the prompt. We started a book and what was printed was the first page. We turned to the next page, and then returned to the previous one. The interesting question is what should happen when we turn to the next page after the last one. Should the navigation report an error, just deliver the last page again or go to the first page? Suppose we decide on the last alternative, namely that the next page after the last one should be the first page, and the previous page before the first one should be the last page. In other words, our book is an instance of a *cyclic doubly-linked list*.

Here is the relevant datatype declaration:

```
data DList a = Cons a (DList a) (DList a)

elem :: DList a -> a
elem (Cons a p n) = a

prev,next :: DList a -> DList a
prev (Cons a p n) = p
next (Cons a p n) = n
```

We print a doubly-linked list by displaying the current entry:

```
instance Show a => Show (DList a)
  where show d = show (elem d)
```

Our book is then a list [p1,p2,p3] of three pages, where

```
p1 = Cons "Page 1" p3 p2
p2 = Cons "Page 2" p1 p3
p3 = Cons "Page 3" p2 p1
```

This example suggests that the function mkCDList :: [a] -> DList a for converting a (nonempty) list as into a doubly-linked list can be specified as the first element in a finite list xs of doubly-linked lists satisfying the following three properties:

```
map elem xs = as
map prev xs = rotr xs
map next xs = rotl xs
```

Here, rotr and rotl (short for *rotate right* and *rotate left*), are defined by

```
rotr xs = [last xs] ++ init xs
rotl xs = tail xs ++ [head xs]
```

Observe now that for any list `xs` of doubly-linked lists we have

```
xs = zipWith3 Cons
        (map elem xs) (map prev xs) (map next xs)
```

where `zipWith3` is like `zipWith` except that it takes three lists instead of two. The standard prelude definition is:

```
zipWith3 f (x:xs) (y:ys) (z:zs)
   = f x y z : zipWith3 f xs ys zs
zipWith3 _ _ _ _ = []
```

We will see another definition in a moment. We can prove the claim above by induction. It clearly holds for the undefined and empty lists. For the inductive case we reason:

```
    x:xs
 =    {since xs is a doubly-linked list}
   Cons (elem x) (prev x) (next x):xs
 =    {induction}
   Cons (elem x) (prev x) (next x):
   (zipWith3 Cons
   (map elem xs) (map prev xs) (map next xs))
 =    {definition of zipWith3 and map}
   zipWith3 Cons
   (map elem (x:xs)) (map prev (x:xs)) (map next (x:xs))
```

Putting this result together with our specification of doubly-linked lists, we arrive at

```
mkCDList as = head xs
   where xs = zipWith3 Cons as (rotr xs) (rotl xs)
```

This definition involves a cyclic list `xs`. Does it work? The answer is: No, it doesn't. The reason is that `zipWith3` as defined above is too eager. We need to make it lazier by not demanding the values of the second two lists until they are really needed:

```
zipWith3 f (x:xs) ys zs
   = f x (head ys) (head zs):
       zipWith3 f xs (tail ys) (tail zs)
zipWith3 _ _ _ _ = []
```

An equivalent way to define this function is to make use of Haskell's *irrefutable patterns*:

```
zipWith3 f (x:xs) ~(y:ys) ~(z:zs)
    = f x y z : zipWith3 f xs ys zs
zipWith3 _ _ _ _ = []
```

An irrefutable pattern is introduced using a tilde, and ~(x:xs) is matched lazily, meaning that no matching is actually performed until either x or xs is needed.

Just to convince ourselves that the above definition of mkCDList with the revised definition of zipWith3 does make progress, let $xs_0 = \perp$ and

$$xs_{n+1} = \text{zipWith3 Cons "A" (rotr } xs_n) \text{ (rotl } xs_n)$$

Then xs_1 is given by

```
    zipWith3 Cons "A" ⊥ ⊥
  = [Cons 'A' ⊥ ⊥]
```

and xs_2 by

```
    zipWith3 Cons "A"
    [Cons 'A' ⊥ ⊥] [Cons 'A' ⊥ ⊥]
  = [Cons 'A' (Cons 'A' ⊥ ⊥) (Cons 'A' ⊥ ⊥)]
```

and so on.

9.7 Exercises

Exercise A

Given three lists xs, ys and zs in strictly increasing order, we have

```
merge (merge xs ys) zs} = merge xs (merge ys zs)
```

Thus merge is associative. Assuming in addition that the first elements of xs, ys and zs are in strictly increasing order, we also have

```
xmerge (xmerge xs ys) zs = xmerge xs (xmerge ys zs)
```

Does it follow that in the expression foldr1 xmerge multiples we could replace foldr1 by foldl1?

Exercise B

The standard prelude function `cycle :: [a] -> [a]` takes a list `xs` and returns a list consisting of an infinite number of repetitions of the elements of `xs`. If `xs` is the empty list, then `cycle []` returns an error message. For instance

```
cycle "hallo" = "hallohallohallo...
```

Define `cycle` using a cyclic list. Ensure that your definition works on empty, finite and infinite lists.

Exercise C

The fibonacci function is defined by

```
fib 0 = 0
fib 1 = 1
fib n = fib (n-1) + fib (n-2)
```

Write down a one-line definition of the list `fibs` that produces the infinite list of Fibonacci numbers.

Exercise D

A well-known problem, due to the mathematician W.R. Hamming, is to write a program that produces an infinite list of numbers with the following properties: (i) the list is in strictly increasing order; (ii) the list begins with the number 1; (iii) if the list contains the number x, then it also contains the numbers $2x$, $3x$ and $5x$; (iv) the list contains no other numbers. Thus, the required list begins with the numbers

$$1, 2, 3, 4, 5, 6, 8, 9, 10, 12, 15, 16, \ldots$$

Write a definition of `hamming` that produces this list.

Exercise E

Prove that `approx n xs` $\sqsubseteq$ `xs` for all n. Now prove that if `approx n xs` $\sqsubseteq$ `ys` for all n, then `xs` $\sqsubseteq$ `ys`. Hence conclude that

$$\lim_{n \to \infty} \text{approx n xs} = \text{xs}.$$

Exercise F

Give a counter-example to the claim that `xs=ys` if `xs!!n=ys!!n` for all n.

Exercise G

Prove that `iterate f x = x: map f (iterate f x)`.

Exercise H

In the definition of `primes` as a cyclic list, could we have defined

```
mergeAll = foldr xmerge []
```

as an alternative to the definition in the text?

Exercise I

Recall that

```
prs n = approx n (2:([3..] \\ crs n))
crs n = mergeAll [map (p*) [p..] | p <- prs n]
```

Given that `prs` $n = p_1 : p_2 : \cdots p_n : \bot$, where p_j is the jth prime, sketch how to show that `crs` $n = c_1 : c_2 : \cdots c_m : \bot$, where c_j is the jth composite number (so $c_1 = 4$) and $m = p_n^2$. Hence show that `primes` does produce the infinite list of primes.

We said in the text that it is not the case that the nth approximation $primes_n$ of `primes` is equal to `approx n primes`. In fact

$$primes_4 = 2 : 3 : 5 : 7 : \cdots : 47 : \bot$$

What list does $primes_5$ produce?

Exercise J

Another way of generating the primes is known as the *Sieve of Sundaram*, after its discoverer S.P. Sundaram in 1934:

```
primes   = 2:[2*n+1 | n <- [1..] \\ sundaram]
sundaram = mergeAll [[i+j+2*i*j | j <- [i..]] | i <- [1..]]
```

To show that the list comprehension in the definition of `primes` generates exactly the odd primes, it is sufficient to prove that the term `2*n+1` is never composite, which is to say that it never factorises into `(2*i+1)*(2*j+1)` for positive integers `i` and `j`. Why is this so?

Exercise K

Is the function f, defined by $f(\bot) = 0$ and $f(x) = 1$ for $x \neq \bot$, computable? How about the function that returns $\bot$ on all finite or partial lists, and 1 on all infinite lists?

Exercise L

By definition, a *torus* is a doubly-cyclic, doubly-doubly-linked list. It is a cyclic doubly-linked list in the left/right direction, and also in the up/down direction. Given a matrix represented as a list of length m of lists, all of length n, construct a definition of

```
mkTorus :: Matrix a -> Torus a
```

where

```
data Torus a = Cell a (Torus a) (Torus a)
                      (Torus a) (Torus a)
elem  (Cell a u d l r) = a
up    (Cell a u d l r) = u
down  (Cell a u d l r) = d
left  (Cell a u d l r) = l
right (Cell a u d l r) = r
```

That looks tricky, but the answer is short enough to be tweeted.

9.8 Answers

Answer to Exercise A

No, since `foldl1 f xs` = undefined for any infinite list `xs`.

Answer to Exercise B

The definition is

```
cycle [] = error "empty list"
cycle xs = ys  where ys = xs ++ ys
```

Note that if `xs` is infinite, then `xs ++ ys` = `xs`, so cycle is the identity function on infinite lists.

Answer to Exercise C

The one-liner is:

```
fibs :: [Integer]
fibs = 0:1:zipWith (+) fibs (tail fibs)
```

Answer to Exercise D

```
hamming :: [Integer]
hamming = 1: merge (map (2*) hamming)
               (merge (map (3*) hamming)
                      (map (5*) hamming))
```

Answer to Exercise E

The proof of `approx n xs` $\sqsubseteq$ `xs` is by induction on `n`. The base case is easy but the induction step involves a sub-induction over `xs`. The base cases (the empty list and the undefined list) of the sub-induction are easy and the inductive case is

$$\text{approx (n+1) (x:xs)}$$

= {definition}

  `x:approx n xs`

$\sqsubseteq$ {induction and monotonicity of `(x:)`}

  `x:xs`.

The proof of

$$(\forall n : \text{approx n xs} \sqsubseteq \text{ys}) \Rightarrow \text{xs} \sqsubseteq \text{ys}$$

is by induction on `xs`. The claim is immediate for the undefined and empty lists, and for the inductive case we have

$$(\forall n : \text{approx n (x:xs)} \sqsubseteq \text{ys})$$

$$\Rightarrow \text{xs} \sqsubseteq \text{head ys} \wedge (\forall n : \text{approx n xs} \sqsubseteq \text{tail ys})$$

by the definitions of `approx` and the approximation ordering on lists. By induction we therefore have

$$\text{x:xs} \sqsubseteq \text{head ys:tail ys} = \text{ys}.$$

It follows that

$$\lim_{n \to \infty} \text{approx n xs} = \text{xs}$$

by the definition of limit.

Answer to Exercise F

The two lists `repeat undefined` and `undefined` are not equal, but

$$(\text{repeat undefined}) \,!!\, n = \text{undefined} \,!!\, n$$

for all `n` because both sides are $\bot$.

Answer to Exercise G

We have to show that

```
approx n (iterate f x) = approx n (x:map f (iterate f x))
```

for all natural numbers n. This claim follows from

```
approx n (iterate f (f x))
            = approx n (map f (iterate f x))
```

which we establish by induction on n. For the inductive step we simplify each side. For the left-hand side:

```
      approx (n+1) (iterate f (f x))
  =   {definition of iterate}
      approx (n+1) (f x:iterate f (f (f x)))
  =   {definition of approx}
      f x: approx n (iterate f (f (f x)))
  =   {induction}
      f x: approx n (map f (iterate f (f x)))
```

For the right-hand side:

```
      approx (n+1) (map f (iterate f x))
  =   {definition of iterate and map}
      approx (n+1) (f x:map f (iterate f (f x)))
  =   {definition of approx}
      f x: approx n (map f (iterate f (f x)))
```

Answer to Exercise H

Yes, since

```
foldr xmerge [] (xs:undefined) = xmerge xs undefined
```

and the right-hand side begins with the first element of xs.

Answer to Exercise I

The proof is by induction. We have first to show that crs (n+1) is the result of merging $c_1 : c_2 : \cdots c_m : \bot$, where $m = p_n^2$ with the infinite list of multiples

$p_{n+1}p_{n+1}, p_{n+1}(p_{n+1}+1), \ldots$ of p_{n+1}. That gives the partial list of all composite numbers up to p_{n+1}^2. Finally, we need the result that $p_{n+2} < p_{n+1}^2$.

The partial list $\texttt{primes}_5$ produces all the primes smaller than $2209 = 47 \times 47$.

Answer to Exercise J

Because an odd integer is excluded from the final list if it takes the form $2n+1$ where n is of the form $i+j+2ij$. But

$$2(i+j+2ij)+1 = (2i+1)(2j+1).$$

Answer to Exercise K

No, f is not monotonic: $\bot \sqsubseteq 1$ but $f(\bot) \not\sqsubseteq f(1)$. For the second function (call it g) we have $\texttt{xs} \sqsubseteq \texttt{ys}$ implies $g(\texttt{xs}) \sqsubseteq g(\texttt{ys})$, so g is monotonic. But g is not continuous, so it's not computable.

Answer to Exercise L

The definition is

```
mkTorus ass = head (head xss)
  where xss = zipWith5 (zipWith5 Cell)
              ass (rotr xss) (rotl xss)
              (map rotr xss) (map rotl xss)
```

Whereas $\texttt{rotr}$ and $\texttt{rotl}$ rotate the rows of a matrix, $\texttt{map rotr}$ and $\texttt{map rotl}$ rotate the columns. The definition of $\texttt{zipWith5}$ has to be made non-strict in its last four arguments.

9.9 Chapter notes

Melissa O'Neill has written a nice pearl on sieve methods for generating primes; see 'The genuine sieve of Eratosthenes', *Journal of Functional Programming* 19 (1), 95–106, 2009. Ben Sijtsma's thesis *Verification and derivation of infinite-list programs* (University of Groningen, the Netherlands, 1988) studies various aspects of infinite-list programs and gives a number of techniques for reasoning about them. One chapter is devoted to the proof of fairness in the paper–rock–scissors game.

My paper, 'On building cyclic and shared data structures in Haskell', *Formal Aspects of Computing* 24(4–6), 609–621, July 2012, contains more examples of the uses of infinite and cyclic lists. See also the article on 'Tying the knot' at `haskell.org/haskellwiki/Tying_the_Knot`

Hamming's problem has been used as an illustration of cyclic programs since the early days of functional programming.

Chapter 10

Imperative functional programming

Back in Chapter 2 we described the function putStrLn as being a Haskell *command*, and IO a as being the type of input–output *computations* that interact with the outside world and deliver values of type a. We also mentioned some syntax, called *do-notation*, for sequencing commands. This chapter explores what is really meant by these words, and introduces a new style of programming called *monadic* programming. Monadic programs provide a simple and attractive way to describe interaction with the outside world, but are also capable of much more: they provide a simple sequencing mechanism for solving a range of problems, including exception handling, destructive array updates, parsing and state-based computation. In a very real sense, a monadic style enables us to write functional programs that mimic the kind of imperative programs one finds in languages such as Python or C.

10.1 The IO monad

The type IO a is an abstract type in the sense described in the previous chapter, so we are not told how its values, which are called *actions* or commands, are represented. But you can think of this type as being

```
type IO a = World -> (a,World)
```

Thus an action is a function that takes a world and delivers a value of type a and a new world. The new world is then used as the input for the next action. Having changed the world with an input–output action, you can't go back to the old world. You can't duplicate the world or inspect its components. All you can do is operate on the world with given primitive actions, and put such actions together in a sequence.

One primitive action is to print a character:

```
putChar :: Char -> IO ()
```

When executed, this action prints a character on the standard output channel, usually the computer screen. For example,

```
ghci> putChar 'x'
xghci>
```

The character x is printed, but nothing else, so the next GHCi prompt follows without additional spaces or newlines. Performing this action produces no value of interest, so the return value is the null tuple ().

Another primitive action is done :: IO (), which does nothing. It leaves the world unchanged and also returns the null tuple ().

One simple operation to sequence actions is denoted by (>>) and has type

```
(>>) :: IO () -> IO () -> IO ()
```

Given actions p and q, the action p >> q first performs action p and then performs action q. For example,

```
ghci> putChar 'x' >> putChar '\n'
x
ghci>
```

This time a newline is printed. Using (>>) we can define the function putStrLn:

```
putStrLn :: String -> IO ()
putStrLn xs = foldr (>>) done (map putChar xs) >>
                 putChar '\n'
```

This action prints all the characters in a string, and then finishes up with an additional newline character. Note that map putChar xs is a list of actions. We are still in the universe of functional programming and its full expressive power, including uses of map and foldr, is still available to us.

Here is another primitive action:

```
getChar :: IO Char
```

When performed, this operation reads a character from the standard input channel. This channel is fed by you typing at the keyboard, so getChar returns the first character you type. For example,

```
ghci> getChar
x
'x'
```

After typing getChar and pressing return, GHCi waits for you to type a character. We typed the character 'x' (and what we typed was echoed), and then that
character was read and printed.

The generalisation of done is an action that does nothing and returns a named
value:

```
    return :: a -> IO a
```

In particular, done = return (). The generalisation of (>>) has type

```
    (>>) :: IO a -> IO b -> IO b
```

Given actions p and q, the action p >> q first does p, and then throws the return
value away, and then does q. For example,

```
ghci> return 1 >> return 2
2
```

It is clear that this action is useful only when the value returned by p is not interesting since there is no way that q can depend on it. What is really wanted is a more
general operator (>>=) with type

```
    (>>=) :: IO a -> (a -> IO b) -> IO b
```

The combination p >>= f is an action that, when performed, first does p, returning
a value x of type a, then does action f x returning a final value y of type b. It is easy
to define (>>) in terms of (>>=) and we leave this as an exercise. The operator
(>>=) is often referred to as *bind*, though one can also pronounce it as 'then apply'.

Using (>>=), we can define a function getLine for reading a line of input, more
precisely, the list of characters up to but not including the first newline character:

```
    getLine :: IO String
    getLine = getChar >>= f
             where f x = if x == '\n' then return []
                         else getLine >>= g
                         where g xs = return (x:xs)
```

This has a straightforward reading: get the first character x; stop if x is a newline
and return the empty list; otherwise get the rest of the line and add x to the front.
Though the reading is straightforward, the use of nested where clauses makes the

definition a little clumsy. One way to make the code smoother is to use anonymous lambda expressions and instead write:

```
getLine = getChar >>= \x ->
          if x == '\n'
          then return []
          else getLine >>= \xs ->
               return (x:xs)
```

Another, arguably superior solution is to use do-notation:

```
getLine = do x <- getChar
             if x == '\n'
             then return []
             else do xs <- getLine
                     return (x:xs)
```

The right-hand side makes use of the Haskell layout convention. Note especially the indentation of the conditional expression, and the last return to show it is part of the inner do. Better in our opinion is to use braces and semicolons to control the layout explicitly:

```
getLine = do {x <- getChar;
             if x == '\n'
             then return []
             else do {xs <- getLine;
                      return (x:xs)}}
```

We return to do-notation below.

The Haskell library System.IO provides many more actions than just putChar and getChar, including actions to open and read files, to write and close files, to buffer output in various ways and so on. We will not go into details in this book. But perhaps two more things need to be said. Firstly, there is no function of type IO a -> a [1]. Once you are in a room performing input–output actions, you stay in the room and can't come out of it. To see one reason this has to be the case, suppose there is such a function, runIO say, and consider

```
int :: Int
int = x - y
      where x = runIO readInt
            y = runIO readInt
```

---

[1] Actually there is, and it's called unsafePerformIO, but it is a very unsafe function.

```
readInt = do {xs <- getLine; return (read xs :: Int)}
```

The action `readInt` reads a line of input and, provided the line consists entirely of digits, interprets it as an integer. Now, what is the value of `int`? The answer depends entirely on which of x and y gets evaluated first. Haskell does not prescribe whether or not x is evaluated before y in the expression x-y. Put it this way: input–output actions have to be sequenced in a deterministic fashion, and Haskell is a lazy functional language in which it is difficult to determine the order in which things happen. Of course, an expression such as x-y is a very simple example (and exactly the same undesirable phenomenon arises in imperative languages) but you can imagine all sorts of confusion that would ensue if we were provided with `runIO`.

The second thing that perhaps should be said is in response to a reader who casts a lazy eye over an expression such as

```
undefined >> return 0 :: IO Int
```

Does this code raise an error or return zero? The answer is: an error. IO is *strict* in the sense that IO actions are performed in order, even though subsequent actions may take no heed of their results.

To return to the main theme, let us summarise. The type `IO a` is an abstract type on which the following operations, at least, are available:

```
return :: a -> IO a
(>>=)  :: IO a -> (a -> IO b) -> IO b

putChar :: Char -> IO ()
getChar :: IO Char
```

The second two functions are specific to input and output, but the first two are not. Indeed they are general sequencing operations that characterise the class of types called *monads*:

```
class Monad m where
  return :: a -> m a
  (>>=)  :: m a -> (a -> m b) -> m b
```

The two monad operations are required to satisfy certain laws, which we will come to in due course. As to the reason for the name 'monad', it is stolen from philosophy, in particular from Leibniz, who in turn borrowed it from Greek philosophy. Don't read anything into the name.

10.2 More monads

If that's all a monad is, then surely lots of things form a monad? Yes, indeed. In particular, the humble list type forms a monad:

```
instance Monad [] where
  return x = [x]
  xs >>= f = concat (map f xs)
```

Of course, we don't yet know what the laws governing the monad operations are, so maybe this instance isn't correct (it is), but at least the operations have the right types. Since do-notation can be used with any monad we can, for example, define the cartesian product function cp :: [[a]] -> [[a]] (see Section 7.3) using the new notation:

```
cp []        = return []
cp (xs:xss) = do {x <- xs;
                  ys <- cp xss;
                  return (x:ys)}
```

Comparing the right-hand side of the second clause to the list comprehension

```
[x:ys | x <- xs, ys <- cp xss]
```

one can appreciate that the two notations are very similar; the only real difference is that with do-notation the result appears at the end rather than at the beginning. If monads and do-notation had been made part of Haskell before list comprehensions, then maybe the latter wouldn't have been needed.

Here is another example. The Maybe type is a monad:

```
instance Monad Maybe where
  return x        = Just x
  Nothing >>= f = Nothing
  Just x >>= f   = f x
```

To appreciate what this monad can bring to the table, consider the Haskell library function

```
lookup :: Eq a => a -> [(a,b)] -> Maybe b
```

The value of lookup x alist is Just y if (x,y) is the first pair in alist with first component x, and Nothing if there is no such pair. Imagine looking up x in alist, then looking up the result y in a second list blist, and then looking up the result z in yet a third list clist. If any of these lookups return Nothing, then

Nothing is the final result. To define such a function we would have to write its defining expression as something like

```
case lookup x alist of
   Nothing -> Nothing
   Just y  -> case lookup y blist of
                   Nothing -> Nothing
                   Just z  -> lookup z clist
```

With a monad we can write

```
do {y <- lookup x alist;
    z <- lookup y blist;
    return (lookup z clist)}
```

Rather than having to write an explicit chain of computations, each of which may return Nothing, and explicitly passing Nothing back up the chain, we can write a simple monadic expression in which handling Nothing is done implicitly under a monadic hood.

do-notation

Just as list comprehensions can be translated into expressions involving map and concat, so do-expressions can be translated into expressions involving return and bind. The three main translation rules are:

```
do {p}               = p
do {p;stmts}         = p >> do {stmts}
do {x <- p;stmts} = p >>= \x -> do {stmts}
```

In these rules p denotes an action, so the first rule says that a do round a single action can be removed. In the second and third rules stmts is a *nonempty* sequence of statements, each of which is either an action or a statement of the form x <- p. The latter is *not* an action; consequently an expression such as

```
do {x <- getChar}
```

is not syntactically correct. Nor, by the way, is an empty do-expression do { }. The last statement in a do-expression must be an action.

On the other hand, the following two expressions are both fine:

```
do {putStrLn "hello "; name <- getLine; putStrLn name}
do {putStrLn "hello "; getLine; putStrLn "there"}
```

The first example prints a greeting, reads a name and completes the greeting. The second prints a greeting, reads a name but immediately forgets it, and then completes the greeting with a 'there'. A bit like being introduced to someone in real life.

Finally, there are two rules that can be proved from the translation rules above:

```
do {do {stmts}} = do {stmts}
do {stmts1; do {stmts2}} = do {stmts1; stmts2}
```

But one has to be careful; the nested dos in

```
do {stmts1;
    if p
    then do {stmts2}
    else do {stmts3}}
```

are necessary if stmts2 and stmts3 contain more than one action.

Monad laws

The monad laws say nothing much more than that expressions involving return and (>>=) simplify in just the way one would expect. There are three laws and we are going to state them in three different ways. The first law states that return is a right identity element of (>>=):

```
(p >>= return) = p
```

In do-notation the law reads:

```
do {x <- p; return x} = do {p}
```

The second law says that return is also a kind of left identity element:

```
(return e >>= f) = f e
```

In do-notation the law reads:

```
do {x <- return e; f x} = do {f e}
```

The third law says that (>>=) is kind of associative:

```
((p >>= f) >>= g) = p >>= (\x -> (f x >>= g))
```

In do-notation the law reads:

```
  do {y <- do {x <- p; f x}; g y}
= do {x <- p; do {y <- f x; g y}}
= do {x <- p; y <- f x; g y}
```

The last line makes use of the un-nesting property of do-notation.

For the third way of stating the monad laws, consider the operator (>=>) defined by

```
(>=>) :: Monad m => (a -> m b) -> (b -> m c) -> (a -> m c)
(f >=> g) x = f x >>= g
```

This operator is just like function composition except that the component functions each have type `x -> m y` for appropriate x and y, and the order of composition is from left to right rather than from right to left. This operator, which is called *(left to right) Kleisli composition*, is defined in the Haskell library `Control.Monad`. There is a dual version, *(right to left) Kleisli composition*,

```
(<=<) :: Monad m => (b -> m c) -> (a -> m b) -> (a -> m c)
```

whose definition we leave as an easy exercise.

The point is that we can define (>>=) in terms of (>=>):

```
(p >>= f) = (id >=> f) p
```

More briefly, `(>>=) = flip (id >=>)`. We also have the *leapfrog* rule:

```
(f >=> g) . h = (f . h) >=> g
```

The proof is left as an exercise.

In terms of (>=>) the three monad laws say simply that (>=>) is associative with identity `return`. Any set of values with an associative binary operation and an identity element is called a *monoid*, and the word 'monad' was probably adopted because of the pun with monoid. Be that as it may, this is certainly the shortest way of stating the monad laws.

One additional and instructive way of describing the monad laws is considered in the exercises.

10.3 The State monad

If it wasn't for the problem of how to sequence input–output actions correctly, monads probably wouldn't have appeared in Haskell. But once it was appreciated what they could do, all kinds of other uses quickly followed. We have seen with the `Maybe` monad how chains of computations that involve passing information back up the chain can be simplified with monadic notation. Another primary use of monads is a way to handle *mutable* structures, such as arrays, that rely for their efficiency on being able to update their values, destroying the original structure in the process.

Mutable structures are introduced through the State-Thread monad `ST s` which we will consider in a subsequent section. Before getting on to the particular properties of this monad, we start by considering a simpler monad, called `State s`, for manipulating an explicit state `s`. You can think of the type `State s a` as being

```
type State s a = s -> (a,s)
```

An action of type `State s a` takes an initial state and returns a value of type `a` and a new state. It is tempting, but wrong, to think of `IO a` as synonymous with `State World a`. The state component `s` in `State s a` can be exposed and manipulated, but we can't expose and manipulate the world.

Specifically, as well as the monad operations `return` and `(>>=)`, five other functions are provided for working with the state monad:

```
put        :: s -> State s ()
get        :: State s s
state      :: (s -> (a,s)) -> State s a
runState   :: State s a -> (s -> (a,s))
evalState  :: State s a -> s -> a
```

The function `put` puts the state into a given configuration, while `get` returns the current state. Each of these two operations can be defined in terms of `state`:

```
put s = state (\_ -> ((),s))
get   = state (\s -> (s,s))
```

On the other hand, `state` can also be defined using `put` and `get`:

```
state f = do {s <- get; let (a,s') = f s;
              put s'; return a}
```

Haskell permits an abbreviated form of `let` expressions in do expressions (and also in list comprehensions). We have

```
do {let decls; stmts} = let decls in do {stmts}
```

The function `runState` is the inverse of `state`: it takes both an action and an initial state and returns the final value and the final state after performing the action (something the IO monad cannot do). The function evalState is defined by

```
evalState m s = fst (runState m s)
```

and returns just the value of the stateful computation.

Here is an example of the use of State. In Section 7.6 we constructed the following program for building a binary tree out of a given nonempty list of values:

```
build :: [a] -> BinTree a
build xs = fst (build2 (length xs) xs)
build2 1 xs = (Leaf (head xs),tail xs)
build2 n xs = (Fork u v, xs'')
              where (u,xs')  = build2 m xs
                    (v,xs'') = build2 (n-m) xs'
                    m        = n `div` 2
```

The point to appreciate here is that build2 is essentially a function that manipulates a state of type [a], returning elements of BinTree a as its result. Another way of writing build is as follows:

```
build xs = evalState (build2 (length xs)) xs

build2 :: Int -> State [a] (BinTree a)
build2 1 = do {x:xs <- get;
               put xs;
               return (Leaf x)}
build2 n = do {u <- build2 m;
               v <- build2 (n-m);
               return (Fork u v)}
          where m = n `div` 2
```

All the work in manipulating the state explicitly is done when building a leaf. The state is accessed and its first element is chosen as the label associated with a Leaf; the remaining list then is installed as the new state. Whereas the first version of build2 n threads the state explicitly, the second version hides this machinery under a monadic hood.

Notice in the first line of build2 we have a statement x:xs <- get in which the left-hand side is a *pattern* rather than a simple variable. If the current state happens to be the empty list, the action fails with a suitable error message. For example,

```
ghci>  runState (do {x:xs <- get; return x}) ""
```

```
*** Exception: Pattern match failure in do expression ...
```

Of course this behaviour cannot arise with `build2 1` because the definition only applies when the state is a singleton list. We leave it as an exercise to say what `build []` does.

As another example, consider the problem of producing a pseudo-random integer in a specified interval. Imagine we have a function

```
random :: (Int,Int) -> Seed -> (Int,Seed)
```

that takes a pair of integers as the specified interval and then a seed, and calculates a random integer and a new seed. The new seed is used for obtaining further random values. Rather than be explicit about what a seed is, suppose there is a function

```
mkSeed :: Int -> Seed
```

that makes a seed from a given integer. Now if we wanted to roll a pair of dice, we could write

```
diceRoll :: Int -> (Int,Int)
diceRoll n = (x,y)
             where (x,s1) = random (1,6) (mkSeed n)
                   (y,s2) = random (1,6) s1
```

But we could also write

```
diceRoll n = evalState (
                do {x <- randomS (1,6);
                    y <- randomS (1,6);
                    return (x,y)}
                ) (mkSeed n)
             where randomS = state . random
```

The function `randomS :: (Int,Int) -> State Seed Int` takes an interval and returns an action. The second version of `diceRoll` is a little longer than the first, but is arguably more easy to write. Imagine that instead of two dice we had five, as in liar dice. The first method would involve a chain of where-clauses expressing the linkage between five values and five seeds, something that would be easy to mistype, but the second version is easily extended and harder to get wrong.

One final point. Consider

```
evalState (do {undefined; return 0}) 1
```

Does this raise an exception, or does it return zero? In other words, is the monad

State strict, as the IO monad is, or is it lazy? The answer is that it can be both. There are two variants of the state monad, one of which is lazy and the other of which is strict. The difference lies in how the operation (>>=) is implemented. Haskell provides the lazy variant by default, in `Control.Monad.State.Lazy`, but you can ask for the strict variant, in `Control.Monad.State.Strict` if you want.

10.4 The ST monad

The state-thread monad, which resides in the library `Control.Monad.ST`, is a different kettle of fish entirely from the state monad, although the kettle itself looks rather similar. Like `State s a` you can think of this monad as the type

```
type ST s a = s -> (a,s)
```

but with one very important difference: the type variable s cannot be instantiated to specific states, such as `Seed` or `[Int]`. Instead it is there only to *name* the state. Think of s as a label that identifies one particular state *thread*. All mutable types are tagged with this thread, so that actions can only affect mutable values in their own state thread.

One kind of mutable value is a *program variable*. Unlike variables in Haskell, or mathematics for that matter, program variables in imperative languages can change their values. They can be thought of as *references* to other values, and in Haskell they are entities of type `STRef s a`. The s means that the reference is local to the state thread s (and no other), and the a is the type of value being referenced. There are operations, defined in `Data.STRef`, to create, read from and write to references:

```
newSTRef    :: a -> ST s (STRef s a)
readSTRef   :: STRef s a -> ST s a
writeSTRef  :: STRef s a -> a -> ST s ()
```

Here is an example. Recall Section 7.6 where we gave the following definition of the Fibonacci function:

```
fib :: Int -> Integer
fib n  = fst (fib2 n)
fib2 0 = (0,1)
fib2 n = (b,a+b)  where (a,b) = fib2 (n-1)
```

Evaluating `fib` takes linear time, but the space involved is not constant (even ignoring the fact that arbitrarily large integers cannot be stored in constant space): each recursive call involves fresh variables a and b. By contrast, here is a definition of `fib` in the imperative language Python:

```python
def fib (n):
    a,b = 0,1
    for i in range (0,n):
        a,b = b,a+b
    return a
```

The definition manipulates two program variables a and b, and runs in constant space (at least, for small integers). We can translate the Python code almost directly into Haskell:

```haskell
fibST :: Int -> ST s Integer
fibST n = do {a <- newSTRef 0;
              b <- newSTRef 1;
              repeatFor n
               (do {x <- readSTRef a;
                    y <- readSTRef b;
                    writeSTRef a y;
                    writeSTRef b $! (x+y)});
              readSTRef a}
```

Note the use of the strict application operator ($!) to force evaluation of the sum. The action `repeatFor` repeats an action a given number of times:

```haskell
repeatFor :: Monad m => Int -> m a -> m ()
repeatFor n = foldr (>>) done . replicate n
```

All well and good, but we end up with an action `ST s Integer` when what we really want is an integer. How do we escape from the monad back into the world of Haskell values?

The answer is to provide a function similar to `runState` for the state monad, Here it is, with its type:

```haskell
runST :: (forall s. ST s a) -> a
```

This type is unlike any other Haskell type we have met so far. It is what is called a *rank 2 polymorphic type*, while all previous polymorphic types have had rank 1. What it says is that the argument of `runST` must be universal in s, so it can't depend on any information about s apart from its name. In particular, every STRef declared in the action has to carry the same thread name s.

To amplify a little on rank 2 types, consider the difference between the two lists

```
list1 :: forall a. [a -> a]
list2 :: [forall a. a -> a]
```

The type of list1 is just what we would have previously written as [a -> a] because in ordinary rank 1 types universal quantification at the outermost level is assumed. For example, [sin,cos,tan] is a possible value of list1 with the instantiation Float for a. But there are only two functions that can be elements of list2, namely id and the undefined function undefined, because these are the only two functions with type forall a. a -> a. If you give me an element x of a type a about which absolutely nothing is known, the only things I can do if I have to give you back an element of a, is either to give you x or ⊥.

Why have a rank 2 type for runST? Well, it prevents us from defining things like

```
let v = runST (newSTRef True)
in runST (readSTRef v)
```

This code is not well-typed because

```
newSTRef True :: ST s (STref s Bool)
```

and in the expression runST (newSTRef Bool) the Haskell type checker cannot match STRef s a with a, the expected result type of runST. Values of type STRef s a cannot be exported from ST s, but only entities whose types do not depend on s. If the code were allowed, then the reference allocated in the first runST would be usable inside the second runST. That would enable reads in one thread to be used in another, and hence the result would depend on the evaluation order used to execute the threads, leading to mayhem and confusion. It is just the same problem that we prevented from occurring in the IO monad.

But we can safely define

```
fib :: Int -> Integer
fib n = runST (fibST n)
```

This version of fib runs in constant space.

For our purposes the main use of the ST monad resides in its ability to handle mutable arrays. The whole question of arrays deserves a section to itself.

10.5 Mutable arrays

It sometimes surprises imperative programmers who meet functional programming for the first time that the emphasis is on lists as the fundamental data structure rather than arrays. The reason is that most uses of arrays (though not all) depend for their efficiency on the fact that updates are destructive. Once you update the value of an array at a particular index the old array is lost. But in functional programming, data structures are *persistent* and any named structure continues to exist. For instance, insert x t may insert a new element x into a tree t, but t continues to refer to the original tree, so it had better not be overwritten.

In Haskell a mutable array is an entity of type STArray s i e. The s names the state thread, i the index type and e the element type. Not every type can be an index; legitimate indices are members of the type class Ix. Instances of this class include Int and Char, things that can be mapped into a contiguous range of integers.

Like STRefs there are operations to create, read from and write to arrays. Without more ado we consider an example, explaining the actions as we go along. Recall the Quicksort algorithm from Section 7.7:

```
qsort :: (Ord a) => [a] -> [a]
qsort []    = []
qsort (x:xs) = qsort [y | y <- xs, y < x] ++ [x] ++
                qsort [y | y <- xs, x <= y]
```

There we said that when Quicksort is implemented in terms of arrays rather than lists, the partitioning phase can be performed *in place* without using any additional space. We now have the tools to write just such an algorithm. We begin with

```
qsort :: (Ord a) => [a] -> [a]
qsort xs = runST $
            do {xa <- newListArray (0,n-1) xs;
                qsortST xa (0,n);
                getElems xa}
            where n = length xs
```

First we create a mutable array with bounds (0,n-1) and fill it with the elements of xs. Sorting the array is done with the action qsortST xa (0,n). At the end, the list of elements of the sorted array is returned. In the code above, the action newListArray has type

```
Ix i => (i, i) -> [e] -> ST s (STArray s i e)
```

and getElems has type

```
Ix i => STArray s i e -> ST s [e]
```

The first constructs a mutable array from a list of elements, and the second returns a list of the elements in a mutable array.

The purpose of qsortST xa (a,b) is to sort the elements in the sub-array of xa in the interval (a,b), where by definition such an interval includes the lower bound but excludes the upper bound; in other words [a .. b-1]. Choosing intervals that are closed on the left but open on the right is almost always the best policy when processing arrays. Here is the definition of qsortST:

```
qsortST :: Ord a => STArray s Int a ->
                     (Int,Int) -> ST s ()
qsortST xa (a,b)
  | a == b    = return ()
  | otherwise = do {m <- partition xa (a,b);
                    qsortST xa (a,m);
                    qsortST xa (m+1,b)}
```

If a==b we have an empty interval and there is nothing to do. Otherwise we rearrange the array so that for some suitable element x in the array all elements in the interval (a,m) are less than x, and all elements in the interval (m+1,b) are at least x. The element x itself is placed in the array at position m. Sorting is then completed by sorting both sub-intervals.

It remains to define partition. The *only* way to find a suitable definition is by formal development using pre- and post-conditions and loop invariants. But this is a book on functional programming, not on the formal development of imperative programs, so we are going to cop out and just record one version:

```
partition xa (a,b)
  = do {x <- readArray xa a;
        let loop (j,k)
              = if j==k
                then do {swap xa a (k-1);
                         return (k-1)}
                else do {y <- readArray xa j;
                         if y < x then loop (j+1,k)
                         else do {swap xa j (k-1);
                                  loop (j,k-1)}}
        in loop (a+1,b)}
```

The action swap is defined by

```
swap :: STArray s Int a -> Int -> Int -> ST s ()
swap xa i j =  do {v <- readArray xa i;
                   w <- readArray xa j;
                   writeArray xa i w;
                   writeArray xa j v}
```

Here is a brief and certainly inadequate explanation of how partition works. We begin by taking the first element x in the interval (a,b) as pivot. We then enter a loop that processes the remaining interval (a+1,b), stopping when the interval becomes empty. We pass over elements that are less than x, shrinking the interval from the left. Encountering a y not less than x, we swap it with the element at the rightmost position in the interval, shrinking the interval from the right. When the interval becomes empty, we place the pivot in its final position, returning that position as a result.

Note that loop is defined as a local procedure within the monad. We could have defined it as a global procedure, though we would have had to add three extra parameters, namely the array xa, the pivot x and the starting position a.

Hash tables

A purely functional Quicksort has the same asymptotic time efficiency as one based on mutable arrays, but there are one or two places where mutable arrays seem to play a crucial role in achieving an asymptotically faster algorithm. One such place is the use of hash tables for an efficient representation of sets.

But let us approach the use of hash tables in the context of a particular problem. Consider a typical puzzle defined in terms of two finite sets, a set of *positions* and a set of *moves*. Given are the following functions:

```
moves  :: Position -> [Move]
move   :: Position -> Move -> Position
solved :: Position -> Bool
```

The function moves describes the set of possible moves that can be made in a given position, move makes a move, and solved determines those positions that are a solution to the puzzle. Solving the puzzle means finding some sequence of moves, preferably a shortest such sequence, that leads from a given starting position to a solved position:

```
solve :: Position -> Maybe [Move]
```

The value `solve p` is `Nothing` if there is no sequence of moves starting in position p that leads to a solved position, and `Just ms` otherwise, where

```
solved (foldl move p ms)
```

We are going to implement `solve` by carrying out a *breadth-first* search. What this means is that we examine all positions one move away from the starting position to see if there is a solution, then all positions two moves away, and so on. Breadth-first will therefore find a shortest solution if one exists. To implement the search we need

```
type Path     = ([Move],Position)
type Frontier = [Path]
```

A path consists of a sequence of moves made from the starting position (in reverse order), and the position that results after making the moves. A frontier is a list of paths waiting to be extended into longer paths. A breadth-first search is then implemented by

```
solve p = bfs [] [([],p)]

bfs :: [Position] -> Frontier -> Maybe [Move]
bfs ps [] = Nothing
bfs ps ((ms,p):mps)
  | solved p    = Just (reverse ms)
  | p `elem` ps = bfs ps mps
  | otherwise   = bfs (p:ps) (mps ++ succs (ms,p))

succs :: Path -> [Path]
succs (ms,p) = [(m:ms,move p m) | m <- moves p]
```

The first argument `ps` of `bfs` represents the set of positions that have already been explored. The second argument is the frontier, which is managed in a queue-like fashion to ensure that paths of the same length are inspected before their successors. Inspecting a path means accepting it if the final position is a solution, rejecting it if the end position has already been explored, and otherwise adding its successors to the end of the current frontier for future exploration. The moves in a successful path are reversed before being returned as the final result of `bfs` simply because, for efficiency, `succs` adds a new move to the front of the list rather than at the end.

There are two major sources of inefficiency with `bfs`, one concerning the use of

(++) and the other concerning elem. Firstly, the size of a frontier can grow expo-
nentially and so concatenating successors to the end of the frontier is slow. Better
is the following alternative to bfs:

```
bfs :: [Position] -> Frontier -> Frontier ->
       Maybe [Move]
bfs ps [] []  = Nothing
bfs ps [] mqs = bfs ps mqs []
bfs ps ((ms,p):mps) mqs
  | solved p   = Just (reverse ms)
  | p `elem` ps = bfs ps mps mqs
  | otherwise  = bfs (p:ps) mps (succs (ms,p) ++ mqs)
```

The additional argument is a temporary frontier used to store successors. When the
first frontier is exhausted the contents of the temporary frontier are installed as the
new frontier. Adding successors to the front of the temporary frontier takes time
proportional to the number of successors, not to the size of the frontier, and that
leads to a faster algorithm. On the other hand, the new version of bfs is not the
same as the old one because successive frontiers are traversed alternately from left
to right and from right to left. Nevertheless a shortest solution will still be found if
one exists.

The second source of inefficiency is the membership test. Use of a list to store
previously explored positions is slow because the membership test can take time
proportional to the number of currently explored positions. It would all be easier
if positions were integers in the range $[0..n-1]$ for some n, for then we could
use a boolean array with bounds $(0, n-1)$ to tick off positions as they arise. The
membership test would then consist of a single array lookup.

One can imagine coding positions as integers, but not as integers in an initial segment of the natural numbers. For instance, a Sudoku position (see Chapter 5) can
be expressed as an integer consisting of 81 digits. So suppose we have a function

```
encode :: Position -> Integer
```

that encodes positions as integers. To reduce the range we can define

```
hash :: Position -> Int
hash p = fromInteger (encode p) `mod` n
```

for some suitable n :: Int. The result of hash is then an integer in the range
[0..n-1].

The one hitch, and it's a big one, is that two distinct positions may hash to the same integer. To solve this problem we abandon the idea of having an array of booleans, and instead have an array of lists of positions. The positions in the array at index k are all those whose hash value is k. There is no guarantee that any of this will improve efficiency in the worst case, but if we allow n to be reasonably large, and trust that the hash function assigns integers to positions in a reasonably evenly distributed way, then the complexity of a membership test is reduced by a factor of n.

With this hashing scheme the revised code for solve is:

```
solve :: Maybe [Move]
solve = runST $
        do {pa <- newArray (0,n-1) [];
            bfs pa [([],start)] []}

bfs :: STArray s Int [Position] -> Frontier ->
        Frontier -> ST s (Maybe [Move])
bfs pa [] []  = return Nothing
bfs pa [] mqs = bfs pa mqs []
bfs pa ((ms,p):mps) mqs
  = if solved p then return (Just (reverse ms))
    else do {ps <- readArray pa k;
             if p `elem` ps
             then bfs pa mps mqs
             else
             do {writeArray pa k (p:ps);
                 bfs pa mps (succs (ms,p) ++ mqs)}}
    where k = hash p
```

10.6 Immutable arrays

We cannot leave the subject of arrays without mentioning a very nice Haskell library Data.Array that provides purely functional operations on immutable arrays. The operations are implemented using mutable arrays, but the interface is purely functional.

The type Array i e is an abstract type of arrays with indices of type i and elements of type e. One basic operation for constructing arrays is

```
array :: Ix i => (i,i) -> [(i,e)] -> Array i e
```

This function take a pair of bounds, the lowest and highest indices in the array, and a list of index-element pairs specifying the array entries. The result is an array with the given bounds and entries. Any entry missing from the association list is deemed to be the undefined entry. If two entries have the same index, or one of the indices is out of bounds, the undefined array is returned. Because of these checks, array construction is strict in the indices, though lazy in the elements. Building the array takes linear time in the number of entries.

A simple variant of `array` is `listArray` which takes just a list of elements:

```
listArray :: Ix i => (i,i) -> [e] -> Array i e
listArray (l,r) xs = array (l,r) (zip [l..r] xs)
```

Finally, there is another way of building arrays called `accumArray` whose type appears rather daunting:

```
Ix i => (e -> v -> e) -> e -> (i,i) -> [(i,v)] -> Array i e
```

The first argument is an 'accumulating' function for transforming array entries and new values into new entries. The second argument is an initial entry for each index. The third argument is a pair of bounds, and the fourth and final argument is an association list of index–value pairs. The result is an array built by processing the association list from left to right, combining entries and values into new entries using the accumulating function. The process takes linear time in the length of the association list, assuming the accumulating function takes constant time.

That's what `accumArray` does in words. In symbols,

```
elems (accumArray f e (l,r) ivs)
   = [foldl f e [v | (i,v) <- ivs, i==j] | j <- [l..r]]
```

where `elems` returns the list of elements of an array in index order. Well, the identity above is not quite true: there is an additional restriction on `ivs`, namely that every index should lie in the specified range. If this condition is not met, then the left-hand side returns an error while the right-hand side does not.

Complicated as `accumArray` seems, it turns out to be a very useful tool for solving certain kinds of problem. Here are two examples. First, consider the problem of representing directed graphs. Directed graphs are usually described in mathematics in terms of a set of *vertices* and a set of *edges*. An edge is an ordered pair (j, k) of vertices signifying that the edge is directed from j to k. We say that k is *adjacent* to j. We will suppose that vertices are named by integers in the range 1 to n for some n. Thus

```
type Vertex = Int
```

```
type Edge    = (Vertex,Vertex)
type Graph   = ([Vertex],[Edge])

vertices g = fst g
edges g    = snd g
```

In computing, directed graphs are often described in terms of adjacency lists:

```
adjs :: Graph -> Vertex -> [Vertex]
adjs g v = [k | (j,k) <- edges g, j==v]
```

The problem with this definition of `adjs` is that it takes time proportional to the number of edges to compute the adjacency list of any particular vertex. Better is to implement `adjs` as an array:

```
adjArray :: Graph -> Array Vertex [Vertex]
```

Then we have

```
adjs g v = (adjArray g)!v
```

where `(!)` denotes the operation of array-indexing. For reasonably sized arrays this operation takes constant time.

The specification of `adjArray` is that

```
elems (adjArray g)
  = [[k | (j,k) <- edges g, j==v] | v <- vertices g]
```

Using this specification we can calculate a direct definition of `adjArray`. To keep each line short, abbreviate `edges g` to `es` and `vertices g` to `vs`, so

```
elems (adjArray g) = [[k | (j,k) <- es, j==v] | v <- vs]
```

Concentrating on the right-hand side, the first step is to rewrite it using the law `foldr (:) [] = id`. That gives the expression

```
[foldr (:) [] [k | (j,k) <- es, j==v] | v <- vs]
```

Next we use the law `foldr f e xs = foldl (flip f) e (reverse xs)` for all finite lists `xs`. Abbreviating `flip (:)` to `(@)`, we obtain

```
[foldl (@) [] (reverse [k | (j,k) <- es, j==v]) | v <- vs]
```

Distributing `reverse` we obtain the expression

```
[foldl (@) [] [k | (j,k) <- reverse es, j==v] | v <- vs]
```

Next we use `swap (j,k) = (k,j)` to obtain

```
    [foldl (@) [] [j | (k,j) <- es', j==v] | v <- vs]
```

where es' = map swap (reverse es). Finally, using n = length vs and the
specification of accumArray, we obtain

```
      elems (adjArray g)
   = elems (accumArray (flip (:)) [] (1,n) es')
```

That means we can define

```
   adjArray g = accumArray (flip (:)) [] (1,n) es
                where n  = length (vertices g)
                      es = map swap (reverse (edges g))
```

This definition of adjArray g computes the successors in time proportional to the
number of edges.

Here is the second example of the use of accumArray. Suppose we are given a list
of n integers, all in the range $(0, m)$ for some m. We can sort this list in $\Theta(m+n)$
steps by counting the number of times each element occurs:

```
   count :: [Int] -> Array Int Int
   count xs = accumArray (+) 0 (0,m) (zip xs (repeat 1))
```

The value repeat 1 is an infinite list of 1s. Counting takes $\Theta(n)$ steps. Having
counted the elements, we can now sort them:

```
   sort xs = concat [replicate c x
                    | (x,c) <- assocs (count xa)]
```

The function assocs is yet another library function and returns the list of index–
element pairs of an array in index order. The sorting is completed in $\Theta(m)$ steps.

As well as the above operations Data.Array contains one or two more, including
the update operation (//):

```
   (//) :: Ix i => Array i e -> [(i,e)] -> Array i e
```

For example, if xa is an $n \times n$ matrix, then

```
   xa // [((i,i),0) | i <- [1..n]]
```

is the same matrix except with zeros along the diagonal. The downside of (//) is
that it takes time proportional to the size of the array, even for an update involving
a single element. The reason is that a completely new array has to be constructed
because the old array xa continues to exist.

We have ended the chapter back in the world of pure functional programming, where equational reasoning can be used both to calculate definitions and to optimise them. Although the monadic style is attractive to programmers who are used to imperative programming, there remains the problem of how to reason about monadic programs. True, equational reasoning is still possible in certain situtations (see Exercise F for an example), but it is not so widely applicable as it is in the pure functional world (witness the correctness of the partition phase of Quicksort). Imperative programmers have the same problem, which they solve (if they bother to) by using predicate calculus, preconditions, postconditions and loop invariants. How to reason directly with monadic code is still a topic of ongoing research.

Our best advice is to use the monadic style sparingly and only when it is really useful; otherwise the most important aspect of functional programming, the ability to reason mathematically about its constructs, is lost.

10.7 Exercises

Exercise A

Recall that

```
putStr = foldr (>>) done . map putChar
```

What does

```
foldl (>>) done . map putChar
```

do? Justify your answer by expressing (>>) in terms of (>>=) and appealing to the monad laws.

Exercise B

Using a pattern-matching style, define a function

```
add3 :: Maybe Int -> Maybe Int -> Maybe Int -> Maybe Int
```

that adds three numbers, provided all of them exist. Now rewrite add3 using the Maybe monad.

Exercise C

The monadic definition of cp in Section 10.1 is still inefficient. We might prefer to write

```
cp (xs:xss) = do {ys <- cp xss;
                  x <- xs;
                  return (x:ys)}
```

By definition a *commutative* monad is one in which the equation

```
  do {x <- p; y <- q; f x y}
= do {y <- q; x <- p; f x y}
```

holds. The IO monad is certainly not commutative, while some other monads are. Is the Maybe monad commutative?

Exercise D

Every monad is a functor. Complete the definition

```
instance Monad m => Functor m where
  fmap :: (a -> b) -> m a -> m b
  fmap f = ...
```

Currently Haskell does not insist that the Monad class should be a subclass of Functor, though there are plans to change this in future releases. Instead, Haskell provides a function liftM equivalent to fmap for monads. Give a definition of liftM in terms of return and >>=.

The function join :: m (m a) -> m a flattens two layers of monadic structure into one. Define join in terms of >>=. What familiar functions do join and liftM give for the list monad?

Finally, using join and liftM, define (>>=). It follows that instead of defining monads in terms of return and >>=, we can also define them in terms of return, liftM and join.

Exercise E

A number of useful monadic functions are provided in the Control.Monad library. For instance:

```
sequence_ :: Monad m => [m a] -> m ()
sequence_ = foldr (>>)  done
```

(The underscore convention is used in a number of places in Haskell to signify that the result of the action is the null tuple.) Define the related function

```
sequence :: Monad m => [m a] -> m [a]
```

Using these two functions, define

```
mapM_ :: Monad m => (a -> m b) -> [a] -> m ()
mapM  :: Monad m => (a -> m b) -> [a] -> m [b]
```

Also, define

```
foldM :: Monad m => (b -> a -> m b) -> b -> [a] -> m b
```

In the text we made use of a function `repeatFor` n that repeated an action n times. Generalise this function to

```
for_ :: Monad m => [a] -> (a -> m b) -> m ()
```

Exercise F

Here is an exercise in monadic equational reasoning. Consider the function

```
add :: Int -> State Int ()
add n = do {m <- get; put (m+n)}
```

The task is to prove that

```
sequence_ . map add = add . sum
```

where `sequence_` was defined in the previous exercise and `sum` sums a list of integers. You will need the fusion law of `foldr`, some simple laws of `put` and `get`, and the monad law

```
do {stmts1} >> do {stmts2} = do {stmts1;stmts2}
```

which is valid provided the variables in `stmts1` and `stmts2` are disjoint.

Exercise G

Prove the leapfrog rule: `(f >=> g) . h = (f . h) >=> g`.

Using this rule, prove: `(return . h) >=> g = g . h`.

Exercise H

Prove that

```
liftM f = id >=> (return . f)
join    = id >=> id
```

A fourth way of describing the monad laws is in terms of the two functions `liftM` and `join` of Exercise D. There are seven laws governing these two functions, all of which have a familiar ring:

```
liftM id     = id
liftM (f . g) = liftM f . liftM g

liftM f . return = return . f
liftM f . join   = join . liftM (liftM f)

join . return       = id
join . liftM return = id
join . liftM join   = join . join
```

Prove the fourth rule.

Exercise I

What does build [] do (see Section 10.3)?

Exercise J

Write an interactive program to play hangman. An example session:

```
ghci> hangman
I am thinking of a word:
-----
Try and guess it.
guess: break
-a---
guess: parties
Wrong number of letters!
guess: party
-appy
guess: happy
You got it!
Play again? (yes or no)
no
Bye!
```

Assume that a list of secret words is stored in a file called Words, so that the action xs <- readFile "Words" reads the file as a list of characters. By the way, readFile is lazy in that its contents are read on demand.

Exercise K

Write another version of fib in terms of a fibST that uses a single STRef.

Exercise L

One way of defining the greatest common divisor (gcd) of two positive integers is:

```
gcd (x,y) | x==y = x
          | x<y  = gcd (x,y-x)
          | x>y  = gcd (x-y,y)
```

Translate this definition into two other programs, one of which uses the State monad and the other the ST monad.

Exercise M

Here is a concrete puzzle you can solve using breadth-first search. A cut-down version of Sam Loyd's famous 15 puzzle is the 8 puzzle. You are given a 3×3 array containing tiles numbered from 1 to 8 and one blank space. You move by sliding an adjacent tile into the blank space. Depending on where the blank space is, you can slide tiles upwards, downwards, to the left or to the right. At the start the blank space is in the top left corner and the tiles read from 1 to 8. At the end the blank space is in the bottom right corner, but the tiles are still neatly arranged in the order 1 to 8.

Your mission, should you choose to accept it, is to settle on a suitable representation of positions and moves, and to define the functions moves, move, solved and encode.

10.8 Answers

Answer to Exercise A

We claim that (>>) :: IO () -> IO () -> IO () is associative with identity element done. That means

```
putStr xs = foldl (>>) done (map putChar xs)
```

for all finite strings xs

We concentrate on the proof of associativity. Firstly, for actions in IO () we have

```
p >> q = p >>= const q
```

where const x y = x. Now we can reason:

$$(p >> q) >> r$$

$$= \quad \{\text{definition of } (>>)\}$$

$$(p >>= \text{const } q) >>= \text{const } r$$

$$= \quad \{\text{third monad law}\}$$

$$p >>= \text{const } (q >>= \text{const } r)$$

$$= \quad \{\text{definition of } (>>)\}$$

$$p >>= \text{const } (q >> r)$$

$$= \quad \{\text{definition of } (>>)\}$$

$$p >> (q >> r)$$

Answer to Exercise B

The direct version uses pattern matching with a wild-card:

```
add3 Nothing _ _              = Nothing
add3 (Just x) Nothing _       = Nothing
add3 (Just x) (Just y) Nothing = Nothing
add3 (Just x) (Just y) (Just z) = Just (x+y+z)
```

This definition ensures that add Nothing undefined = Nothing.

The monadic version reads:

```
add3 mx my mz
 = do {x <- mx; y <- my; z <- mz;
       return (x + y + z)}
```

Answer to Exercise C

Yes. The commutative law states that

```
  p >>= \x -> q >>= \y -> f x y
= q >>= \y -> p >>= \x -> f x y
```

In the Maybe monad there are four possible cases to check. For example, both sides simplify to Nothing if p = Nothing and q = Just y, . The other cases are similar.

Answer to Exercise D

We have

```
fmap f p = p >>= (return . f)
join p   = p >>= id
```

For the list monad we have liftM = map and join = concat.

In the other direction

```
p >>= f = join (liftM f p)
```

Answer to Exercise E

The function sequence is defined by

```
sequence :: Monad m => [m a] -> m [a]
sequence = foldr k (return [])
  where k p q = do {x <- p; xs <- q; return (x:xs)}
```

The two new map functions are:

```
mapM_ f = sequence_ . map f
mapM f  = sequence . map f
```

The function foldM is defined by

```
foldM :: Monad m => (b -> a -> m b) ->
         b -> [a] -> m b
foldM f e []     = return e
foldM f e (x:xs) = do {y <- f e x; foldM f y xs}
```

Note that foldM is analogous to foldl in that it works from left to right. Finally for = flip mapM_.

Answer to Exercise F

The first thing to note is that

```
  sequence_ . map add
= foldr (>>) done . map add
= foldr ((>>) . add) done
```

using the fusion law of foldr and map given in Section 6.3. Moreover,

```
((>>) . add) n p = add n >> p
```

Since sum = foldr (+) 0 that means we have to prove

```
foldr (\ n p -> add n >> p) = add . foldr (+) 0
```

That looks like an instance of the fusion law of foldr. We therefore have to show that add is strict (which it is), and

```
add 0 = done
add (n + n') = add n >> add n'
```

Here goes:

$$
\begin{aligned}
&\texttt{add 0} \\
=\ &\{\text{definition}\} \\
&\texttt{do \{m <- get; put (m+0)\}} \\
=\ &\{\text{arithmetic}\} \\
&\texttt{do \{m <- get; put m\}} \\
=\ &\{\text{simple law of put and get}\} \\
&\texttt{done}
\end{aligned}
$$

That disposes of the first condition. For the second we start with the more complicated side and reason:

$$
\begin{aligned}
&\texttt{add n >> add n'} \\
=\ &\{\text{definition}\} \\
&\texttt{do \{l <- get; put (l + n) \} >>} \\
&\texttt{do \{m <- get; put (m + n')\}} \\
=\ &\{\text{monad law}\} \\
&\texttt{do \{l <- get; put (l + n); m <- get; put (m + n')\}} \\
=\ &\{\text{simple law of put and get}\} \\
&\texttt{do \{l <- get; put ((l + n) + n')\}} \\
=\ &\{\text{associativity of (+); definition of add}\} \\
&\texttt{add (n + n')}
\end{aligned}
$$

Answer to Exercise G

We can reason:

$$
\begin{aligned}
&\texttt{(f >=> g) (h x)} \\
=\ &\{\text{definition of (>=>)}\} \\
&\texttt{f (h x) >>= g} \\
=\ &\{\text{definition of (>=>)}\} \\
&\texttt{(f . h >=> g) x}
\end{aligned}
$$

For the second part:

$$(\texttt{return . h}) \texttt{ >=> } \texttt{g}$$

$$= \quad \{\text{leapfrog rule}\}$$

$$(\texttt{return >=> g}) \texttt{ . h}$$

$$= \quad \{\text{monad law}\}$$

$$\texttt{g . h}$$

Answer to Exercise H

For the fourth rule we simplify both sides. For the left-hand side:

$$\texttt{liftM f . join}$$

$$= \quad \{\text{definitions}\}$$

$$(\texttt{id >=> (return . f)) . (id >=> id)}$$

$$= \quad \{\text{leapfrog rule and } \texttt{id . f = f}\}$$

$$(\texttt{id >=> id}) \texttt{ >=> (return . f)}$$

For the right-hand side:

$$\texttt{join . liftM (liftM f)}$$

$$= \quad \{\text{definitions}\}$$

$$(\texttt{id >=> id}) \texttt{ . (id >=> return . (id >=> (return . f)))}$$

$$= \quad \{\text{leapfrog rule, and associativity of } (\texttt{>=>})\}$$

$$\texttt{id >=> (return . (id >=> (return . f))) >=> id}$$

$$= \quad \{\text{since } (\texttt{return . h}) \texttt{ >=> g = g . h}\}$$

$$\texttt{id >=> id >=> (return . f)}$$

The two sides are equal because (>=>) is associative.

Answer to Exercise I

build [] causes an infinite loop, so its value is $\bot$.

Answer to Exercise J

For the main function we can define

```
hangman :: IO ()
hangman = do {xs <- readFile "Words";
              play (words xs)}
```

The function `play` plays as many rounds of the game as desired with different words from the file (which we quietly suppose always has enough words):

```
play (w:ws)
= do {putStrLn "I am thinking of a word:";
      putStrLn (replicate (length w) '-');
      putStrLn "Try and guess it.";
      guess w ws}
```

The function guess deals with a single guess, but keeps the remaining words for any subsequent round of play:

```
guess w ws
= do {putStr "guess: ";
      w' <- getLine;
      if length w' /= length w then
      do {putStrLn "Wrong number of letters!";
          guess w ws}
      else if w' == w
      then
      do {putStrLn "You got it!";
          putStrLn "Play again? (yes or no)";
          ans <- getLine;
          if ans == "yes"
          then play ws
          else putStrLn "Bye!"}
      else do {putStrLn (match w' w);
               guess w ws}}
```

Finally we program match:

```
match w' w = map check w
  where
  check x = if x `elem` w' then x else '-'
```

Answer to Exercise K

The following program is correct but doesn't run in constant space:

```
fib n = fst $ runST (fibST n)

fibST :: Int -> ST s (Integer,Integer)
fibST n = do {ab <- newSTRef (0,1);
```

```
        repeatFor n
         (do {(a,b) <- readSTRef ab;
                 writeSTRef ab $! (b,a+b)});
       readSTRef ab}
```

The reason is that (b,a+b) is already in head-normal form, so strict-apply has no effect. The penultimate line needs to be changed to

```
    b `seq` (a+b) `seq` writeSTRef ab (b,a+b)
```

in order to force evaluation of the components.

Answer to Exercise L

The version that uses the State monad:

```
    gcd (x,y) = fst $ runState loop (x,y)

    loop :: State (Int,Int) Int
    loop = do {(x,y) <- get;
               if x == y
               then return x
               else if x < y
               then do {put (x,y-x); loop}
               else do {put (x-y,y); loop}}
```

The version that uses the ST monad:

```
    gcd (x,y) = runST $
              do {a <- newSTRef x;
                  b <- newSTRef y;
                  loop a b}

    loop :: STRef s Int -> STRef s Int -> ST s Int
    loop a b
     = do {x <- readSTRef a;
           y <- readSTRef b;
           if x==y
           then return x
           else if x<y
           then do {writeSTRef b (y-x);loop a b}
           else do {writeSTRef a (x-y);loop a b}}
```

Answer to Exercise M

There are, of course, many possible answers. The one I chose was to represent the array of tiles by a list of nine digits $[0 .. 8]$ with zero representing the space. To avoid recalculation, a position is represented by a pair (j, ks) with j as the position of the zero in ks, where ks was some permutation of $[0 .. 8]$. Thus:

```
type Position = (Int,[Int])
data Move     = Up | Down | Left | Right

encode :: Position -> Integer
encode (j,ks) = foldl op 0 ks
  where op x d = 10*x + fromIntegral d

start :: Position
start = (0,[0..8])
```

The function moves can be defined by

```
moves :: Position -> [Move]
moves (j,ks)
  = [Up    | j `notElem` [6,7,8]] ++
    [Down  | j `notElem` [0,1,2]] ++
    [Left  | j `notElem` [2,5,8]] ++
    [Right | j `notElem` [0,3,6]]
```

Up moves are allowed except for a blank in the bottom row; down moves except for a blank in the top row, left moves except for a blank in the rightmost column, and right moves except for a blank in the leftmost column.

The function move can be defined by:

```
move :: Position -> Move -> Position
move (j,ks) Up    = (j+3,swap (j,j+3) ks)
move (j,ks) Down  = (j-3,swap (j-3,j) ks)
move (j,ks) Left  = (j+1,swap (j,j+1) ks)
move (j,ks) Right = (j-1,swap (j-1,j) ks)

swap (j,k) ks = ks1 ++ y:ks3 ++ x:ks4
  where (ks1,x:ks2) = splitAt j ks
        (ks3,y:ks4) = splitAt (k-j-1) ks2
```

Finally,

```
solved :: Position -> Bool
solved p = p == (8,[1,2,3,4,5,6,7,8,0])
```

My computer produced:

```
ghci> solve start
Just [Left,Up,Right,Up,Left,Left,Down,
      Right,Right,Up,Left,Down,Down,Left,
      Up,Up,Right,Right,Down,Left,Left,Up]
(4.84 secs, 599740496 bytes)
```

10.9 Chapter notes

Read *The History of Haskell* to see how monads came to be an integral part of Haskell, and why this idea has been mainly responsible for the increasing use of Haskell in the real world. Monads are used to structure GHC, which itself is written in Haskell. Each phase of the compiler uses a monad for book-keeping information. For instance, the type checker uses a monad that combines state (to maintain a current substitution), a name supply (for fresh type variable names) and exceptions.

Use of do-notation in preference to (>>=) was suggested by John Launchbury in 1993 and was first implemented by Mark Jones in Gofer.

The number of tutorials on monads has increased steadily over the years; see

```
haskell.org/haskellwiki/Monad_tutorials
```

for a reasonably comprehensive list.

The example (in Exercise F) of monadic equational reasoning can be found in the paper 'Unifying theories of programming with monads', (UTP Symposium, August 2012) by Jeremy Gibbons. For additional material on reasoning equationally with monads, read 'Just do it: simple monadic equational reasoning' by Jeremy Gibbons and Ralf Hinze, which appeared in the proceedings of the 2011 International Conference of Functional Programming. Both papers can be found at

```
www.cs.ox.ac.uk/people/jeremy.gibbons/publications/
```

Chapter 11

Parsing

A *parser* is a function that analyses a piece of text to determine its logical structure. The text is a string of characters describing some value of interest, such as an arithmetic expression, a poem or a spreadsheet. The output of a parser is a representation of the value, such as a tree of some kind for an arithmetic expression, a list of verses for a poem, or something more complicated for a spreadsheet. Most programming tasks involve decoding the input in some way, so parsing is a pervasive component of computer programming. In this chapter we will describe a monadic approach to parsing, mainly designing simple parsers for expressions of various kinds. We will also say a little more about the converse process of encoding the output as a string; in other words, more about the type class Show. This material will be used in the final chapter.

11.1 Parsers as monads

Parsers return different values of interest, so as a first cut we can think of a parser as a function that takes a string and returns a value:

```
type Parser a = String -> a
```

This type is basically the same as that of the standard prelude function

```
read :: Read a => String -> a
```

Indeed, read is a parser, though not a very flexible one. One reason is that all the input must be consumed. Thus:

```
ghci> read "123" :: Int
123
```

```
ghci> read "123+51" :: Int
*** Exception: Prelude.read: no parse
```

With read there is no obvious way of reading two or more things in sequence. For example, in a parser for arithmetic expressions we may want to look in the input stream for a numeral, then an operator and then another numeral. The first parser for a numeral will consume some prefix of the input, the parser for an operator some prefix of the remaining input, and the third parser yet more input. A better idea is to define a parser as a function that consumes a prefix of the input and returns both a value of interest and the unconsumed suffix:

```
type Parser a = String -> (a,String)
```

We are not quite there yet. It can happen that a parser may *fail* on some input. It is not a mistake to construct parsers that can fail. For example, in a parser for arithmetic expressions, we may want to look for either a numeral or an opening parenthesis. One or either of these subsidiary parsers will certainly fail. Failure should not be thought of as an error that terminates the parsing process; rather it acts like an identity element for an operation that chooses between alternatives. More generally, a parser may find a number of different ways that some prefix of the input can be structured. Failure then corresponds to the particular case of the empty sequence of parses. In order to handle these various possibilities, we change our definition yet again and define

```
type Parser a = String -> [(a,String)]
```

The standard prelude provides exactly this type synonym, except that it is called ReadS, not Parser. And it also provides a function

```
reads :: Read a => ReadS a
```

as a subsidiary method in the type class Read. For example,

```
ghci> reads "-123+51" :: [(Int,String)]
[(-123,"+51")]
ghci> reads "+51" :: [(Int,String)]
[]
```

As with the function read you have to tell reads the type you are expecting. The second example fails, returning no parses, because a Haskell integer can be preceded by an optional minus sign but not by an optional plus sign. By definition, a parser is *deterministic* if it returns an empty or singleton list of parses in all possible cases. In particular, instances of reads ought to be deterministic parsers.

There is one further change we have to make to the definition of `Parser`. We would like to install this type as an instance of the `Monad` class, but that is not possible. The reason is that `Parser` is declared as a type synonym, and type synonyms cannot be made members of any type class: they inherit whatever instances are declared for the underlying type. A type synonym is there simply to improve readability in type declarations; no new types are involved and we cannot construct two different type class instances for what is essentially the same type.

One way to construct a new type is by a data declaration:

```
data Parser a = Parser (String -> [(a,String)])
```

The identifier `Parser` on the right is a constructor, while on the left it is the name of a new type. Most people are happy with the pun; others would rename the constructor as something like `MkParser` or just P.

There is a better way to create a new type for `Parser` and that is to use a `newtype` declaration:

```
newtype Parser a = Parser (String -> [(a,String)])
```

We have not needed `newtype` declarations up to now, so let us digress a little to explain them. The price paid for using a `data` declaration for `Parser` is that operations to examine parsers have to be constantly unwrapped and rewrapped with the constructor `Parser`, and this adds to the running time of parser operations. In addition there is an unwanted element of `Parser`, namely `Parser undefined`. In other words, `Parser a` and `String -> [(a,String)]` are not *isomorphic* types. Recognising this, Haskell allows a `newtype` declaration for types defined with a *single* constructor taking a *single* argument. It differs from a type synonym in that it creates a genuinely new type whose values must be expressed using the `Parser` wrapper. But these coercions, though they have to appear in the program text, do not add to the execution time of the program because the Haskell compiler eliminates them before evaluation begins. The values of the new type are systematically replaced by the values in the underlying type. Consequently, `Parser a` and `String -> [(a,String)]` describe isomorphic types, and `Parser undefined` and `undefined` are isomorphic values sharing the same representation. New types, as distinct from synonym types, can be made members of type classes in different ways from the underlying type.

With either kind of declaration we have to provide some way of applying the parsing function, so we define

```
apply :: Parser a -> String -> [(a,String)]
apply (Parser p) s = p s
```

The functions `apply` and `Parser` are mutual inverses and witness the isomorphism.

We also define

```
parse :: Parser a -> String -> a
parse p = fst . head . apply p
```

The function `parse p` returns the first object of the first parse, causing an error if the parser p fails. This is the only place an error might occur.

Now we can define

```
instance Monad Parser where
   return x = Parser (\s -> [(x,s)])
   p >>= q  = Parser (\s -> [(y,s'')
                           | (x,s') <- apply p s,
                             (y,s'') <- apply (q x) s'])
```

In the definition of p `>>=` q the parser p is applied to an input string, producing a list of possible parses each of which is paired with the corresponding unconsumed portion of the input. The parser q is then applied to each parse to produce a list of results whose concatenation provides the final answer. One should also show that the three monad laws hold, a task we will leave as an exercise.

11.2 Basic parsers

Perhaps the simplest basic parser is

```
getc :: Parser Char
getc = Parser f
       where f []     = []
             f (c:cs) = [(c,cs)]
```

This parser returns the first character of the input if there is one. It plays exactly the same role for parsers as `getChar` does for the input–output monad of the previous chapter.

Next, here is a parser for recognising a character that satisfies a given condition:

```
sat :: (Char -> Bool) -> Parser Char
sat p = do {c <- getc;
            if p c then return c
            else fail}
```

where `fail` is defined by

```
fail = Parser (\s -> [])
```

The parser `fail` is another basic parser that returns no parses. The parser `sat p` reads a character and, if it satisfies p, returns the character as the result. The definition of `sat` can be written more briefly by using a little combinator called `guard`:

```
sat p = do {c <- getc; guard (p c); return c}

guard :: Parser ()
guard True  = return ()
guard False = fail
```

To see that these two definitions are the same, observe that if p c is false, then

```
guard (p c) >> return c = fail >> return c = fail
```

Note the use of the law `fail >> p = fail`, whose proof we leave as an exercise. If p c is true, then

```
  guard (p c) >> return c
= return () >> return c
= return c
```

Using *sat* we can define a number of other parsers; for instance

```
char :: Char -> Parser ()
char x = do {c <- sat (==x); return ()}

string :: String -> Parser ()
string []     = return ()
string (x:xs) = do {char x; string xs; return ()}

lower :: Parser Char
lower = sat isLower

digit :: Parser Int
digit = do {d <- sat isDigit; return (cvt d)}
        where cvt d = fromEnum d - fromEnum '0'
```

The parser `char x` looks for the specific character x as the next item in the input string, while `string xs` looks for a specific string; both parsers return () if successful. For example,

```
ghci> apply (string "hell") "hello"
[((),"o")]
```

The parser `digit` looks for a digit character and returns the corresponding integer if successful. The parser `lower` looks for a lowercase letter, returning such a letter if found.

11.3 Choice and repetition

In order to define more sophisticated parsers we need operations for choosing between alternative parsers and for repeating parsers. One such alternation operator is (<|>), defined by

```
    (<|>) :: Parser a -> Parser a -> Parser a
    p <|> q = Parser f
             where f s = let ps = apply p s in
                           if null ps then apply q s
                           else ps
```

Thus p <|> q returns the same parses as p unless p fails, in which case the parses of q are returned. If both p and q are deterministic, then so is p <|> q. For another choice of <|> see the exercises. We claim that <|> is associative with `fail` as its identity element, but again we relegate the proof as an exercise.

Here is a parser for recognising a string of lowercase letters:

```
    lowers :: Parser String
    lowers = do {c <- lower; cs <- lowers; return (c:cs)}
             <|> return ""
```

To see how this parser works, suppose the input is the string 'Upper'. In this case the parser on the left of <|> fails because 'U' is not a lowercase letter. However, the parser on the right succeeds, so

```
ghci> apply lowers "Upper"
[("","Upper")]
```

With input string 'isUpper', the left-hand parser succeeds, so

```
ghci> apply lowers "isUpper"
[("is","Upper")]
```

Use of the choice operator < | > requires care. For example, consider a very simple form of arithmetic expression that consists of either a single digit or a digit followed by a plus sign followed by another digit. Here is a possible parser:

```
wrong :: Parser Int
wrong = digit <|> addition

addition :: Parser Int
addition = do {m <- digit; char '+'; n <- digit;
               return (m+n)}
```

We have

```
ghci> apply wrong "1+2"
[(1,"+2")]
```

The parser `digit` succeeds, so `addition` is not invoked. But what we really wanted was to return `[(3,"")]`, absorbing as much of the input as possible. One way to correct `wrong` is to rewrite it in the form

```
better = addition <|> digit
```

Then on 1+2 the parser `addition` succeeds, returning the result we want. What is wrong with `better` is that it is inefficient: applied to the input 1 it parses the digit but fails to find a subsequent plus sign, so parser `addition` fails. As a result `digit` is invoked and the input is parsed again from scratch. Not really a problem with a single digit, but the repetition of effort could be costly if we were parsing for a numeral that could contain many digits.

The best solution is to *factor* the parser for digits out of the two component parsers:

```
best   = digit >>= rest
rest m = do {char '+'; n <- digit; return (m+n)}
         <|> return m
```

The argument to `rest` is just an accumulating parameter. We saw essentially the same solution in the chapter on pretty-printing. Factoring parsers to bring out common prefixes is a Good Idea to improve efficiency.

Generalising from the definition of `lowers`, we can define a parser combinator that repeats a parser zero or more times:

```
many :: Parser a -> Parser [a]
many p = do {x <- p; xs <- many p; return (x:xs)}
         <|> none
```

```
none = return []
```

The value none is different from fail (why?). We can now define

```
lowers = many lower
```

In many applications, so-called *white space* (sequences of space, newline and tab characters) can appear between *tokens* (identifiers, numbers, opening and closing parentheses, and so on) just to make the text easier to read. The parser space recognises white space:

```
space :: Parser ()
space = many (sat isSpace) >> return ()
```

The function isSpace is defined in the library Data.Char. The function

```
symbol :: String -> Parser ()
symbol xs = space >> string xs
```

ignores white space before recognising a given string. More generally we can define

```
token :: Parser a -> Parser a
token p =  space >> p
```

for ignoring white space before invoking a parser. Note that

```
token p <|> token q = token (p <|> q)
```

but the right-hand parser is more efficient as it does not look for white space twice if the first parser fails.

Sometimes we want to repeat a parser one or more times rather than zero or more times. This can be done by a combinator which we will call some (it is also called many1 in some parser libraries):

```
some :: Parser a -> Parser [a]
some p = do {x <- p; xs <- many p; return (x:xs)}
```

This definition repeats that of the first parser in the definition of many, a fact we can take into account by redefining many in terms of some:

```
many :: Parser a -> Parser [a]
many p = optional (some p)

optional :: Parser [a] -> Parser [a]
optional p = p <|> none
```

The parsers many and some are now mutually recursive.

Here is a parser for natural numbers, one that allows white space before the number:

```
natural :: Parser Int
natural = token nat
nat = do {ds <- some digit;
          return (foldl1 shiftl ds)}
      where shiftl m n = 10*m+n
```

The subsidiary parser nat does not allow white space before the number.

Consider now how to define a parser for an *integer* numeral, which by definition is a nonempty string of digits possibly prefixed by a minus sign. You might think that the parser

```
int :: Parser Int
int = do {symbol "-"; n <- natural; return (-n)}
      <|> natural
```

does the job, but it is inefficient (see Exercise H) and may or may not be what we want. For example,

```
ghci> apply int "  -34"
[(-34,"")]
ghci> apply int "  - 34"
[(-34,"")]
```

Whereas we are quite happy with white space before a numeral, we may not want any white space to appear between the minus sign and the ensuing digits. If that is the case, then the above parser will not do. It is easy to modify the given definition of int to give what we want:

```
int :: Parser Int
int = do {symbol "-"; n <- nat; return (-n)}
      <|> natural
```

This parser is still inefficient, and a better alternative is to define

```
int :: Parser Int
int = do {space; f <- minus; n <- nat; return (f n)}
  where
  minus = (char '-' >> return negate) <|> return id
```

The parser minus returns a function, either negate if the first symbol is a minus sign, or the identity function otherwise.

Next, let us parse a list of integers, separated by commas and enclosed in square brackets. White space is allowed before and after commas and brackets though not of course between the digits of the integers. Here is a very short definition:

```
ints :: Parser [Int]
ints = bracket (manywith (symbol ",") int)
```

The subsidiary parser bracket deals with the brackets:

```
bracket :: Parser a -> Parser a
bracket p = do {symbol "[";
                x <- p;
                symbol "]";
                return x}
```

The function manywith sep p acts a bit like many p but differs in that the instances of p are separated by instances of sep whose results are ignored. The definition is

```
manywith :: Parser b -> Parser a -> Parser [a]
manywith q p = optional (somewith q p)

somewith :: Parser b -> Parser a -> Parser [a]
somewith q p = do {x <- p;
                   xs <- many (q >> p);
                   return (x:xs)}
```

For example,

```
ghci> apply ints "[2, -3, 4]"
[([2,-3,4],"")]
ghci> apply ints "[2, -3, +4]"
[]
ghci> apply ints "[]"
[([],"")]
```

Integers cannot be preceded by a plus sign, so parsing the second expression fails.

11.4 Grammars and expressions

The combinators described so far are sufficiently powerful for translating a structural description of what is required directly into a functional parser. Such a struc-

tural description is provided by a *grammar*. We will illustrate some typical gram-
mars by looking at parsers for various kinds of arithmetic expression.

Let us start by building a parser for the type `Expr`, defined by

```
data Expr = Con Int | Bin Op Expr Expr
data Op   = Plus | Minus
```

Here is a grammar for fully parenthesised expressions, expressed in what is known
as *Backus-Naur form*, or BNF for short:

```
expr  ::= nat | '(' expr op expr ')'
op    ::= '+' | '-'
nat   ::= {digit}+
digit ::= '0' | '1' | ... | '9'
```

This grammar defines four *syntactic categories*. Symbols enclosed in quotes are
called *terminal* symbols and describe themselves; these are symbols that actually
occur in the text. There are ten possible characters for a digit, and a `nat` is defined
as a sequence of one or more digits. The meta-symbol `{-}+` describes a non-zero
repetition of a syntactic category. Note that we do not allow an optional minus
sign before a sequence of digits, so constants are natural numbers, not arbitrary
integers. The grammar states that an expression is either a natural number or else
a compound expression consisting of an opening parenthesis, followed by an expression, followed by either a plus or minus sign, followed by another expression,
and finally followed by a closing parenthesis. It is implicitly understood in the description that white space is ignored between terminal symbols except between the
digits of a number. The grammar translates directly into a parser for expressions:

```
expr :: Parser Expr
expr = token (constant <|> paren binary)
constant = do {n <- nat; return (Con n)}
binary = do {e1 <- expr;
             p <- op;
             e2 <- expr;
             return (Bin p e1 e2)}
op = (symbol "+" >> return Plus) <|>
     (symbol "-" >> return Minus)
```

For readability we have made use of a subsidiary parser `binary`; the parser `paren`
is left as an exercise.

Now suppose we want a parser that also works for expressions that are not fully
parenthesised, things like `6-2-3` and `6-(2-3)` and `(6-2)-3`. In such a case, `(+)`

and (-) should associate to the left in expressions, as is normal with arithmetic. One way to express such a grammar in BNF is to write

```
expr ::= expr op term | term
term ::= nat | '(' expr ')'
```

This grammar says that an expression is a sequence of one or more terms separated by operators. A term is either a number or a parenthesised expression. In particular, 6-2-3 will be parsed as the expression 6-2 followed by a minus operator, followed by the term 3. In other words, the same as (6-2)-3, as required. This grammar also translates directly into a parser:

```
expr = token (binary <|> term)
binary = do {e1 <- expr;
             p  <- op;
             e2 <- term;
             return (Bin p e1 e2)}
term = token (constant <|> paren expr)
```

However, there is a fatal flaw with this parser: it falls into an infinite loop. After ignoring initial white space the first action of expr is to invoke the parser binary, whose first action is to invoke the parser expr again. Whoops!

Furthermore, it will not do to rewrite expr as

```
expr = token (term <|> binary)
```

because, for example,

```
Main*> apply expr "3+4"
[(Con 3,"+4")]
```

Only the first term is parsed. The problem is called the *left recursion* problem and is a difficulty with all recursive parsers, functional or otherwise.

One solution is to rewrite the grammar in the following equivalent form:

```
expr ::= term {op term}*
```

The meta-symbol {-}* indicates a syntactic category that can be repeated zero or more times. The new parser then takes the form

```
expr = token (term >>= rest)
rest e1 = do {p <- op;
              e2 <- term;
              rest (Bin p e1 e2)} <|> return e1
```

The parser `rest` corresponds to the category {op term}* and takes an argument (an accumulating parameter) whose value is the expression parsed so far.

Finally, let us design a parser for arithmetic expressions that may contain multiplication and division, changing the definition of Op to

```
data Op = Plus | Minus | Mul | Div
```

The usual rules apply in that multiplication and division take precedence over addition and subtraction, and operations of the same precedence associate to the left. Here is a grammar:

```
expr ::= term {addop term}*
term ::= factor {mulop factor}*
factor ::= nat | '(' expr ')'
addop ::= '+' | '-'
mulop ::= '*' | '/'
```

And here is the parser:

```
expr = token (term >>= rest)
rest e1 = do {p <- addop;
              e2 <- term;
              rest (Bin p e1 e2)}
         <|> return e1
term = token (factor >>= more)
more e1 = do {p <- mulop;
              e2 <- factor;
              more (Bin p e1 e2)}
         <|> return e1
factor = token (constant <|> paren expr)
```

The definitions of addop and mulop are left as exercises.

11.5 Showing expressions

Our final question is: how can we install `Expr` as a member of the type class `Show` so that the function `show` is the inverse of parsing? More precisely, we want to define `show` so that

```
parse expr (show e) = e
```

Recall that `parse p` extracts the first parse returned by `apply p`.

As a warm-up, here is the instance of Show when expr is the parser for fully parenthesised expressions involving addition and subtraction only:

```
instance Show Expr where
  show (Con n) = show n
  show (Bin op e1 e2) =
    = "(" ++ show e1 ++
      " " ++ showop op ++
      " " ++ show e2 ++ ")"
showop Plus = "+"
showop Minus = "-"
```

Clear enough, but there is a problem with efficiency. Because (++) has time complexity linear in the length of its left argument, the cost of evaluating show is, in the worst case, quadratic in the size of the expression.

The solution, yet again, is to use an accumulating parameter. Haskell provides a type synonym ShowS:

```
type ShowS = String -> String
```

and also the following subsidiary functions

```
showChar   :: Char -> ShowS
showString :: String -> ShowS
showParen  :: Bool -> ShowS -> ShowS
```

These functions are defined by

```
showChar      = (:)
showString    = (++)
showParen p x = if b then
                  showChar '(' . p . showChar ')'
                else p
```

Now we can define show for expressions by

```
show e = shows e ""
  where
  shows (Con n) = showString (show n)
  shows (Bin op e1 e2)
    = showParen True (shows e1 . showSpace .
      showsop op . showSpace  . shows e2)
  showsop Plus  = showChar '+'
  showsop Minus = showChar '-'
```

```
showSpace      = showChar ' '
```

This version, which contains no explicit concatenation operations, takes linear time in the size of the expression.

Now suppose we want to display expressions that are not fully parenthesised. There is no need for parentheses around left-hand expressions, but we do need parentheses around right-hand expressions. That leads to

```
show = shows False e ""
 where
 shows b (Con n) = showString (show n)
 shows b (Bin op e1 e2)
  = showParen p (shows False e1 . showSpace .
     showsop op . showSpace . shows True e2)
```

This definition takes no account of associativity; for example, 1+(2+3) is not shown as 1+2+3.

Finally, let's tackle expressions involving all four arithmetic operations. The difference here is that:

1. With expressions e1 + e2 or e1 - e2 we will never need parentheses around e1 (just as above), nor will we need parentheses around e2 if e2 is a compound expression with a multiplication or division at the root.

2. On the other hand, with expressions e1 * e2 or e1 / e2 we will need parentheses around e1 if e1 is a compound expression with a plus or minus at the root, and we will always need parentheses around e2.

One way to codify these rules is to introduce precedence levels (for another way, see Exercise L). Define

```
prec :: Op -> Int
prec Mul   = 2
prec Div   = 2
prec Plus  = 1
prec Minus = 1
```

Consider now how to define a function showsPrec with type

```
showsPrec :: Int -> Expr -> ShowS
```

such that showsPrec p e shows the expression e assuming that the parent of e is a compound expression with an operator of precedence p. We will define show by

```
show e = showsPrec 0 e ""
```

so the enclosing *context* of e is an operator with fictitious precedence 0. We can at once define

```
showsPrec p (Con n) = showString (show n)
```

because constants are never enclosed in parentheses. The interesting case is when we have a compound expression. We give the definition first and explain it afterwards:

```
showsPrec p (Bin op e1 e2)
  = showParen (p>q) (showsPrec q e1 . showSpace .
    showsop op . showSpace . showsPrec (q+1) e2)
    where q = prec op
```

We put parentheses around an expression if the parent operator has greater precedence than the current one. To display the expression e1 it is therefore sufficient to pass the current precedence as the new parent precedence. But we need parentheses around e2 if the root operator of e2 has precedence less than *or equal to* q; so we have to increment q in the second call.

Admittedly, the above definition of showsPrec requires a little thought, but there is a payoff. The type class Show has a *second* method in it, namely showsPrec. Moreover, the default definition of show is just the one above. So to install expressions as a member of Show we merely have to give the definition of showsPrec.

11.6 Exercises

Exercise A

Consider the synonym

```
type Angle = Float
```

Suppose we want to define equality on angles to be equality modulo a multiple of 2π. Why can't we use (==) for this test? Now consider

```
newtype Angle = Angle Float
```

Install Angle as a member of Eq, thereby allowing (==) as an equality test between angles.

Exercise B

We could have defined

```
newtype Parser a = Parser (String -> Maybe (a,String))
```

Give the monad instance of this kind of parser.

Exercise C

Prove that `fail >> p = fail`.

Exercise D

Could we have defined `<|>` in the following way?

```
p <|> q = Parser (\s -> parse p s ++ parse q s)
```

When is the result a deterministic parser? Define a function

```
limit :: Parser a -> Parser a
```

such that `limit (p <|> q)` is a deterministic parser, even if p and q are not.

Exercise E

Parsers are not only instances of monads, they can also be made instances of a more restricted class, called `MonadPlus`, a class we could have introduced in the previous chapter. Basically, these are monads that support choice and failure. The Haskell definition is

```
class Monad m => MonadPlus m where
  mzero :: m a
  mplus :: m a -> m a -> m a
```

As examples, both `[]` and `Maybe` can be made members of `MonadPlus`:

```
instance MonadPlus [] where
  mzero = []
  mplus = (++)

instance MonadPlus Maybe where
  mzero = Nothing
  Nothing `mplus` y = y
  Just x  `mplus` y = Just x
```

Install `Parser` as an instance of `MonadPlus`.

Exercise F

Continuing from the previous exercise, the new methods `mzero` and `mplus` are expected to satisfy some equational laws, as is usually the case with the methods of a type class. But currently the precise set of rules that these methods should obey is not agreed on by the Haskell designers! Uncontroversial are the laws that `mplus` should be associative with identity element `mzero`. That's three equations. Another reasonable law is the *left-zero* law

```
mzero >>= f = mzero
```

The corresponding *right-zero* law, namely

```
p >> mzero = mzero
```

can also be imposed. Does the `MonadPlus` instance of the list monad satisfy these five laws? How about the `Maybe` monad?

Finally, the really contentious law is the following one:

```
(p `mplus` q) >>= f = (p >>= f) `mplus` (q >>= f)
```

This law is call the *left-distribution* law. Why can't `Maybe` be installed as a member of `MonadPlus` if the left-distribution is imposed?

Exercise G

Design a parser for recognising Haskell floating-point numbers. Bear in mind that `.314` is not a legitimate number (no digits before the decimal point) and that `3 . 14` is not legitimate either (because no spaces are allowed before or after the decimal point).

Exercise H

Why are the first and second definitions of `int` given in the text inefficient, compared to the third definition?

Exercise I

Is `"(3)"` a fully parenthesised expression? Is it a non-fully parenthesised expression? Haskell allows parenthesised constants:

```
ghci> (3)+4
7
```

Design a parser for fully parenthesised expressions that allows parentheses around constants.

Exercise J

Consider the grammar `expr ::= term {op term}*`. Define `pair` and `shunt` so that the following parser is legitimate:

```
expr = do {e1 <- term;
           pes <- many (pair op term);
           return (foldl shunt e1 pes)}
```

Exercise K

Define the parsers `addop` and `mulop`.

Exercise L

Consider again the showing of expressions with all four arithmetic operations. The rules for putting in parentheses come down to: we need parentheses around `e1` in `e1 op e2` if `op` is a multiplication operator, and the root of `e1` isn't. Dually we will need parentheses around `e2` if either `op` is a multiplication operator or the root of `e2` isn't. Defining

```
isMulOp Mul = True
isMulOp Div = True
isMulOp _   = False
```

construct an alternative definition of `show` involving a subsidiary function

```
showsF :: (Op -> Bool) -> Expr -> ShowS
```

11.7 Answers

Answer to Exercise A

Because `(==)` is the equality test on floating-point numbers, and different numbers cannot be equal.

```
instance Eq Angle where
  Angle x == Angle y = reduce x == reduce y
  where
  reduce x | x<0 = reduce (x + r)
           | x>r = reduce (x - r)
           | otherwise = x
           where r = 2*pi
```

Answer to Exercise B

```
instance Monad Parser where
  return x = Parser (\s -> Just (x,s))
  P >>= q  = Parser (\s -> case apply p s of
                           Nothing -> apply q s
                           Just (x,s') -> Just (x,s'))
```

Answer to Exercise C

```
   fail >> p
 = fail >>= const p
 = fail
```

The fact that `fail >>= p = fail` is immediate from the definition of `fail` and the definition of `p >>= q`.

Answer to Exercise D

Yes, but the result is only a deterministic parser when either p or q is `fail`. The function `limit` can be defined by

```
   limit p = Parser (take 1 . apply p)
```

Answer to Exercise E

```
   mzero = fail
   mplus = (<|>)
```

Answer to Exercise F

Yes, both the list monad and the `Maybe` monad satisfy the five laws. For example, in the list monad

```
   mzero >>= f = concat (map f []) = [] = mzero
   xs >> mzero = concat (map (const []) xs) = [] = mzero
```

With Maybe the left-distribution law doesn't hold. We have

```
   (Just x `mplus` q) >>= (\x -> Nothing)
 = Just x >>= (\x -> Nothing)
 = Nothing
```

but

```
    (Just x >> \x -> Nothing) `mplus`
    (q >>= \x -> Nothing)
  = Nothing `mplus` (q >>= \x -> Nothing)
  = q >>= \x -> Nothing
```

The two resulting expressions are not equal (take q = undefined).

Answer to Exercise G

```
    float :: Parser Float
    float = do {ds <- some digit;
                char '.';
                fs <- some digit;
                return (foldl shiftl 0 ds +
                        foldr shiftr 0 fs)}
          where shiftl n d = 10*n + fromIntegral d
                shiftr f x = (fromIntegral f+x)/10
```

The parser digit returns an Int, which has to be converted to a number (in this case a Float).

Answer to Exercise H

White space is parsed twice. For example, calling the first version int1 and the third int3 we have

```
ghci> apply int3 $ replicate 100000 ' ' ++ "3"
[(3,"")]
(1.40 secs, 216871916 bytes)
ghci> apply int1 $ replicate 100000 ' ' ++ "3"
[(3,"")]
(2.68 secs, 427751932 bytes)
```

Answer to Exercise I

No, according to the first grammar for expr, only binary expressions can be parenthesised. Yes, according to the second grammar as arbitrary expressions can be parenthesised.

The revised grammar is

```
    expr ::= term | '(' expr op expr ')'
    term ::= nat | '(' expr ')'
```

The corresponding parser is

```
expr = token (term <|> paren binary)
  where
  term = token (constant <|> paren expr)
  binary = do {e1 <- expr;
               p <- op;
               e2 <- expr;
               return (Bin p e1 e2)}
```

Answer to Exercise J

```
pair :: Parser a -> Parser b -> Parser (a,b)
pair p q = do {x <- p; y <- q; return (x,y)}

shunt e1 (p,e2) = Bin p e1 e2
```

Answer to Exercise K

```
addop = (symbol "+" >> return Plus) <|>
        (symbol "-" >> return Minus)
mulop = (symbol "*" >> return Mul) <|>
        (symbol "/" >> return Div)
```

Answer to Exercise L

```
show e = showsF (const False) e ""
  where
  showsF f (Con n) = showString (show n)
  showsF f (Bin op e1 e2)
   = showParen (f op) (showsF f1 e1 . showSpace .
     showsop op . showSpace . showsF f2 e2)
     where f1 x = isMulOp op && not (isMulOp x)
           f2 x = isMulOp op || not (isMulOp x)
```

11.8 Chapter notes

The design of functional parsers in a monadic setting has long been a favourite application of functional programming. Our presentation follows that of 'Monadic parsing in Haskell' by Graham Hutton and Erik Meijer, which appears in *The Journal of Functional Programming* 8(4), 437–144, 1998.

Chapter 12

A simple equational calculator

This final chapter is devoted to a single programming project, the design and implementation of a simple calculator for carrying out point-free equational proofs. Although the calculator provides only a small subset of the facilities one might want in an automatic proof assistant, and is highly restrictive in a number of other ways, it will nevertheless be powerful enough to prove many of the point-free laws described in previous chapters – well, provided we are prepared to give it a nudge in the right direction if necessary. The project is also a case study in the use of modules. Each component of the calculator, its associated types and functions, is defined in an appropriate module and linked to other modules through explicit import and export lists.

12.1 Basic considerations

The basic idea is to construct a single function `calculate` with type

```
calculate :: [Law] -> Expr -> Calculation
```

The first argument of `calculate` is a list of laws that may be applied. Each law consists of a descriptive name and an equation. The second argument is an expression and the result is a calculation. A calculation consists of a starting expression and a sequence of steps. Each step consists of the name of a law and the expression that results by applying the left-hand side of the law to the current expression. The calculation ends when no more laws can be applied, and the final expression is the conclusion. The entire process is automatic, requiring no intervention on the part of the user.

Laws, expressions and calculations are each elements of appropriate data types to be defined in the following sections. But for now let us plunge straight in with an example to show the framework we have in mind.

Here are some laws (we use a smaller font to avoid breaking lines):

```
definition filter:   filter p = concat . map (box p)
definition box:      box p = if p one nil

if after dot:        if p f g . h = if (p . h) (f . h) (g . h)
dot after if:        h . if p f g = if p (h . f) (h . g)

nil constant:        nil . f = nil
map after nil:       map f . nil = nil
map after one:       map f . one = one . f

map after concat:    map f . concat = concat . map (map f)

map functor:         map f . map g = map (f . g)
map functor:         map id = id
```

Each law consists of a name and an equation. The name of the law is terminated by a colon sign, and an equation consists of two expressions separated by an equals sign. Each expression describes a function; our calculator will be one that simplifies functional expressions only (yes, it's a pointless calculator). Expressions are built from constants, like one and map, and variables, like f and g. The precise syntax will be given in due course. Note that there are no conditional laws, equations that are valid only if some subsidiary conditions are met. That will limit what we can do with the calculator, but it still leaves enough to be interesting.

Suppose we want to simplify the expression filter p . map f. Here is one possible calculation:

```
    filter p . map f
=   {definition filter}
    concat . map (box p) . map f
=   {map functor}
    concat . map (box p . f)
=   {definition box}
    concat . map (if p one nil . f)
=   {if after dot}
    concat . map (if (p . f) (one . f) (nil . f))
=   {nil constant}
    concat . map (if (p . f) (one . f) nil)
```

The steps of the calculation are displayed in the conventional format with the name of the law being invoked printed in braces between the two expressions to which it applies. No more laws apply to the final expression, so that is the result of the calculation. It is certainly not simpler than the expression we started out with.

The calculator could have applied some of the laws in a different order; for example, the definition of box could have been applied at the second step rather than at the third. But the conclusion would have been the same. It is also possible, though not with this particular set of laws, that an expression could be simplified to different conclusions by different calculations. However, at the outset we make the decision that calculate returns just one calculation, not a tree of possible calculations.

Notice what is happening at each step. Some left-hand side of some law is *matched* against some subexpression of the current expression. If a match is successful the result is a *substitution* for the variables occurring in the law. For example, in the second step, the subexpression map (box p) . map f is successfully matched with the first map functor law, resulting in a substitution in which the variable f of the functor law is bound to the expression box p, and the variable g is bound to f. The result of the step involves *rewriting* the subexpression with the corresponding instance of the right-hand side of the law in which each variable is replaced by its binding expression. Matching, substitutions and rewriting are all fundamental components of the calculator.

Now suppose that with the same set of laws as above we want to simplify the expression map f . filter (p . f). Here is the calculation:

```
  map f . filter (p . f)
=   {definition filter}
  map f . concat . map (box (p . f))
=   {map after concat}
  concat . map (map f) . map (box (p . f))
=   {map functor}
  concat . map (map f . box (p . f))
=   {definition box}
  concat . map (map f . if (p . f) one nil)
=   {dot after if}
  concat . map (if (p . f) (map f . one) (map f . nil))
=   {map after nil}
  concat . map (if (p . f) (map f . one) nil)
=   {map after one}
  concat . map (if (p . f) (one . f) nil)
```

Again, some of the laws could have been applied in a different order. No more laws apply to the final expression so that is the result of the calculation.

The point about these two calculations is that the two final expressions are the same, so we have proved

```
filter p . map f = map f . filter (p . f)
```

This is the way we will conduct equational proofs, simplifying both sides to the same conclusion. Rather than show two calculations, one after the other, the two results can be *pasted* together by recording the first calculation and then appending the steps of the second calculation in reverse. The main advantage of this scheme is simplicity; we do not have to invent a new format for proofs, and we do not have to apply laws from right to left in order to reach the desired goal. Accordingly, we will also define a function

```
prove :: [Law] -> Equation -> Calculation
```

for proving equations.

Further considerations

It is a basic constraint of our calculator that laws are applied in one direction only, namely from left to right. This is primarily to prevent calculations from looping. If laws could be applied in both directions, then the calculator could oscillate by applying a law in one direction and then immediately applying it in the reverse direction.

Even with a left-to-right rule, some laws can lead to infinite calculations. Typically, these laws are the definitions of recursive functions. For example, consider the definition of `iterate`:

```
defn iterate: iterate f = cons . fork id (iterate f . f)
```

This is the definition of `iterate` expressed in point-free form. The functions `cons` and `fork` are defined by

```
cons (x,xs) = x:xs
fork f g x  = (f x,g x)
```

We have met `fork` before in the exercises in Chapters 4 and 6, except that we wrote `fork (f,g)` instead of `fork f g`. In what follows, all our functions will be curried. The appearance of the term `iterate f` on both sides of the law means that any calculation that can apply the definition of `iterate` once can, potentially, apply it infinitely often. But not necessarily. Here is a calculation (produced by the calculator) that avoids infinite regress:

```
   head . iterate f
=    {defn iterate}
   head . cons . fork id (iterate f . f)
```

```
=    {head after cons}
   fst . fork id (iterate f . f)
=    {fst after fork}
   id
```

The calculation makes use of the two laws:

```
head after cons:  head . cons = fst
fst after fork:   first . fork f g = f
```

The reason non-termination is avoided is that these two laws are given preference over definitions in calculations, a wrinkle that we will elaborate on below.

In order to appreciate just what the calculator can and cannot do, here is another example of rendering a recursive definition into point-free form. Consider the definition of concatenation:

```
[] ++ ys      = ys
(x:xs) ++ ys = x:(xs ++ ys)
```

We will use cat to stand for (++). We will also need nil, cons and the function cross (f,g), which we will now write as f * g. Thus,

```
(f * g) (x,y) = (f x, g y)
```

Finally we will need a combinator assocr (short for 'associate-right'), defined by

```
assocr ((x,y),z) = (x,(y,z))
```

Here are the translations of the two defining equations of cat in point-free form:

```
cat . (nil * id)  = snd
cat . (cons * id) = cons . (id * cat) . assocr
```

We cannot prove that cat is associative with our calculator, for that would involve a proof by induction, but we can state it as a law:

```
cat associative: cat . (cat * id) = cat . (id * cat) . assocr
```

Continuing with this example for a bit longer, here are the two bifunctor laws of (*):

```
bifunctor *:    id * id = id
bifunctor *:    (f * g) . (h * k) = (f . h) * (g . k)
```

And here is a law about assocr:

```
assocr law:  assocr . ((f * g) * h) = (f * (g * h)) . assocr
```

Now for the point of the example: our calculator *cannot* perform the following valid calculation:

```
  cat . ((cat . (f * g)) * h)
=   {identity law, in backwards direction}
  cat . ((cat . (f * g)) * (id . h))
=   {bifunctor *, in backwards direction}
  cat . (cat * id) . ((f * g) * h)
=   {cat associative}
  cat . (id * cat) . assocr . ((f * g) * h)
=   {assoc law}
  cat . (id * cat) . (f * (g * h)) . assocr
=   {bifunctor *}
  cat . ((id . f) * (cat . (g * h))) . assocr
=   {identity law}
  cat . (f * (cat . (g * h))) . assocr
```

The problem here is that we have to apply the identity and bifunctor laws in *both* directions, and the calculator is simply not up to the task. Observe that the essence of the proof is the simplification of the expression

```
  cat . (id * cat) . assocr . ((f * g) * h)
```

in two different ways, one by using the associativity of `cat`, written in the form

```
  cat associative: cat . (id * cat) . assocr = cat . (cat * id)
```

and one by using the `assocr` law. Even if we generalised `calculate` to return a tree of possible calculations, it would not be obvious what expression we would have to start out with in order to achieve the calculation above, so we abandon any attempt to get the calculator to produce it.

It is not just the functor laws that sometimes have to be applied in both directions. For an example, see Section 12.8. Sometimes we can get around the problem by stating a law in a more general form than necessary, sometimes by using a hack, and sometimes not at all. As we said at the outset, our calculator is a limited one.

In the scheme of automatic calculation that we are envisaging there are only two degrees of freedom: the choice of which law to apply, and the choice of which subexpression to be changed. The first degree of freedom can be embodied in the order in which laws are presented to the calculator: if two different laws are applicable, then the one earlier in the list is chosen.

Certainly some laws should be tried before others; these are laws that reduce the complexity of intermediate expressions. Good examples are the laws `f.id = f` and `id.f = f`. The naive definition of complexity is that there are fewer compositions on the right than on the left. It is unlikely to be a mistake to apply these laws as soon as the opportunity arises. Indeed the fact that id is the identity element of composition can and will be built into the calculator, so the two identity laws will be taken care of automatically. Similarly, early application of laws like nil.f = nil and map f.nil = nil (and indeed the two laws used in the calculation about iterate), all of which reduce the number of compositions, help to reduce the sizes of intermediate expressions. For the sake of a word, let us call these the *simple* laws.

On the other hand, some laws should be applied only as a last resort. Typically, these laws are definitions, such as the definition of filter or iterate. For example, in the expression

```
map f . concat . map (filter p)
```

we really don't want to apply the definition of filter too early; rather we would prefer to apply the map after concat law first, and only apply the definition of filter later on if and when it becomes necessary. Apart from anything else, intermediate expressions will be shorter.

In summary it looks sensible to sort our laws into the simple laws, followed the non-simple laws that are not definitions, followed by the definitions.

The second degree of freedom is represented by the order in which the subexpressions of a given expression are presented as candidates for instances of laws: if laws are applicable to two different subexpressions, then the subexpression coming earlier in the enumeration is chosen.

That still leaves open the decision whether to give preference to laws or to subexpressions in calculations. Do we start with a subexpression and try every law in turn, or start with a law and see if it applies anywhere? Does it really matter which of these alternatives is chosen? While it is true that, having applied some law at some subexpression, the next law to be applied is likely to be at a 'nearby' expression, it is not clear how to formalise this notion of nearness, nor is it clear whether it would contribute significantly to the efficiency of calculations, either in the computation time or in the length of the result.

12.2 Expressions

At the heart of the calculator is the data type Expr of expressions. Most of the components of the calculator are concerned with analysing and manipulating expressions in one way or the other. Expressions are built from (function) variables and constants, using functional composition as the basic combining form. Variables take no arguments, but constants can take any number of arguments, which are themselves expressions. We will suppose all functions are curried and there are no tuples; for example we write `pair f g` instead of `pair (f,g)`. There is no particular reason for avoiding tuples, it is just that most functions we have discussed in the book are curried and we don't really need both.

To compensate, we will also allow ourselves binary infix operators, writing, for example, `f * g` instead of `cross f g`. Except for functional composition we will not assume any order of precedence or association between binary operators, insisting that expressions involving such operators be fully parenthesised. That still leaves open the question of the precedence of composition. Does `f * g . h` mean `(f * g) . h` or `f * (g . h)`? Haskell puts composition at a high level of precedence and we will adopt the same convention. Thus `f * g . h` will be parsed as `f * (g . h)`. But we will always write such expressions using parentheses to avoid ambiguity.

Here is the proposed BNF grammar for expressions:

```
expr   ::= simple {op simple}
simple ::= term {'.' term}*
term   ::= var | con {arg}* | '(' expr ')'
arg    ::= var | con | '(' expr ')'
var    ::= letter {digit}
con    ::= letter letter {letter | digit}*
op     ::= {symbol}+
```

Variable names consist of single letters only, possibly followed by a single digit. Thus `f` and `f1` are legitimate variable names. Constant names are sequences of at least two alphanumeric characters beginning with two letters, such as `map` or `lhs2tex`, while operator names are nonempty sequences of non-alphanumeric symbols, such as `*` and `<+>`. The first line says that an expression is a simple expression, possibly followed by an operator and another simple expression. Simple expressions are compositions of terms. The remaining lines are, we trust, self-explanatory.

Here is the definition of Expr we will use:

```
newtype Expr = Compose [Atom] deriving Eq
data Atom    = Var VarName | Con ConName [Expr]
                deriving Eq
type VarName = String
type ConName = String
```

Expressions and atoms are declared to be members of the class Eq because we will need to test expressions for equality. Later on we will install expressions as an instance of Show for printing them at the terminal.

Here are some examples of expressions and their representations:

```
f . g . h   => Compose [Var "f",Var "g",Var "h"]
id          => Compose []
fst         => Compose [Con "fst" []]
fst . f     => Compose [Con "fst" [],Var "f"]
(f * g) . h => Compose [Con "*" [Var "f",Var "g"],Var "h"]
f * g . h   => Compose [Con "*" [Compose [Var "f"],
                                 Compose [Var "g",Var "h"]]]
```

The fact that composition is an associative operation is built into the design of Expr. The particular constant id is reserved and will always be interpreted as the identity element of composition.

The parsing combinators described in the previous chapter enable us to parse expressions. Following the BNF, we start with

```
expr :: Parser Expr
expr = simple >>= rest
  where
  rest s1 = do {op <- operator;
                s2 <- simple;
                return (Compose [Con op [s1,s2]])}
            <|> return s1
```

An operator is a sequence of one or more operator symbols, as long as it is neither the composition operator nor an equals sign:

```
operator :: Parser String
operator = do {op <- token (some (sat symbolic));
               Parsing.guard (op /= "." && op /= "=");
               return op}

symbolic = (`elem` opsymbols)
opsymbols = "!@#$%&*+./<=>?\\^|:-~"
```

The function Parsing.guard is an example of a *qualified* name. The Haskell Prelude also provides a function guard, but we want the function of the same name from a module Parsing that includes all our parsing functions. A qualified name consists of a module name followed by a period followed by the name of the qualified value.

A simple expression is a sequence of one or more terms separated by composition:

```
simple :: Parser Expr
simple = do {es <- somewith (symbol "."); term;
             return (Compose (concatMap deCompose es))}
```

The function concatMap f as an alternative to concat . map f is provided in the standard prelude, and deCompose is defined by

```
deCompose :: Expr -> [Atom]
deCompose (Compose as) = as
```

Next, a term is an identifier, either a variable or a constant, possibly with arguments, or a parenthesised expression:

```
term :: Parser Expr
term = ident args <|> paren expr
args = many (ident none <|> paren expr)
```

The parser ident takes a parser for a list of expressions and returns a parser for expressions:

```
ident :: Parser [Expr] -> Parser Exp
ident args
  = do {x <- token (some (sat isAlphaNum));
        Parsing.guard (isAlpha (head x));
        if isVar x
        then return (Compose [Var x])
        else if (x == "id")
        then return (Compose [])
        else
        do {as <- args;
            return (Compose [Con x as])}}
```

The test for being a variable is implemented by

```
isVar [x]   = True
isVar [x,d] = isDigit d
isVar _     = False
```

Note that any identifier consisting entirely of alphanumeric characters and beginning with a letter and which is not a variable is a constant.

Next, we make Expr and Atom instances of Show. As in the previous chapter we will do this by defining `showsPrec` p for each type. A little thought reveals that we need three values for p:

- At top level, there is no need for parentheses. For example, we write all of `map f . map g`, `foo * baz`, and `bar bie doll` without parentheses. We assign p=0 to this case.

- When an expression is a composition of terms, or an operator expression, occurring as an argument to a constant, we need to parenthesise it. For example, parentheses are necessary in the expression

  ```
  map (f . g) . foo f g . (bar * bar)
  ```

  But we don't have to parenthesise the middle term. We assign p=1 to this case.

- Finally, p=2 means we should parenthesise compositions of terms, operator expressions and curried functions of at least one argument, as in

  ```
  map (f . g) . foo (foldr f e) g . (bar * bar)
  ```

Here goes. We start with

```
instance Show Expr where
 showsPrec p (Compose []) = showString "id"
 showsPrec p (Compose [a]) = showsPrec p a
 showsPrec p (Compose as)
  = showParen (p>0) (showSep " . " (showsPrec 1) as)
```

The last line makes use of the function `showSep`, defined by

```
showSep :: String -> (a -> ShowS) -> [a] -> ShowS
showSep sep f
 = compose . intersperse (showString sep) . map f
```

The utility function `compose` is defined by `compose = foldr (.) id`. The function `intersperse :: a -> [a] -> [a]` can be found in `Data.List` and intersperses its first argument between elements of its second. For example,

```
intersperse ',' "abcde" == "a,b,c,d,e"
```

The two occurrences of `showsPrec` on the right-hand sides of the second two clauses of `showsPrec` refer to the corresponding function for atoms:

```
instance Show Atom where
 showsPrec p (Var v)    = showString v
 showsPrec p (Con f []) = showString f
 showsPrec p (Con f [e1,e2])
```

```
    | isOp f = showParen (p>0) (showsPrec 1 e1 . showSpace .
                  showString f . showSpace . showsPrec 1 e2)
  showsPrec p (Con f es)
    = showParen (p>1) (showString f . showSpace .
        showSep " " (showsPrec 2) es)


  isOp f = all symbolic f
```

The value p=2 is needed in the final clause because we want parentheses in, for example, foo (bar bie) doll. Variables and nullary constants never need parentheses.

A module structure

The final step is to install these definitions, and possibly others, in a module for expressions. Such a module will include all the functions specifically related to expressions.

Creating such a module is not immediate because we do not yet know what other functions on expressions we may need in other modules, modules that deal with laws, calculations and so on. But for the moment we declare

```
module Expressions
  (Expr (Compose), Atom (Var,Con),
   VarName, ConName, deCompose, expr)
where
import Parsing
import Data.List (intersperse)
import Utilities (compose)
import Data.Char (isAlphaNum,isAlpha,isDigit)
```

The module Expressions has to be stored in a file Expressions.lhs to enable Haskell to find out where it resides. It exports the types Expr and Atom along with their constructors. It also exports the type synonyms VarName and ConName, as well as the functions deCompose and expr, all of which are likely to be needed in the module that deals with laws. Later on we might add more functions on expressions to this export list.

Next comes the imports. We import the module Parsing that contains the parsing functions, and also some functions from Data.List and Data.Char. We will also set up a module Utilities containing general utility functions. A good example of a utility function is `compose`, defined above. It is not specific to expressions and may be needed in other places, so we put it into the utilities module.

12.3 Laws

We define laws in the following way:

```
data Law      = Law LawName Equation
type LawName  = String
type Equation = (Expr,Expr)
```

A law consists of a descriptive name and an equation. To parse a law we define:

```
law :: Parser Law
law = do {name <- upto ':';
          eqn <- equation;
          return (Law name eqn)}
```

The parsing function `upto c` returns the string up to but not including the character c, and then discards c if found. It wasn't included among the parsing functions of the previous chapter, but we will put it into the module `Parsing` to avoid breaking the parser abstraction. One definition is:

```
upto :: Char -> Parser String
upto c
 = Parser (\s ->
           let (xs,ys) = break (==c) s in
           if null ys then []
           else [(xs,tail ys)])
```

The parser `equation` is defined by

```
equation :: Parser Equation
equation = do {e1 <- expr;
               symbol "=";
               e2 <- expr;
               return (e1,e2)}
```

We probably don't need to show laws, but here is the definition anyway:

```
instance Show Law where
 showsPrec _ (Law name (e1,e2))
    = showString name .
```

```
            showString ": " .
            shows e1 .
            showString " = " .
            shows e2
```

The precedence number is not needed to define showPrec so it is made a don't care pattern. Recall that shows takes a printable value, here an expression, and returns a function of type ShowS, a synonym for String -> String.

Finally we sort the laws:

```
    sortLaws :: [Law] -> [Law]
    sortLaws laws = simple ++ others ++ defns
      where
      (simple,nonsimple) = partition isSimple laws
      (defns,others)     = partition isDefn nonsimple
```

This definition makes use of a Data.List function partition that partitions a list:

```
    partition p xs = (filter p xs, filter (not . p) xs)
```

The various tests are defined by

```
    isSimple (Law _ (Compose as1,Compose as2))
            = length as1 > length as2
    isDefn (Law _ (Compose [Con f es], _))
            = all isVar es
    isDefn _ = False
    isVar (Compose [Var _]) = True
    isVar _                 = False
```

The test isVar also appears in the module Expressions though with a different definition. There is no problem though since that function is not exported from the expressions module.

Here is the module declaration for laws:

```
    module Laws
      (Law (Law), LawName, law, sortLaws,
       Equation, equation)
    where
    import Expressions
    import Parsing
    import Data.List (partition)
```

Having shown how to parse and print expressions and laws, we can now define two functions, one a version of `calculate` that consumes strings rather than laws and expressions:

```
simplify :: [String] -> String -> Calculation
simplify strings string
  = let laws = map (parse law) strings
        e = parse expr string
    in calculate laws e
```

In a similar vein we can define

```
prove :: [String] -> String -> Calculation
prove strings string
  = let laws = map (parse law) strings
        (e1,e2) = parse equation string
    in paste (calculate laws e1) (calculate laws e2)
```

These two functions can be put in a module `Main`. We put `paste` and `calculate` into a module concerned solely with calculations, and we turn to this module next.

12.4 Calculations

Calculations are defined by

```
data Calculation = Calc Expr [Step]
type Step        = (LawName,Expr)
```

Let's begin with the key definition of the calculator, that of `calculate`:

```
calculate :: [Law] -> Expr -> Calculation
calculate laws e = Calc e (manyStep rws e)
  where rws e = [(name,e')
                | Law name eqn <- sortedlaws,
                  e' <- rewrites eqn e,
                  e' /= e]
        sortedlaws = sortLaws laws
```

The function `rewrites :: Equation -> Expr -> [Expr]` returns a list of all the possible ways of rewriting an expression using a given equation, a function that will be defined in a separate module. It may be the case that an expression can be rewritten to itself (see Exercise H), but such rewrites are disallowed because they would lead to infinite calculations. The function `rws :: Expr -> [Step]` returns a list of all the single steps, leading to new expressions, that can arise by using the laws in all possible ways. This list is defined by taking each law in turn and generating all the rewrites associated with the law. That means we give preference to laws over subexpressions in calculations, resolving one of the issues we worried about in the first section. Only experimentation will show if we have made the right decision.

The function `manyStep` uses `rws` to construct as many steps as possible:

```
manyStep :: (Expr -> [Step]) -> Expr -> [Step]
manyStep rws e
  = if null steps then []
    else step : manyStep rws (snd step)
    where steps = rws e
          step  = head steps
```

The calculation ends if `rws e` is the empty list; otherwise the head of the list is used to continue the calculation.

The remaining functions of the calculations module deal with showing and pasting calculations. We show a calculation as follows:

```
instance Show Calculation where
   showsPrec _ (Calc e steps)
     = showString "\n   " .
       shows e .
       showChar '\n' .
       compose (map showStep steps)
```

Each individual step is shown as follows:

```
showStep :: Step -> ShowS
showStep (why,e)
  = showString "=   {" .
    showString why .
    showString "}\n   " .
    shows e .
    showChar '\n'
```

In order to paste two calculations together we have to reverse the steps of a calculation. For example, the calculation

```
Calc e0 [(why1,e1),(why2,e2),(why3,e3)]
```

has to be turned into

```
Calc e3 [(why3,e2),(why2,e1),(why1,e0)]
```

In particular, the conclusion of a calculation is the first expression in the reversed calculation. Here is how to reverse a calculation:

```
reverseCalc :: Calculation -> Calculation
reverseCalc (Calc e steps)
 = foldl shunt (Calc e []) steps
   where shunt (Calc e1 steps) (why,e2)
           = Calc e2 ((why,e1):steps)
```

In order to paste two calculations together we first have to check that their conclusions are the same. If they are not, then we go ahead and paste the calculations anyway with an indication of failure:

```
   conc1
 = {... ??? ...}
   conc2
```

If the two conclusions are the same, we can be a little smarter than just stitching the calculations together. If the penultimate conclusion of one calculation also matches the penultimate conclusion of the other, then we can cut out the final steps altogether. And so on. Here, then, is how we paste two calculations:

```
paste :: Calculation -> Calculation -> Calculation
paste calc1@(Calc e1 steps1) calc2
  = if conc1 == conc2
    then Calc e1 (prune conc1 rsteps1 rsteps2)
    else Calc e1 (steps1 ++ (gap,conc2):rsteps2)
    where Calc conc1 rsteps1 = reverseCalc calc1
          Calc conc2 rsteps2 = reverseCalc calc2
          gap = "... ??? ..."
```

The function prune is defined by:

```
prune :: Expr -> [Step] -> [Step] -> [Step]
prune e ((_,e1):steps1) ((_,e2):steps2)
 | e1==e2 = prune e1 steps1 steps2
prune e steps1 steps2 = rsteps ++ steps2
  where Calc _ rsteps = reverseCalc (Calc e steps1)
```

Finally, here is the module declaration of Calculations:

```
module Calculations
  (Calculation (Calc), Step, calculate, paste)
```

```
where
import Expressions
import Laws
import Rewrites
import Utilities (compose)
```

The exports are those types and functions needed to define `simplify` and `prove` in the main module.

12.5 Rewrites

The sole purpose of the module `Rewrites` is to provide a definition of the function `rewrites` that appears in the definition of `calculate`. Recall that the expression `rewrites eqn e` returns a list of all expressions that can arise by matching some subexpression of e against the left-hand expression of `eqn` and replacing the subexpression with the appropriate instance of the right-hand expression of `eqn`.

The fun is in figuring out how to define `rewrites`. Suppose we construct a list of all possible subexpressions of an expression. We can match the given equation against each subexpression, get the substitutions that do the matching (of which there may be none, one or more than one; see the section on matching below) and compute the new subexpressions. But how do we replace an old subexpression with a new one in the original expression? The simple answer is that we can't, at least not without determining alongside each subexpression its *context* or *location* in the original expression. The new subexpression can then be inserted at this location.

Rather than introducing contexts explicitly, we take another approach. The idea is to burrow into an expression, applying a rewrite to some subexpression at some point, and then to build the rewritten expression as we climb back out of the burrow. We will need a utility function `anyOne` that takes a function yielding a choice of alternatives, and a list, and installs a single choice for one of the elements. The definition is

```
anyOne :: (a -> [a]) -> [a] -> [[a]]
anyOne f []     = []
anyOne f (x:xs) = [x':xs | x' <- f x] ++
                  [x:xs' | xs' <- anyOne f xs]
```

For example, if `f 1 = [-1,-2]` and `f 2 = [-3,-4]`, then

```
anyOne f [1,2] = [[-1,2],[-2,2],[1,-3],[1,-4]]
```

Either one of the choices for the first element is installed, or one of the choices for the second, but not both at the same time.

Here is our definition of `rewrites`:

```
rewrites :: Equation -> Expr -> [Expr]
rewrites eqn (Compose as) = map Compose (
    rewritesSeg eqn as ++ anyOne (rewritesA eqn) as)
rewritesA eqn (Var v) = []
rewritesA eqn (Con k es)
    = map (Con k) (anyOne (rewrites eqn) es)
```

In the first line we concatenate the rewrites for a *segment* of the current expression with the rewrites for any one of its proper subexpressions. Only constants with arguments have subexpressions. Note that the two uses of `anyOne` have different types, one taking a list of atoms, and one taking a list of expressions.

It remains to define `rewritesSeg`:

```
rewritesSeg :: Equation -> [Atom] -> [[Atom]]
rewritesSeg (e1,e2) as
    = [as1 ++ deCompose (apply sub e2) ++ as3
       | (as1,as2,as3) <- segments as,
         sub <- match (e1,Compose as2)]
```

The function `segments` splits a list into segments:

```
segments as = [(as1,as2,as3)
               | (as1,bs)  <- splits as,
                 (as2,as3) <- splits bs]
```

The utility function `splits` splits a list in all possible ways:

```
splits :: [a] -> [([a],[a])]
splits []     = [([],[])]
splits (a:as) = [([],a:as)] ++
                [(a:as1,as2) | (as1,as2) <- splits as]
```

For example,

```
ghci> splits "abc"
[("","abc"),("a","bc"),("ab","c"),("abc","")]
```

The remaining functions `apply` and `match` have types

```
apply :: Subst -> Expr -> Expr
```

```
match :: (Expr,Expr) -> [Subst]
```

Each will be defined in their own modules, `Substitutions` and `Matchings`. Finally, here is the module declaration for `Rewrites`:

```
module Rewrites (rewrites)
where
import Expressions
import Laws (Equation)
import Matchings (match)
import Substitutions (apply)
import Utilities (anyOne, segments)
```


12.6 Matchings

The sole purpose of the module `Matchings` is to define the function `match`. This function takes two expressions and returns a list of substitutions under which the first expression can be transformed into the second. Matching two expressions produces no substitutions if they don't match, but possibly many if they do. Consider matching the expression `foo (f . g)` against `foo (a . b . c)`. There are four substitutions that do the trick: `f` may be bound to any of the expressions

```
id,    a,    a . b,    a . b . c
```

with four corresponding bindings for `g`. Although the calculator will select a single substitution at each step, it is important to take account of multiple substitutions in the process of obtaining the valid matchings. For example, in matching `foo (f . g) . bar g` against `foo (a . b . c) . bar c`, the subexpression `f . g` is matched against `a . b . c`, resulting in four possible substitutions. Only when `bar g` is matched against `bar c` are three of the substitutions rejected. A premature commitment to a single substitution for the first match may result in a successful match being missed.

The most straightforward way of defining `match (e1,e2)` is to first line up the atoms of `e1` with a partition of the atoms of `e2`; the first atom is associated with the first segment of the partition, the second with the second segment, and so on. The function `alignments` has type

```
alignments :: (Expr,Expr) -> [[(Atom,Expr)]]
```

and does the alignments. To define it we need a function `parts` that partitions a list into a given number of segments:

```
parts :: Int -> [a] -> [[[a]]]
parts 0 [] = [[]]
parts 0 as = []
parts n as = [bs:bss
                | (bs,cs) <- splits as,
                  bss <- parts (n-1) cs]
```

The interesting clauses are the first two: there is one partition of the empty list into 0 segments, namely the empty partition, but there are no partitions of a nonempty list into 0 segments. For example,

```
ghci> parts 3 "ab"
[["","","ab"],["","a","b"],["","ab",""],
 ["a","","b"],["a","b",""],["ab","",""]]
```

Now we can define

```
alignments (Compose as,Compose bs)
  = [zip as (map Compose bss) | bss <- parts n bs]
    where n = length as
```

Having aligned each atom with a subexpression, we define `matchA` that matches atoms with expressions:

```
matchA :: (Atom,Expr) -> [Subst]
matchA (Var v,e) = [unitSub v e]
matchA (Con k1 es1,Compose [Con k2 es2])
    | k1==k2 = combine (map match (zip es1 es2))
matchA _ = []
```

Matching a variable always succeeds and results in a single substitution. Matching two constants succeeds only if the two constants are the same. In all other cases `matchA` returns an empty list of substitutions. The function `matchA` depends on `match`, which we can now define by

```
match :: (Expr,Expr) -> [Subst]
match = concatMap (combine . map matchA) . alignments
```

The final ingredient is the function `combine :: [[Subst]] -> [Subst]`. Each component list of substitutions in the argument of `combine` represents alternatives, so `combine` has to combine alternatives by selecting, in all possible ways, one substitution from each list and then unifying the result. We will return to this function in the module for substitutions. This completes the definition of `matches`. The module declaration is

```
module Matchings (match)
where
import Expressions
import Substitutions (Subst, unitSub, combine)
import Utilities (parts)
```

We place parts in the utilities module because it is not specific to expressions.

12.7 Substitutions

A substitution is a finite mapping associating variables with expressions. A simple representation as an association list suffices:

```
type Subst = [(VarName,Expr)]
```

The empty and unit substitutions are then defined by

```
emptySub     = []
unitSub v e = [(v,e)]
```

We can apply a substitution to an expression to get another expression by defining

```
apply :: Subst -> Expr -> Expr
apply sub (Compose as)
       = Compose (concatMap (applyA sub) as)
applyA sub (Var v)    = deCompose (binding sub v)
applyA sub (Con k es) = [Con k (map (apply sub) es)]
```

The function binding looks up a nonempty substitution for the binding for a variable:

```
binding :: Subst -> VarName -> Expr
binding sub v = fromJust (lookup v sub)
```

The function lookup is supplied in the Haskell Prelude and returns Nothing if no binding is found, and Just e if v is bound to e. The function fromJust is in the library Data.Maybe and removes the wrapper Just.

Next we tackle combine. This function has to combine alternative substitutions by selecting, in all possible ways, one substitution from each component list and then unifying each resulting list of substitutions:

```
combine = concatMap unifyAll . cp
```

The utility function cp, which we have seen many times before, computes the cartesian product of a list of lists.

The function unifyAll takes a list of substitutions and unifies them. To define it we first show how to unify two substitutions. The result of unification is either the union of the two substitutions if they are compatible, or no substitution if they are incompatible. To handle the possibility of failure, we can use the Maybe type, or simply return either an empty list or a singleton list. We choose the latter simply because in the following section we are going to calculate another version of the calculator, and it is simplest to stick with list-based functions:

```
unify :: Subst -> Subst -> [Subst]
unify sub1 sub2 = if compatible sub1 sub2
                     then [union sub1 sub2]
                     else []
```

In order to define compatible and union we will suppose that substitutions are maintained as lists in lexicographic order of variable name. Two substitutions are incompatible if they associate different expressions with one and the same variable:

```
compatible [] sub2 = True
compatible sub1 [] = True
compatible sub1@((v1,e1):sub1') sub2@((v2,e2):sub2')
  | v1<v2  = compatible sub1' sub2
  | v1==v2 = if e1==e2 then compatible sub1' sub2'
             else False
  | v1>v2  = compatible sub1 sub2'
```

The union operation is defined in a similar style:

```
union [] sub2 = sub2
union sub1 [] = sub1
union sub1@((v1,e1):sub1') sub2@((v2,e2):sub2')
  | v1<v2  = (v1,e1):union sub1' sub2
  | v1==v2 = (v1,e1):union sub1' sub2'
  | v1>v2  = (v2,e2):union sub1  sub2'
```

The function unifyAll returns either an empty list or a singleton list:

```
unifyAll :: [Subst] -> [Subst]
unifyAll = foldr f [emptySub]
   where f sub subs = concatMap (unify sub) subs
```

That completes the definitions we need. Here is the module declaration:

```
module Substitutions
   (Subst, unitSub, combine, apply)
where
import Expressions
import Utilities (cp)
import Data.Maybe (fromJust)
```

That makes nine modules in total for our calculator.

12.8 Testing the calculator

How useful is the calculator in practice? The only way to answer this question is to try it out on some examples. We are going to record just two. The first is the calculation we performed in Chapter 5 about pruning the matrix of choices in Sudoku. In effect we want to prove

```
filter (all nodups . boxs) . expand . pruneBy boxs
        = filter (all nodups . boxs) . expand
```

from the laws

```
defn pruneBy:      pruneBy f = f . map pruneRow . f
expand after boxs: expand . boxs = map boxs . expand
filter with boxs:  filter (p . boxs)
                        = map boxs . filter p . map boxs
boxs involution:   boxs . boxs = id
map functor:       map f . map g = map (f.g)
map functor:       map id = id
defn expand:       expand = cp . map cp
filter after cp:   filter (all p) . cp = cp . map (filter p)
law of pruneRow:   filter nodups . cp . pruneRow
                        = filter nodups . cp
```

Here is the calculation exactly as performed by the calculator, except that we have broken some expressions across two lines, a task that should be left to a pretty-printer. Don't bother to study it in detail, just note the important bit towards the end:

```
  filter (all nodups . boxs) . expand . pruneBy boxs
=   {filter with boxs}
  map boxs . filter (all nodups) . map boxs . expand .
  pruneBy boxs
=   {defn pruneBy}
  map boxs . filter (all nodups) . map boxs . expand .
  boxs . map pruneRow . boxs
=   {expand after boxs}
```

```
  map boxs . filter (all nodups) . map boxs . map boxs .
  expand . map pruneRow . boxs
=   {map functor}
  map boxs . filter (all nodups) . map (boxs . boxs) . expand .
  map pruneRow . boxs
=   {boxs involution}
  map boxs . filter (all nodups) . map id . expand .
  map pruneRow . boxs
=   {map functor}
  map boxs . filter (all nodups) . expand . map pruneRow . boxs
=   {defn expand}
  map boxs . filter (all nodups) . cp . map cp . map pruneRow . boxs
=   {map functor}
  map boxs . filter (all nodups) . cp . map (cp . pruneRow) . boxs
=   {filter after cp}
  map boxs . cp . map (filter nodups) . map (cp . pruneRow) . boxs
=   {map functor}
  map boxs . cp . map (filter nodups . cp . pruneRow) . boxs
=   {law of pruneRow}
  map boxs . cp . map (filter nodups . cp) . boxs
=   {... ??? ...}
  map boxs . filter (all nodups) . map boxs . cp . map cp
=   {defn expand}
  map boxs . filter (all nodups) . map boxs . expand
=   {filter with boxs}
  filter (all nodups . boxs) . expand
```

Yes, the calculation fails. The reason is not hard to spot: we need to apply the law

```
    expand after boxs:    expand . boxs = map boxs . expand
```

in both directions, and the calculator simply cannot do that.

The solution is a hack. We add in the extra law

```
    hack:    map boxs . cp . map cp = cp . map cp . boxs
```

which is just the expand after boxs law written in the opposite direction and with expand replaced by its definition. Then the calculator is happy, producing the conclusion

```
....
  map boxs . cp . map (filter nodups . cp) . boxs
=   {map functor}
  map boxs . cp . map (filter nodups) . map cp . boxs
=   {filter after cp}
  map boxs . filter (all nodups) . cp . map cp . boxs
=   {hack}
  map boxs . filter (all nodups) . map boxs . cp . map cp
=   {defn expand}
  map boxs . filter (all nodups) . map boxs . expand
```

```
=    {filter with boxs}
   filter (all nodups . boxs) . expand
```

In both cases the calculations were performed in a fraction of a second, so efficiency does not seem to be an issue. And, apart from the hack, the calculations pass muster, being almost exactly what a good human calculator would produce.

Improving the calculator

Our second example is more ambitious: we are going to use the calculator to derive another version of the calculator. Look again at the definition of match. This relies on combine, which in turn involves a messy appeal to the unification of two substitutions, with all the paraphernalia of having to test them for compatibility and computing the union. A better idea is to compute the union of two substitutions only when one of them is a unit substitution. Then everything becomes simpler and probably faster. And the technique which describes this optimisation? Yes, it's another example of accumulating parameters. Just as an accumulating parameter can avoid expensive uses of ++ operations, our hope is to avoid expensive unify operations.

First of all, here is the definition of match again, written with a couple of new subsidiary functions:

```
match = concatMap matchesA . alignments
matchesA = combine . map matchA
matchA (Var v,e) = [unitSub v e]
matchA (Con k1 es1,Compose [Con k2 es2])
   | k1==k2 = matches (zip es1 es2)
matchA _ = []
matches = combine . map match
```

Note the cycle of dependencies of these functions:

```
match --> matchesA --> matchA --> matches --> match
```

These four functions are generalised as follows:

```
xmatch sub    = concatMap (unify sub) . match
xmatchA sub   = concatMap (unify sub) . matchA
xmatches sub  = concatMap (unify sub) . matches
xmatchesA sub = concatMap (unify sub) . matchesA
```

The additional argument in each case is an accumulating parameter. Our aim will be to obtain new versions of these definitions, whose cycle of dependencies is the same as the one above:

For the first calculation, we want to rewrite `match` in terms of `xmatch`, thereby linking the two groups of definitions. To save a lot of ink, we henceforth abbreviate `concatMap` to `cmap`. The three laws we need are

```
defn xmatch:      xmatch s = cmap (unify s) . match
unify of empty:   unify emptySub = one
cmap of one:      cmap one = id
```

In the first law we have to write s rather than `sub` (why?); the second two laws are the pointless versions of the facts that

```
unify emptySub sub = [sub]
cmap one xs = concat [[x] | x <- xs] = xs
```

The calculator is hardly stretched to give:

```
   xmatch emptySub
=  {defn xmatch}
   cmap (unify emptySub) . match
=  {unify of empty}
   cmap one . match
=  {cmap of one}
   match
```

Let us next deal with `xmatchA`. Because of the awkward pattern-matching style of definition of `matchA`, we simply record the following result of an easy (human) calculation:

```
xmatchA sub (Var v,e) = concat [unify sub (unitSub v e)]
xmatchA sub (Con k1 es1,Compose [Con k2 es2])
     | k1==k2 = xmatches sub (zip es1 es2)
xmatchA _ = []
```

If we introduce

```
extend sub v e = concat [unify sub (unitSub v e)]
```

then it is easy to derive

```
extend sub v e
  = case lookup v sub of
      Nothing -> [(v,e):sub]
      Just e' -> if e==e' then [sub]
                 else []
```

No elaborate compatibility test, and no general union of two substitutions. Instead, as we promised earlier, we unify substitutions only with unit substitutions.

Having disposed of xmatchA we concentrate on the other three members of the quartet. Just as xmatchA is defined in terms of xmatches, so xmatch can be defined in terms of xmatchesA. Specifically, we want to prove that

```
xmatch s = cmap (xmatchesA s) . alignments
```

Here are the laws we need:

```
defn match:       match = cmap matchesA . alignments
defn xmatch:      xmatch s = cmap (unify s) . match
defn xmatchesA:   xmatchesA s = cmap (unify s) . matchesA
cmap after cmap:  cmap f . cmap g = cmap (cmap f . g)
```

The last, purely combinatorial law is new; we leave verification as an exercise. The calculator produces:

```
  xmatch s
=   {defn xmatch}
  cmap (unify s) . match
=   {defn match}
  cmap (unify s) . cmap matchesA . alignments
=   {cmap after cmap}
  cmap (cmap (unify s) . matchesA) . alignments
=   {defn xmatchesA}
  cmap (xmatchesA s) . alignments
```

So far, so good. That leaves us with the two remaining members of the quartet, xmatches and xmatchesA. In each case we want to obtain recursive definitions, ones that do not involve unify. The two functions are defined in a very similar way, and it is likely that any calculation about one can be adapted immediately to the other. This kind of meta-calculational thought is, of course, beyond the reaches of the calculator.

Let us concentrate on xmatchesA. We first make xmatchesA entirely pointless, removing the parameter s in the definition above. The revised definition is:

```
xmatchesA :: (Subst,[(Atom,Expr)]) -> Subst
xmatchesA = cup . (one * matchesA)
cup = cmap unify . cpp
```

where the combinator cpp is defined by

```
cpp (xs,ys) = [(x,y) | x <- xs, y <- ys]
```

Thus

```
    xmatchesA (sub,aes)
  = cup ([sub],aes)
  = concat [unify (s,ae) | s <- [sub],ae <- matchesA aes]
  = concat [unify (sub,ae) | ae <- matchesA aes]
```

Apart from the fact that unify is now assumed to be a non-curried function, this is a faithful rendition of the definition of xmatchesA in pointless form.

The new function cup has type [Subst] -> [Subst] -> [Subst]. Later on we will exploit the fact that cup is an associative function, something that unify could never be (why not?). As we saw in Chapter 7 the accumulating parameter technique depends on the operation of interest being associative.

The first thing to check is that the previous calculation is still valid with the new definitions. Suppose we set up the laws

```
    defn match:     match = cmap matchesA . alignments
    defn xmatch:    xmatch = cup . (one * match)
    defn xmatchesA: xmatchesA = cup . (one * matchesA)
```

The calculator then produces

```
    xmatch
  =   {defn xmatch}
    cup . (one * match)
  =   {defn match}
    cup . (one * (cmap matchesA . alignments))
  =   {... ??? ...}
    cmap (cup . (one * matchesA)) . cpp . (one * alignments)
  =   {defn xmatchesA}
    cmap xmatchesA . cpp . (one * alignments)
```

Ah, it doesn't go through. Inspecting the gap in the calculation, it seems we need both the bifunctor law of * and a claim relating cmap and cup:

```
    cross bifunctor: (f * g) . (h * k) = (f . h) * (g . k)
    cmap-cup: cmap (cup . (one * g)) . cpp = cup . (id * cmap g)
```

The calculator is then happy:

```
    xmatch
  =   {defn xmatch}
    cup . (one * match)
  =   {defn match}
    cup . (one * (cmap matchesA . alignments))
  =   {cross bifunctor}
    cup . (id * cmap matchesA) . (one * alignments)
  =   {cmap-cup}
    cmap (cup . (one * matchesA)) . cpp . (one * alignments)
  =   {defn xmatchesA}
```

```
cmap xmatchesA . cpp . (one * alignments)
```

That still leaves us with the claim; apart from the fact that it works we have no reason to suppose it is true. However, we can get the calculator to prove it by using another law that is not specific to matching. We leave the proof as Exercise M. Define the additional laws

```
defn cup:     cup = cmap unify . cpp
cmap-cpp: cmap (cpp . (one * f)) . cpp = cpp . (id * cmap f)
```

The calculator then produces

```
  cmap (cup . (one * g)) . cpp
=   {defn cup}
  cmap (cmap unify . cpp . (one * g)) . cpp
=   {cmap after cmap}
  cmap unify . cmap (cpp . (one * g)) . cpp
=   {cmap-cpp}
  cmap unify . cpp . (id * cmap g)
=   {defn cup}
  cup . (id * cmap g)
```

Good. It seems that the cmap-cup law is valid, and it even might be useful again later on. Now let us return to the main point, which is to express xmatchesA recursively by two equations of the form

```
xmatchesA . (id * nil)  = ...
xmatchesA . (id * cons) = ...
```

The hope is that such a definition will not involve unify.

It is not at all clear what laws we need for this purpose. Instead, we will write down every law we can think of that might prove useful. The first group consists of our main definitions:

```
defn match:      match = cmap matchesA . alignments
defn matchesA:   matchesA = combine . map matchA
defn xmatch:     xmatch   = cup . (one * match)
defn xmatchesA:  xmatchesA = cup . (one * matchesA)
defn xmatchA:    xmatchA   = cup . (one * matchA)
defn combine:    combine = cmap unifyAll . cp
```

The second group are some new laws about cmap:

```
cmap after map:     cmap f . map g = cmap (f . g)
cmap after concat:  cmap f . concat = cmap (cmap f)
cmap after nil:     cmap f . nil = nil
cmap after one:     cmap f . one = f
```

The third group are some new laws about map:

```
map after nil: map f . nil = nil
map after one: map f . one = one . f
map after cons: map f . cons = cons . (f * map f)
map after concat: map f . concat = concat . map (map f)
```

The fourth group concerns cup:

```
cup assoc:  cup . (id * cup) = cup . (cup * id) . assocl
cup ident:  cup . (f * (one . nil)) = f . fst
cup ident:  cup . ((one . nil) * g) = g . snd
assocl: assocl. (f * (g * h)) = ((f * g) * h) . assocl
```

Finally we add in various other definitions and laws:

```
cross bifunctor: (f * g) . (h * k) = (f . h) * (g . k)
cross bifunctor: (id * id) = id
defn cp:  cp . nil = one . nil
defn cp:  cp . cons = map cons . cpp . (id * cp)
defn unifyAll: unifyAll . nil = one . nil
defn unifyAll: unifyAll . cons = cup . (one * unifyAll)
unify after nil:  unify . (id * nil) = one . fst
```

That's a total of 30 laws (including the two map functor laws and three laws about cmap that we haven't repeated). We cross our fingers and hope:

```
  xmatchesA . (id * nil)
=   {defn xmatchesA}
  cup . (one * matchesA) . (id * nil)
=   {cross bifunctor}
  cup . (one * (matchesA . nil))
=   {defn matchesA}
  cup . (one * (combine . map matchA . nil))
=   {map after nil}
  cup . (one * (combine . nil))
=   {defn combine}
  cup . (one * (cmap unifyAll . cp . nil))
=   {defn cp}
  cup . (one * (cmap unifyAll . one . nil))
=   {cmap after one}
  cup . (one * (unifyAll . nil))
=   {defn unifyAll}
  cup . (one * (one . nil))
=   {cup ident}
  one . fst
```

That's gratifying. We have shown that xmatchesA sub [] = [sub]. However, the recursive case cannot be established so easily. Instead we have to guess the result and then try to prove it. Here is the desired result, first expressed in pointed form and then in pointless form:

```
xmatchesA sub (ae:aes)
```

```
          = concat [xmatchesA sub' aes | sub' <- xmatchA sub ae]
```

```
  xmatchesA . (id * cons)
    = cmap xmatchesA . cpp . (xmatchA * one) . assocl
```

We can perform simplification with the right-hand side (we temporarily remove the definitions of xmatchA and matchesA from laws2):

```
    cmap xmatchesA . cpp . (xmatchA * one) . assocl
=   {defn xmatchesA}
    cmap (cup . (one * matchesA)) . cpp . (xmatchA * one) . assocl
=   {cmap-cup}
    cup . (id * cmap matchesA) . (xmatchA * one) . assocl
=   {cross bifunctor}
    cup . (xmatchA * (cmap matchesA . one)) . assocl
=   {cmap after one}
    cup . (xmatchA * matchesA) . assocl
```

Now we would like to show

```
  xmatchesA . (id * cons)
        = cup . (xmatchA * matchesA) . assocl
```

But unfortunately the calculator can't quite make it. The gap appears here:

```
    cup . ((cup . (one * matchA)) * matchesA)
=   {... ??? ...}
    cup . (one * (cup . (matchA * matchesA))) . assocl
```

The gap is easily eliminable by hand:

```
    cup . ((cup . (one * matchA)) * matchesA)
=   {cross bifunctor (backwards)}
    cup . (cup * id) . ((one * matchA) * matchesA)
=   {cup assoc}
    cup . (id * cup) . assocl . ((one * matchA) * matchesA)
=   {assocl}
    cup . (id * cup) . (one * (matchA * matchesA)) . assocl
=   {cross bifunctor}
    cup . (one * (cup . (matchA * matchesA))) . assocl
```

Once again, the inability to apply laws in both directions is the culprit. Instead of trying to force the laws into a form that would be acceptable to the calculator, we leave it here with the comment 'A hand-finished product!'.

To round off the example, here is the program we have calculated:

```
  match = xmatch emptySub
  xmatch sub (e1,e2)
    = concat [xmatchesA sub aes | aes <- alignments (e1,e2)]
```

```
xmatchesA sub [] = [sub]
xmatchesA sub (ae:aes)
 = concat [xmatchesA sub' aes | sub' <- xmatchA sub ae]

xmatchA sub (Var v,e) = extend sub v e
xmatchA sub (Con k1 es1,Compose [Con k2 es2])
    | k1==k2 = xmatches sub (zip es1 es2)
xmatchA _ = []
```

The missing definition is that of xmatches. But exactly the same treatment for xmatchesA goes through for matches, and we end up with

```
xmatches sub [] = [sub]
xmatches sub ((e1,e2):es)
 = concat [xmatches sub' es | sub' <- xmatch sub (e1,e2)]
```

Conclusions

The positive conclusion of these two exercises is that one can indeed get the calculator to assist in the construction of formal proofs. But there remains the need for substantial human input to the process, to set up appropriate laws, to identify subsidiary claims and to control the order in which calculations are carried out. The major negative conclusion is that it is a significant failing of the calculator to be unable to apply laws in both directions. The functor laws are the major culprits, but there are others as well (see the exercises for some examples). The calculator can be improved in a number of ways, but we leave further discussion to the exercises.

There are three other aspects worth mentioning about the calculator. Firstly, the complete calculator is only about 450 lines of Haskell, and the improved version is even shorter. That alone is a testament to the expressive power of functional programming. Secondly, it does seem a viable approach to express laws as purely functional equations and to use a simple equational logic for conducting proofs. To be sure, some work has to be done to express definitions in point-free form, but once this is achieved, equational logic can be surprisingly effective.

The third aspect is that, apart from parsing, no monadic code appears in the calculator. In fact, earlier versions of the calculator did use monads, but gradually they were weeded out. One reason was that we found the code became simpler without monads, without significant loss of efficiency; another was that we wanted to set things up for the extended exercise in improving the calculator. Monads are absolutely necessary for many applications involving interacting with the world, but they can be overused in places where a purely functional approach would be smoother.

On that note, we end.

12.9 Exercises

Exercise A

Suppose we did want `calculate` to return a tree of possible calculations. What would be a suitable tree to use?

Exercise B

Why should the laws

```
map (f . g)  = map f . map g
cmap (f . g) = cmap f . map g
```

never be used in calculations, at least if they are given in the form above?

Exercise C

Here is a calculation, as recorded by the calculator

```
  map f . map g h
=    {map functor}
  map (f . g)
```

Explain this strange and clearly nonsensical result. What simple change to the calculator would prevent the calculation from being valid?

Exercise D

On the same general theme as the previous question, one serious criticism of the calculator is that error messages are totally opaque. For example, both

```
parse law "map f . map g = map (f . g)"
parse law "map functor: map f . map g   map (f . g)"
```

cause the same cryptic error message. What is it? What would be the effect of using the law

```
strange: map f . map g = map h
```

in a calculation?

Again, what change to the calculator would prevent such a law from being acceptable?

Exercise E

The definition of `showsPrec` for atoms makes use of a fact about Haskell that we haven't needed before. And the same device is used in later calculator functions that mix a pattern-matching style with guarded equations. What is the fact?

Exercise F

Define

```
e1 = foo (f . g) . g
e2 = bar f . baz g
```

List the expressions that `rewrites (e1,e2)` produces when applied to the expression `foo (a . b . c) . c`. Which one would the calculator pick?

Exercise G

Can the calculator successfully match `foo f . foo f` with the expression

```
foo (bar g h) . foo (bar (daz a) b) ?
```

Exercise H

It was claimed in the text that it is possible to apply a perfectly valid non-trivial law that will leave some expressions unchanged. Give an example of such a law and an expression that is rewritten to itself.

Exercise I

The function `anyOne` used in the definition of `rewrites` installs a single choice, but why not use `everyOne` that installs every choice at the same time? Thus if `f 1 = [-1,-2]` and `f 2 = [-3,-4]`, then

```
everyOne f [1,2] = [[-1,-3],[-1,-4],[-2,-3],[-3,-4]]
```

Using `everyOne` instead of `anyOne` would mean that a rewrite would be applied to every possible subexpression that matches a law. Give a definition of `everyOne`.

Exercise J

How many segments of a list of length n are there? The definition of `rewritesSeg` is inefficient because the empty segment appears $n+1$ times as the middle component of the segments of a list of length n. That means matching with `id` is performed $n+1$ times instead of just once. How would you rewrite `segments` to eliminate these duplicates?

Exercise K

Prove that `cmap f . cmap g = cmap (cmap f . g)`. The laws needed are:

```
defn cmap:        cmap f = concat . map f
map functor:      map f . map g = map (f.g)
map after concat: map f . concat = concat . map (map f)
concat twice:     concat . concat = concat . map concat
```

Exercise L

The `cmap-cpp` law is as follows:

```
cmap (cpp . (one * f)) . cpp = cpp . (id * cmap f)
```

Prove it from the laws

```
cmap after cmap:  cmap f . map g = cmap (f . g)
cmap after cpp:   cmap cpp . cpp = cpp . (concat * concat)
cross bifunctor:  (f * g) . (h * k) = (f . h) * (g . k)
map after cpp:    map (f * g) . cpp = cpp . (map f * map g)
defn cmap:        cmap f = concat . map f
concat after id:  concat . map one = id
```

Can a calculator conduct the proof?

12.10 Answers

Answer to Exercise A

We would want expressions as labels of nodes and law names as labels of edges. That gives

```
type Calculation = Tree Expr LawName
data Tree a b    = Node a [(b,Tree a b)]
```

Answer to Exercise B

They would both cause the calculator to spin off into an infinite calculation. For example,

```
  map foo
= {map functor}
  map foo . map id
= {map functor}
  map foo . map id . map id
```

and so on.

Answer to Exercise C

The expression map f . map g h is perfectly valid by the rules of syntax, but of course it shouldn't be. The evaluator does not force the restriction that each appearance of one and the same constant should possess the same number of arguments. The reason the functor law can be matched successfully against the expression is that in the definition of matchA the function zip truncates the two arguments to the second map to one. A better calculator should check that each constant has a fixed arity.

Answer to Exercise D

The cryptic message is 'head of empty list'. The first parse fails because the law is missing its name, and the second is missing an equals sign. Use of the strange law would cause the calculator to fall over because pattern-matching with the left-hand side would not bind h to any expression, causing an error when the binding for h is requested. The calculator should have checked that every variable on the right-hand side of a law appears somewhere on the left-hand side.

Answer to Exercise E

The code for showsPrec takes the form

```
    showsPrec p (Con f [e1,e2])
      | isOp f   = expression1 e1 e2
    showsPrec p (Con f es)
      = expression2 es
```

A more 'mathematical' style would have been to write

```
    showsPrec p (Con f [e1,e2])
      | isOp f    = expression1 e1 e2
      | otherwise = expression2 [e1,e2]
```

```
showsPrec p (Con f es) = expression2 es
```

The point is this: in a given clause if a pattern does not match the argument, or if it does but the guard fails to be true, the clause is abandoned and the next clause is chosen.

Answer to Exercise F

There are two rewrites, not one:

```
bar (a . b . c) . baz id . c
bar (a . b) . baz c
```

The calculator would pick the first subexpression that matches, and that means the first rewrite is chosen. Perhaps it would be better to arrange that rewritesSeg is applied to longer segments before shorter ones.

Answer to Exercise G

No, not with our definition of match. They can be matched by binding f to the expression bar (daz a) b provided g is bound to daz a and h to b, but our definition of match does not perform full unification.

Answer to Exercise H

To take just one example out of many, consider the law

```
if p f g . h = if (p . h) (f . h) (g . h)
```

The left-hand side matches if a b c with h bound to id, and the result is again the same expression.

Answer to Exercise I

The temptation is to define

```
everyOne f = cp . map f
```

but that doesn't work if f returns no alternatives for some element. Instead we have to define

```
everyOne :: (a -> [a]) -> [a] -> [[a]]
everyOne f   = cp . map (possibly f)
possibly f x = if null xs then [x] else xs
               where xs = f x
```

In this version, f returns a nonempty list of alternatives.

Answer to Exercise J

There are $(n+1)(n+2)/2$ segments of a list of length n. The improved definition is

```
segments xs = [([],[],xs] ++
                [(as,bs,cs)
                | (as,ys) <- splits xs,
                  (bs,cs) <- tail (splits ys)]
```

Answer to Exercise K

The calculator produced:

```
    cmap f . cmap g
=    {defn cmap}
    concat . map f . cmap g
=    {defn cmap}
    concat . map f . concat . map g
=    {map after concat}
    concat . concat . map (map f) . map g
=    {map functor}
    concat . concat . map (map f . g)
=    {concat after concat}
    concat . map concat . map (map f . g)
=    {map functor}
    concat . map (concat . map f . g)
=    {defn cmap}
    concat . map (cmap f . g)
=    {defn cmap}
    cmap (cmap f . g)
```

Answer to Exercise L

The human proof is:

```
    cmap (cpp . (one * g)) . cpp
=    {cmap after cmap (backwards)}
    cmap cpp . map (one * g) . cpp
=    {map after cpp}
    cmap cpp . cpp . (map one * map g)
=    {cmap after cpp}
    cpp . (concat * concat) . (map one * map g)
=    {cross bifunctor}
    cpp . ((concat . map one) * concat (map g))
=    {defn cmap (backwards)}
    cpp . ((concat . map one) * cmap g)
=    {concat after id}
    cpp . (id * cmap g)
```

No, the calculation cannot be performed automatically. The cmap after cmap law cannot be installed in the backwards direction without causing the calculator to loop (see Exercise B).

12.11 Chapter notes

The calculator in this chapter is based on an undocumented theorem prover by Mike Spivey, a colleague at Oxford. Ross Paterson of City University, London, has produced a version with built-in functor laws that can be applied in both directions when necessary.

One state-of-the-art proof assistant is Coq; see `http://coq.inria.fr/`.

Index